ASIAN PACIFIC AMERICAN YOUTH MINISTRY

PLANNING HELPS AND PROGRAMS

DONALD NG,
EDITOR

Judson Press ® Valley Forge

LIBRARY OF CONGRESS
Library of Congress Cataloging-in-Publication Data

Asian Pacific American youth ministry / edited by Don Ng.
      p.   cm.
    Includes bibliographies.
    ISBN 0-8170-1132-3 : $10.95
    1. Church work with Asian Americans. 2. Church work with Oceanian
Americans. 3. Church work with youth.   I. Ng, Don.
BV4468.2.A74A85 1988   88-23453
259.2'08995073—dc19   CIP

Contents

The Writers

(Listed alphabetically)

BRANDON I. CHO is pastor of North Long Beach United Methodist Church, Long Beach, California, and president of the Transgeneration Fellowship of Korean United Methodists. He formerly served as pastor of Orange St. Paul's United Methodist Church and as associate pastor of San Gabriel First United Methodist Church. He is a graduate of Hawaii Loa College and holds Master of Divinity and Doctor of Ministry degrees from the School of Theology at Claremont.

KATHRYN CHOY-WONG is minister of public ministries for the American Baptist Churches of the West, having formerly served as director of Asian Ministries for American Baptist National Ministries. She is a graduate of San Francisco State University and the American Baptist Seminary of the West, and an ordained American Baptist minister.

CAROLE CHUCK is an English as a Second Language (ESL) teacher of adults at Alemany Community College and a member of the Presbyterian Church of the Mission in San Francisco, California. She is a graduate of the University of California in Berkeley, California State, and San Francisco State University.

JOAN MAY CORDOVA is a bilingual resource teacher in the Sacramento City Unified School District. She holds a B.A. degree in community studies/social change from the University of California, Santa Cruz, and an M.A. degree in multicultural education from the University of San Francisco.

DAVID NG is professor of Christian education at San Francisco Theological Seminary. He has also taught at Austin Presbyterian Theological Seminary, has been a youth curriculum editor for the Presbyterian Church (U.S.A.), an associate general secretary of the National Council of Churches, and a pastor in Mendocino and in Chinatown, San Francisco, both in California.

DONALD NG is director of the Department of Ministry with Youth, American Baptist Educational Ministries. He has previously served as associate pastor of the First Chinese Baptist Church in San Francisco. A graduate of Gordon College and Andover Newton Theological School, he is currently a doctoral candidate at Temple University.

RODGER Y. NISHIOKA is associate for Leader Development for Youth for the Education and Congregational Nurture Unit of the Presbyterian Church (U.S.A.). He holds degrees in English and history from Seattle Pacific University and in curriculum instruction from the University of Washington. He lives in Louisville, Kentucky.

TIM TSENG, a graduate of New York University and Union Theological Seminary, New York, is a Ph.D. candidate at Union. He is also serving as assistant pastor at the Brooklyn Chinese Christian Church and associate staff for Chinese Ministries at ABC of Metropolitan New York.

WESLEY S. WOO is coordinator for Asian Justice Ministries, Presbyterian Church (U.S.A.), having formerly served as director for the Council for Pacific Asian American Ministries, Reformed Church in America, and associate pastor for St. John's Presbyterian Church, San Francisco. He holds an A.B. degree from San Francisco State College, a Master of Divinity degree from San Francisco Theological Seminary, and a Ph.D. degree from the Graduate Theological Union (Berkeley).

Introduction

Is what we are doing meaningful to the youth with whom we are in ministry? This is the basic question for those engaged in working with youth. Although most American youth are experiencing similar life situations as the result of common education, shared youth culture, and common exposure to the American media, there are also different and usually unique life experiences related to specific racial/ethnic cultural traditions. Ministering with Asian Pacific American youth calls for an understanding of the rich histories and traditions of Asians and Asian Pacific Americans.

The term "Asian Pacific Americans" as used in this book generally refers to people whose heritage is primarily rooted along the Asian continent bordering on the Pacific Ocean or in the Pacific islands. This, of course, is obviously not an exact description of this growing group of Americans. Some Asian Pacific Americans have been in the United States for several generations, contributing in their own unique ways in the making of nineteenth- and twentieth-century America. In addition, there are new Asian groups today who are fleeing war, poverty, and political unrest in search for a better life. Therefore, "Asian Pacific Americans" is an umbrella term to represent the great diversity of Asian groups in America. It takes into account the fact that each Asian Pacific group has its own particular gifts that are joined together in forming a new American expression of life. Rather than only referring to oneself as a Chinese American or a Korean American, a person may say, "I am an Asian Pacific American," thus affirming the various threads of the Asian Pacific American groups as one's own. This book is written with this collective perspective in mind.

This book is designed primarily for three kinds of users. First, it is a resource for local Asian Pacific American churches. In addition to the background materials pertinent to their ministry, youth and youth leaders will be able to use the twenty step-by-step program sessions with their church youth groups. The activities and supplies needed are geared for sessions about an hour long. The four units focus on themes of youth interest and Christian responsibility within the context of the Asian Pacific American experience. Second, this resource will be useful to more broadly based local churches that minister with Asian Pacific American youth in their communities. The program sessions can be effective materials for responding to youth's personal and social needs as well as means to share the Christian message. In both types of churches, understanding the Part I: "Foundations for Ministry" materials and then using the Part II: "Ministry with Asian Pacific American Youth" section will enable users to create and plan their own programs and activities to be more appropriate to their particular situations. The third group of users for this book is theological students preparing for ministry with Asian Pacific Americans. The "Foundations for Ministry" section contains theological, historical and cultural, developmental, and educational materials useful in understanding Asian Pacific American youth.

This first major resource in the field of Asian Pacific American youth ministry was the product of efforts by many persons committed to youth ministry. The project was partly funded by the Lilly Endowment through the Youth Ministry and Theological Schools Project at Union Theological Seminary in Virginia. The sponsoring organization is the Pacific-Asian American Christian Education Project (PAACE), related to Education for Christian Life and Mission of the National Council of Churches in Christ. Funding and support were received from PAACE's participating denominations: American Baptist Churches in the USA, Church of the Brethren, Christian Church (Disciples), Episcopal Church, Evangelical Lutheran Church in America, Presbyterian Church (U.S.A.), Reformed Church in America, United Church of Canada, United Church of Christ, and United Methodist Church.

The publication of this book is a dream come true. Wesley Woo, David Ng, and I brought together our hopes of what such a resource might look like. We talked, shared, and imagined its significance and values in enabling effective Asian Pacific American youth ministry. If it adds something meaningful to the group you are working with, our hopes and prayers will have been fulfilled.

Special appreciation is due to our support staff member Shirley Reifsnyder, who typed the manuscript, to Frank Hoadley and to Laura Alden and Kristy Arnesen Pullen, of Judson Press, who believed that we could do it.

Donald Ng, *Editor*

PART 1

Foundations for Ministry with Asian Pacific American Youth

Theological Dimensions, *by Wesley S. Woo*
Historical and Cultural Context, *by Joan May Cordova*
Developmental Characteristics of Youth,
    by Rodger Y. Nishioka
How Youth Learn, *by David Ng*

Theological Dimensions

by Wesley S. Woo

How does theology relate to the critical issues that Asian Pacific American young people are experiencing in their development?

What are some of the key theological principles that govern Asian Pacific American youth ministries?

How does the kingdom of God as a biblical vision guide our faith and practice?

What are some of the issues of identity, community, and vocation which relate to that biblical vision?

However abstract they may seem, such questions as these are basic to our thinking when we are planning a ministry with Asian Pacific American youth. We need to think about underlying philosophical themes and ideas, as well as recent theological reflections on racial and ethnic experiences in America. We need to look at some of the Asian Pacific American theological insights and understandings that have emerged in recent years. These are key elements in what might be called "Asian Pacific American theology."

Theology and the Asian Pacific American Experience

How does theology relate to race and ethnicity? Answers to this question may help us to think creatively about faith, theology, and our own particular racial ethnic experiences. (While recognizing that the definitions of "race" and "ethnicity" and the distinctions between the two concepts are controversial, we shall use both terms as shorthand for the experiences of blacks, Hispanics, Native Americans, and Asians in America.)

Theology

Theology is reflection about the nature of God, God's relationship to all of creation, and our response to God. It is also the attempt to understand and practice faith and discipleship in accordance with God's desire and will for God's creation.

Some people view theology as the *scientific* study of God and ultimate reality. To them it is purely rational and objective, unaffected by the environment or by the theologian's own conscious and unconscious perspec-

tives. They may presume that theology is unrelated to contemporary issues and conditions, except in a secondary or applied sense. Such people generally believe that theology deals almost solely with absolute and unchanging truths.

Such a "scientific" view, however, is flat; it denies its own history; it misreads the fundamental nature of the Christian faith. It incorrectly denies that the God of the Bible is a God who enters into human history and responds to the various conditions in which we find ourselves. Such a view also leaves unchallenged the various cultural, social, political, or economic biases that usually creep into our theological thinking.

In recent years we have seen that theology is dynamic. Liberation theology from Latin America, as well as black, Native American, Hispanic, and Asian American theologies in the United States, as well as feminist theology and various other liberation-type theologies from the Third World, have made a difference. They have provided the critical input needed to help redirect and reshape the field of theology so that it could be more faithful to the Bible and better able to unmask, and therefore correct, various distorting and dehumanizing biases. Without delving in detail into any of these systems of thought and practice, nor attempting to consider the differences between them, we can identify three key points that are relevant to our concerns here:

First is the fact that faith and action go hand in hand. This point is made clear in James 2:14-26. Our beliefs must be translated into action: "So faith by itself, if it has no works, is dead" (James 2:17). Our actions must reflect our beliefs and be consistent with them. On the one hand, faith understandings cannot be genuine or relevant if they do not lead to appropriate faith actions. On the other hand, faith actions lack depth, direction, and effectiveness unless they are grounded in faith understandings. Moreover, as much as understanding shapes action, action—properly reflected upon—shapes understanding. Leaders in youth ministries certainly understand this latter point, since youth programs are often based on giving young persons opportunities to practice discipleship even before they have knowledge and understanding. Practical experiences often serve as laboratories for reflection and for grasping the meaning of Sunday school illustrations. Many of us learned about forgiveness and reconciliation from having to deal in conflict situations with others at a youth camp or ball game. Later, we learned the underlying principles of God's grace and reconciling activities. Authentic discipleship thus requires both faith and action, integrally related. A key tenet of effective Asian Pacific American youth ministries is that discipleship is to be nurtured in settings in which the opportunity both to practice and to explore faith is available.

The second point is that faith and action, together, must address the sinful and oppressive condition of the world. James 2:1-7 ties faith to the ethical principle of impartiality between the rich and the poor. Our faith requires us to make similar judgments about the world in light of God's desire for the reign of love, peace, justice, and righteousness. Such judgments are not easy to make and should be made humbly, corporately, and prayerfully. Without getting into the question of *how* judgments can be made, we see that they *must* be made—for the God we acknowledge as ruler of our lives not only judges, but creates the standards by which we must judge. Moreover, we must voice our judgments and act upon them. We need to be bold, unequivocal, and prophetic in speaking out against injustice, dehumanization, and oppression however and whenever they occur.

We must also translate our judgments into action and seek effective means for overcoming unjust conditions. This effort, of course, necessitates dealing with such conditions on manageable scales. Leaders in youth ministry need to take overwhelming issues—such as institutional racism, poverty, or international peace—and break them down into manageable, "digestible" pieces that young people can understand and do something about in their own settings. For Asian Pacific American youth this might mean focusing on specific and local Asian Pacific American community aspects of larger issues.

This approach means that we need to spend much time studying, analyzing, and understanding the state of our world, again perhaps in manageable pieces. We cannot transform what we do not know or understand. But knowledge and understanding do not need to come solely from study or reading. They can also come from reflecting on our own and other people's experiences. We can learn from honestly listening to other people's individual and community stories. For Asian Pacific Americans, all this means active reflection on Asian Pacific American experiences and race dynamics in American society. Such reflection can greatly inform and direct our faith activities.

The third point is that our context, the world around us, can interact with theology in both positive and negative ways. A negative way would be to make the church captive to the prevailing culture, thus using theology to justify a particular social order. Such a process would serve unworthy ideological functions, as did the Baal religion of early Palestine. Baal religion gave religious legitimation to a political system that served the interests of a small elitist ruling class, while oppressing the large numbers of peasantry. Thus it justified an oppressive world of status quo. In contrast, the religion of the Hebrews was based on faithfulness to God alone. It would not allow loyalty to finite and sinful human institutions (which was considered idolatry), and made justice, compassion, and equality before God the basis of society.[1]

A positive interaction, on the other hand, would be to use history and culture to unfold or reveal dimensions of God's being and involvements in creation. For example, racial ethnic peoples in North America can see their own existence as expressions of the pluralistic nature of God and of God's love for all people. In the same way, feminist concerns can expand our images of God beyond traditional masculine categories. So too, liberation theology, because of its grounding in the sufferings of the poor, tells us of God's active and passionate love for the poor and oppressed. Likewise, the importance of family and community for Asians, when contrasted with the brokenness that exists in much of Asian and Asian Pacific American society, can help us to see the corporate dimension of reconciliation and redemption in Christ. All of these examples also demand that we respond ethically.

Asian Pacific American Experience

The reference to "Asian Pacific American" experience points to the range of historical, psychosocial, cultural, and political issues that Asian Pacific Americans have experienced and that have shaped their collective and individual identities and community characteristics. (See Chapter 2, "Historical and Cultural Context," for more detail.) This experience involves a blending of East and West, but also goes beyond that to include new forms of culture and identity growing out of the United States experience. The term "culture" is used loosely and broadly in this analysis and somewhat interchangeably with the term "experience." Culture is not a matter of tourist-shop trinkets, "oriental" restaurants, or romanticized notions of an exotic "Asiatic" civilization. Rather, it is the expression of the soul of a people, shaped and expressed in complex ways. The singular word "experience" in this chapter refers to the issues and characteristics held in common by the various Asian Pacific American national ancestry groups. The plural "experiences" is used to acknowledge the differences and uniquenesses that exist among the various groups.

Interaction Between Theology and the Asian Pacific American Experience

Historically, in the United States, theology has been shaped by a white "Anglo" Protestant establishment that was attempting to create a perfect Christian (that is, Protestant) nation and society. For this reason Asian immigrants were seen as a potential threat to American society unless they were quickly converted. At the same time, this nation was perceived to be God's agent for Christianizing the rest of the world. Asian immigrants were therefore also seen as a opportunity, since they could (if won to Christianity) bring this newfound faith back to their homelands. However, the American Protestant establishment mixed the concepts of being Christian, being American, and being civilized, thus confusing feelings of nationalistic and cultural superiority with religious faith. This "American cultural Christianity" is another example of the negative interaction between faith and culture. American Protestants generally thought that these two factors were virtually synonymous and interchangeable, and that being one (i.e., Christian, American, or civilized) was essentially the same as being the others—or, at least, one would also automatically lead to the others. Therefore, evangelistic missionary work could involve Americanizing and "civilizing" activities, since they would lead to the same end. This concept explains why schools were a favorite form of missionary work with Asians in America. Given this understanding, historian Arthur Schlesinger, Jr.'s conclusion that the nineteenth-century American Protestant missionary enterprise in China was a form of cultural imperialism is credible. For him, cultural imperialism was the purposeful aggression by one culture against the ideas and values of another.[2] Theological underpinning for such perspectives and worldview came in the form of widely held assumptions about the special calling, higher role, and more perfect identity of America. "Manifest Destiny," the nineteenth-century ideological doctrine that America was destined and expected by God to expand westward, was one of these assumptions.

In recent years there have been various challenges to these notions. The civil rights movement in the United States and various liberation movements in the Third World, paralleled by companion theological movements, have exposed the class, race, nationalistic, and cultural biases in American theological and missionary

thought. For example, the development of black theology, as a religious dimension of the civil rights and black power movements, was instrumental in affirming blackness and the black experience as positive. Likewise, liberation theology in Latin America unmasked the class bias and cultural captivity of traditional western theology. Both of these theological movements were also instrumental in generating new postures and tools for doing theology. They made it possible to approach theology from new perspectives, or to see faith issues with a different set of lenses.

Theological reflection on Asian Pacific American experiences emerged in the early 1970s as counterpart to black, Native American, and Hispanic theological developments. It was also a response by Asian Pacific American Christians to the growing Asian civil rights, "yellow power," and ethnic-identity movements that emerged among Asian Pacific American students on many college campuses and in Asian American communities in the late 1960s. These theological reflections have been, and continue to be, shaped primarily in Asian Pacific American congregations and gatherings and in the context of Asian Pacific American communities. Moreover, the insights that have emerged have been conveyed and shared largely through sermons, church education curriculum and activities, liturgies, occasional local writing projects, and sporadically sponsored denominational events. The Pacific and Asian American Center for Theology and Strategies (PACTS), an ecumenical venture established in this same period of time and located in the San Francisco Bay area, is one of the few agencies to collect and disseminate Asian Pacific American theological writings on a national basis.

Three aspects of Asian Pacific American theological reflection that are important for youth ministries are highlighted here. First, this theology affirms Asian Pacific American identity and experiences as positive, legitimate, and not unchristian. Issues of identity continue to be a primary concern among Asian Pacific Americans and remain a major theme in most Asian Pacific American theological thought, in large part because the forces of cultural alienation and racism in American society persist. Asian Pacific American theology has sought to break the chain of oppression with respect to identity and culture. Whereas Asian Pacific American Christians have oftentimes felt guilty about asserting their ethnicity and thought it to be somehow incompatible with Christianity, current reworkings of biblical and theological themes suggest that such guilt is neither necessary nor appropriate. On the contrary, there is theological depth and integrity in asserting one's racial identity. More will be said about this fact later. For now, we are reminded that all peoples are made in the image of God, without qualification, and all are to be affirmed in their particularities.

Second, along with having uplifted the dignity of Asian Pacific Americans, current theological activities have reminded us of God's special love for the marginal, poor, and oppressed and of our responsibility to respond in like manner. In a sense, there has been a recovery (or discovery) of ethical commitments to the world around us on the part of many Asian Pacific American Christians. On one level there is a new responsibility for dealing with issues faced by Asian Pacific American communities and a commitment to address these issues with greater depth of analysis and resolution. On another level there has emerged a commitment to issues beyond the Asian Pacific American community. This can be seen in Asian Pacific American coalitional activities with blacks, Native Americans, and Hispanics. It also appears in Asian Pacific American involvements in peace issues, antiapartheid activities, and a variety of other social and political agendas. It can be seen, too, in the attention given to democratic and human rights issues in Asia. Of course, concern for the homeland has always been a part of the Asian Pacific American community, particularly within the immigrant generation, but for many younger Asian Pacific Americans, this is a new commitment.

Third, recent theological reflections have helped Asian Pacific American Christians to appreciate the role of ethnicity and culture in the task of trying to discern God's nature and will as revealed in the Bible. Thus we see an expression of the positive interaction between our theology and our context. Asian Pacific American experiences can serve as a tool for interpreting the Bible. For example, Asian Pacific Americans have found, in the struggle for positive identity, that the God of the Bible is a God who gives us our identity and celebrates it, while at the same time calling us to use it for the sake of others. For another example, Asian Pacific Americans, along with other racial ethnic people, are in the position to help the rest of the church understand and appreciate the corporate and communal nature of faith. For a third example, Methodist Bishop Roy Sano tells how the Asian Pacific American experience has led to a new understanding of the nature of God's saving work. According to Sano, European and North American Christian thought on salvation has focused largely on reconciliation. But the oppression experienced by Asian Pacific Americans and others helps us to see that liberation from domination must occur first. If we are to participate in God's saving actions, therefore, we are not only called to experience reconciliation, along with forgiveness and ongoing maturation in faith; "We are called to participate with God in the redemptive events of deliverance,

liberation, and emancipation from domination under intermediaries."[3]

The Kingdom of God

The kingdom (reign) of God is the fundamental biblical theme and vision of our ministry. As described in Scripture, the kingdom provides us with a vision of the fullness of time, when all creation is reconciled to God and when peace, justice, and wholeness reign. The kingdom of God is also a goal that guides and shapes the way we should order society and our lives as part of a holy community. It serves as a plumb line with which we measure the world and its existing orders, institutions, and activities. In Scripture there are many metaphors and poetic images of the kingdom. For example, theologian Nicholas Wolterstorff cites Isaiah 11:6-9 as descriptive of shalom, which is the peace and wholeness of the kingdom:[4]

The wolf shall dwell with the lamb,
    and the leopard shall lie down with the kid,
and the calf and the lion and the fatling together,
    and a little child shall lead them.
The cow and the bear shall feed;
    their young shall lie down together;
    and the lion shall eat straw like the ox.
The sucking child shall play over the hole of the asp,
    and the weaned child shall put his hand on
        the adder's den.
They shall not hurt or destroy
    in all my holy mountain;
for the earth shall be full of the knowledge of the Lord
    as the waters cover the sea.

Poetically imaged, such will be the nature of the new order in God's kingdom. God's reign is also revealed in the stories of acts of compassion as described in Matthew 25:31-40, in Jesus' reading from the book of Isaiah as recorded in Luke 4:18-19, and in many of the parables of Jesus. All these passages also suggest activities and actions appropriate to fulfilling the eschatological vision.

Scriptural references point to the kingdom of God as a state of just, peaceful, and righteous existence in loving and obedient relationship to our Lord, and thus also to all of creation. This state of existence transcends death and history (i.e., it goes *beyond* time and space), but it also encompasses an ideal historical condition (i.e., *within* time and space). While the kingdom cannot, and should not, be reduced to a social or political program, it nevertheless includes social and political dimensions. Theologian Walter Brueggemann says that, although we cannot turn the Bible into a tract for lution, nevertheless biblical understandings of the kingdom of God and resurrection do require us to pay attention to concrete life in community. New life as promised in the Bible is linked to the just reordering of our life together.[5] Brazilian priest and theologian

Leonardo Boff, speaking of liberation theology perspectives, talks about this in terms of the difference between salvation and liberation. Our understanding of salvation, as a theological term, refers to fullness of life in the kingdom of God in eternity, beyond history. Yet salvation is anticipated, prepared for, and situated within history and therefore involves liberation. According to Boff:

> The kingdom, although not of this world in its origin—it comes from God—is nevertheless among us, manifesting itself in processes of liberation. Liberation is the act of gradually delivering reality from the various captivities to which it is historically subject and which run counter to God's historical project—which is the upbuilding of the kingdom, a kingdom in which everything is orientated to God, penetrated by God's presence, and glorified, on the cosmic level as on the personal level.[6]

It is clear that God cares passionately about the world and desires wholeness for all of creation. As people of God who are called to disciple, we respond to God's grace by acting out our commitments to love, justice, peace, compassion, and righteousness. We are called to work for the transformation of the world so that it can approximate the vision of the kingdom. As Boff states, "Liberations [sic] show forth the activity of eschatological salvation by anticipation, as the leaven of today in the dough of a reality fully to be transfigured in the eschaton."

This calling means that we as Christians ought not to withdraw from the world; we should neither be afraid of contamination nor seek merely to pass through it with our eyes focused on the other side. Rather, because we are freed and made whole in Christ, we seek to engage the world, transform it to conform to God's word, and celebrate this transformation. As we learn from the song of Deborah (Judges 5), God marches forth and actively sides with the oppressed, as does all of creation, in the fight for justice. Moreover, this rallying song makes it clear that God requires us to choose sides instead of making excuses. Praise is given to those who "offered themselves willingly among the people" even at the risk of death (vv. 2, 9, 14-15a, 18, 24), while condemnation and curse is called on those who stood back or made excuses for not entering the fray (vv. 15b-17, 23).

While speaking of the antiapartheid struggle, the words of South African theologian Allan Boesak are a challenge to all of us:

> In the heat of the struggle Christians today are called to be the light of the world. In the midst of the struggle we are called to be the embodiment of God's ideal for this broken world. Christians must be there to represent God's possibilities for authentic love, meaningful reconciliation, and genuine peace.[7]

Christians may not necessarily be the only ones who lead the quest for justice, since God sometimes uses outsiders like Cyrus (Isaiah 45), but Christians are certainly called to participate in it. As Boesak states, "It is not a Christian struggle I am pleading for, but a Christian presence in the struggle." This involves the ability to see God's liberating hand in human acts of liberation. Boesak's words reflect a grounding in the Reformed tradition, a tradition that one theologian describes as representing, in its emergence in the sixteenth century, ". . . a fundamental alteration in Christian sensibility, from the vision and practice of turning away from the social world in order to seek closer union with God to the vision and practice of working to reform the social world in obedience to God."[8]

Asian Pacific Americans ought to find this a welcome, albeit challenging, message, for there is a fundamental pain and pathos in the Asian Pacific American experience that such a message addresses. Asian Pacific Americans have experienced suffering and injustice in their individual and collective lives. Dislocation, alienation, and brokenness are common denominators, collectively speaking, even today. For example, countless numbers of families continue to be torn asunder by war and political oppression in their homelands or by discriminatory immigration legislation in America. Therefore, it is good to hear that God cares and that healing and restoration to wholeness is possible. The challenge is for us to be active in the godly task of bringing about wholeness, not just spiritually but also materially, for all of creation.

Based on our understanding of the kingdom of God, we now turn to the issues of identity, community, and vocation—three concerns faced by Asian Pacific American young persons.

Identity

Central to all youth development is the matter of identity formation. For Asian Pacific American young people, the establishment of identity includes the issue of ethnicity and the bewildering and pressure-laden complex of forces pulling and pushing them in various directions. We shall consider this from a theological perspective which is informed by contemporary psychosociological understandings.

American Protestantism, as we have seen, has confounded the concepts of being Christian and being American and presumed the two to be virtually the same. This intermingling of ideas and values has been racially and culturally oppressive in suggesting that one could not be Christian or American and hold on to one's own cultural values and traditions. Thus many Asian Pacific American Christians have felt ashamed or guilty at worst, or uncomfortable at best, about their racial identity and cultural heritage. It seemed that becoming Christian required rejection and separation from one's cultural roots. As Violet Masuda, a Japanese American woman, once said in describing her experience as a woman and as a member of a minority group:

> When one is asked to forget personal experiences and feel as another, how can I believe I am created in God's image? I cannot pretend; I cannot live in contradiction; I cannot play a dual role. This is the conflict of identity which plagues many minority people.[9]

Asian Pacific American Christians have had to contend with ideological readings of scriptural passages like Galatians 3:28, "There is neither Jew nor Greek, there is neither slave nor free, there is neither male nor female; for you are all one in Christ Jesus." One interpretation has been that there ought not to be any assertion of racial or ethnic identity, for such an assertion is both unchristian and separatist. In this same vein, the Bible story of Ruth has been cited to show how leaving one's people can be an act of faith. As Ruth said to her mother-in-law: "Entreat me not to leave you or to return from following you; for where you go I will go, and where you lodge I will lodge; your people shall be my people, and your God my God; where you die I will die, and there will I be buried" (Ruth 1:16–17).

Such a theological understanding has its parallels in sociology. It is not surprising, then, that sociologist Rose Hum Lee argued that religious conversion was an important and final stage in the assimilation process and signaled the victory of the host society over the immigrant society.[10] Likewise, Leonard Cain, Jr. saw the existence of ethnic Japanese American churches after World War II as a barrier to the assimilation of Japanese Americans into American society.[11] Protestant denominations also held this view and attempted, after World War II, to close Japanese American churches and integrate Japanese Americans into white churches after they returned to their communities from internment camps. Japanese American Christians themselves debated this issue.

This theological understanding of assimilation reflects not only the confused intermingling of Christian faith and American identity but also the culture-bound and racially biased sociological models and race and ethnic interaction in America. It is not possible to discuss and critique the history of theories of race and ethnicity in America here, but a brief word does need to be said. Essentially, perhaps the most prevalent sociological model since the 1920s has presumed a natural movement of racial and ethnic groups towards assimilation, integration, and/or cultural pluralism. Of course there would be conflict, but the model presumed that conflict would eventually be overcome and disappear. This model and its variations have been heavily criticized in recent years—for example, as reflecting only white ethnic immigrant experience and ignoring the persistence of racism. Another criticism is that this model presumes the existence of a static host society to which all others need to adapt, without ever asking if that host society itself has not been shaped along racial lines and might yet be further shaped. As one critic, Jesse Vazquez, puts it:

> The most commonly held belief on ethnic change suggests that individuals and groups move from a traditional point of reference—identity or orientation—to an Anglo-American point of reference: an inevitable unidirectional process to assimilation . . . . The premise upon which ethnic change theory is based is the notion that time and continuous contact with the dominant society will eventually wash away all traces of cultural differences.[12]

It is not surprising, therefore, that many white Christians are still troubled by the existence of racial ethnic churches, feeling that these should be transitional at best until the day when integrated or multiethnic churches replace them. Such viewpoints, however, are naive with respect to racism and racial dynamics in American society. They ignore the importance of collective identities and their formation and maintenance in community; they lend themselves to what Vazquez terms "Disneyworld" views of race and culture. They also tend to place the blame on racial ethnic groups for not integrating and for choosing to be "different." They do not consider the way institutional racism makes authentic and just pluralism impossible under the existing structures and conditions of society. Moreover, such viewpoints ignore the profound shift in direction that racial ethnic groups have decided to take since the 1950s. As sociologists Michael Omi and Howard Winant argue, the upsurge in racially based movements which began in the 1950s reflects a contest over the social meaning of race.[13] Racial ethnic groups found it both imperative and more meaningful to assert racially based self-definitions. In the end, self-survival and self-dignity for racial ethnic individuals and groups were at stake. As such, the enduring legacy of the past three decades has been the forging and affirmation of collective racial identities. In churches this trend is reflected in the perpetuation of racial ethnic churches and the formation of racial ethnic caucuses.

Along with the affirmation of their identity, racial ethnic groups have found renewed meaning in the scriptural teaching that all peoples are equally children of God, made in the image of God. There are to be no hierarchies based on race and ethnicity. In the story of Peter's dream and encounter with Cornelius (Acts 10) we are told that God shows no partiality and that we are not to treat anyone as "common or unclean." As church educator David Ng (one of the co-authors of this book) has stated, in the Eucharist God declares that all are welcome at the table of the Lord, just as they are. There are no insiders or outsiders. All are invited. The true meaning of Galatians 3:28, then, is not that we must leave our particularities behind or get rid of them, but rather that they do not stand in our way. They cannot be used to block us from participation in God's kingdom. In *One in Christ: The Letter to the Galatians from an Asian American Perspective,* writers Bradford Woo and Michael Angevine show how this Epistle teaches us that we do not have to conform to white church standards to be Christian.[14] The apostle Paul fought against requiring the rite of circumcision of Gentiles who wished to be Christian. That is, they did not have to become Jewish first in order to be Christian (see Acts 15). So too, Asian Pacific Americans need not become "white" or "American" to be Christian.

Asian Pacific American Christians realize that their ethnicity is not a barrier, but rather a gift from God. As we are made in God's image, our ethnic particularities are gifts to celebrate and share. They are also given to us to use for the sake of others. For example, this affirmation of our identity can free others to affirm *their* identities. Different racial ethnic perspectives and resources can help the church to break free from cultural captivity and stale homogeneity. Moreover, such perspectives include social issues that help the church to be more faithful to the vision of the kingdom of God. For example, Asian Pacific American Christians have provided their respective denominations with the opportunity to respond to various racial and civil rights issues, including redress for Japanese Americans interned during World War II, bilingual education, anti-Asian violence, human rights issues in Asia, and the particular concerns of Asian Pacific American women.

In asserting their racial ethnic identity Asian Pacific American Christians have also been able to give new theological meaning to various aspects of their historical experiences. For example, Professor Sang Hyun Lee finds the theological notion of the "pilgrim" particularly meaningful for Korean immigrants. Lee states:

We [Koreans] are a pilgrim people who are on a sacred journey. We have been freed from the hold of one culture or one society; we have been called "to go out" with visions for "a better country" which would be a true homeland not only for ourselves but for all mankind.[15]

Similarly, Japanese American Christians have found this theme expressive of their own experience in America. It is also helpful and significant to look, from a biblical perspective, at the Chinese experience of sojourning in America. In this light, what whites in

nineteenth-century America used as a criticism of the Chinese—i.e., that they were sojourners—could be regarded as a sacred calling. Theologically speaking, a sojourner is called to break free from acceptance of the status quo and the prevailing worldview when seeking the city of God. Bishop Roy Sano explores this theme even further in a study of the Letter to Hebrews and suggests that all of us are called to be "outside the gate."[16]

For Asian Pacific American young people, a major lesson of our discussion of identity is that racial ethnic identity need not be negative. More importantly, at least from a theological perspective, it means that a choice can be made. Some psychologists agree with this matter of choices. Jesse Vazquez states:

We are faced continuously with certain choices which involve a facet or an aspect of our ethnicity: our ethnic selves . . . . These ethnic choices operate on many levels and carry with them varying degrees of psychological and social meaning and consequence. At times, these choices may be quite mundane, routine, and of little consequence. At other times, the choice may produce a deeply significant impact on our ethnicity and ultimately result in a push towards an acculturative life pattern. The choices, whether petty or profound, build upon a lifetime of options which ultimately enhance our ethnic associations (psychologically and socially), or reduce ethnicity in a cumulative sense. New patterns emerge from the choices, and these patterns in turn create new sets of choices on the ethnic continuum.[17]

Sociologist Bok-Lim C. Kim says that what is lacking in the school and home environment of Asian Pacific Americans is "a *conscious articulation* of the decisions, choices, and compromises" that must be made [emphasis mine]. Psychologists Stanley Sue and James Morishima feel that the question of whether one can choose one's identity, or identity is primarily shaped by environmental conditions, has yet to be addressed.[18] No doubt there are various forces pulling and pushing in different directions, some of which can be controlled, some not. For example, genetic characteristics cannot be changed, but some forms of family and societal pressures can. Moreover, one generation can try to change some of these relevant conditions and forces, including racism, so that succeeding generations can at least have better choices and possibilities.

Whatever the answer to Sue and Morishima's question is, with respect to sociology and psychology, the theological breakthrough is that we are children of God, free to be fully human and to make choices based on our Christian values. We are not just historically and sociologically determined and shaped. In this light, we can make choices about ethnic identity, whether to affirm it, reject it, or create new forms of identity. We can negotiate our choice of who we want to be. The decision may not be easy to make or live out, but at least we have a new measuring stick and standard by which to make it. Throughout history Asian Pacific Americans were pressured to assimilate and become "American." The contradiction was that those who tried were never really allowed to succeed, nor were they genuinely accepted into American society. In the late 1960s and early 1970s pressure came from the other side as Asian American militants pushed other Asian Americans to become more conscious about their racial ethnic identities and at times tried to force them into narrow understandings of what being "Asian American" meant. Both pressures were oppressive. The gospel message tells us that there is freedom to make one's own decision about ethnic identity. Whatever the choice, we are still children of God.

Community

While Asian Pacific American identity formation is, to a degree, a matter of individual choice, it is never totally free from influence or pressure. For example, identity can never be individualistically defined. In Asian societies individual identities are formed in the context of community, particularly that of the nuclear and extended family.[19] In Asian societies the group is more important than the individual and the individual is always related to a community. Both of these notions give shape to certain styles of relationship, communications patterns, and formal and informal modes of interaction, including living arrangements (the extended family usually lived together under one roof). Moreover, at least for the Chinese, not only was the family the locus of identity, but the family system served as a prototype for the human community. The state was seen as a superfamily, as the projection of the patriarchal family, and the cosmic order was viewed the same way.[20]

The notion that one's individual identity is inherently and inextricably related to the family or the larger community continues to be taught today. Many Asian Pacific Americans were taught that, in everything they did, they represented their family, their community, and their race. They were admonished never to do anything that would bring shame on their people. In the same vein, many Asian Pacific Americans seldom refer to their individual selves as "I," but use the collective "we." The same dynamic makes them hesitant to assert themselves. It is considered undignified and a bad reflection on the family to be showy. This attitude contrasts with that of western culture, in which individualism and assertiveness are more dominant values. For example, in Western society there is a tendency to validate all experiences in terms of the self—e.g., "I've got to do what is right for me." As another exam-

ple, Asians are more concerned about shame (a collective mechanism) and possible embarrassment to the community than guilt, which is a more important and individualistic mechanism for Westerners. The matter of geographical mobility provides us with another example of the difference between Asians and Westerners. In America, geographical mobility is encouraged and persons are not considered "grown up" until they "leave the nest." In Asian Pacific American communities, however, individuals are encouraged to stay near the rest of the family. Of course there are positive and negative aspects of both the Western emphasis on individualism and the Asian emphasis on familial relationship. Here we are not being judgmental; we are merely pointing out the contrast.

Individualism has been an ingredient in Western Christian theology, perhaps too much so. In contrast, Old Testament thought and psychosocial understandings about the individual were corporate in tone. The whole group, including persons in the past, present, and future, could function as a single individual through any one of its members. Likewise, the individual could represent the whole group, as when Adam's sin led to the condemnation of the human race. So too, we see how Israel is often talked about as if it were a single person, rather than as a nation or people. Corporateness was also a major teaching of the New Testament. There was no ambivalence in Paul's description of the body of Christ and our incorporation into that body. Nor was there hesitation to point out the way the body functions interdependently. An expression of community and corporateness is also recorded in Acts 2:44ff. The church is essentially understood as a community, although modern congregations are sometimes little more than a collection of individuals who happen to be in the same place. The kingdom of God is essentially a corporate and communal state. We also find in the parable of the rich young man (Matthew 19:16-22) a call to move from concern for the self (individual) to concern for others (community) as the requisite move for salvation. Then too, the "cloud of witnesses" mentioned in Hebrews 12:1 might be viewed as community extended back through time (which may be the way Asians understand their ancestors). These biblical views shaped Reformation understandings too. For example, the covenant theme (i.e., that God enters into a covenant relationship with humanity through Jesus Christ), which was central to Puritan teachings, presumed a social dimension in which the individual was part of a holy community. For Asian Pacific American Christians (and to others as well), then, participation in, and commitment to, community is integral to individual identities. In a way, Asian Pacific Americans should have an ingrained cultural predisposition to appreciate biblical teachings about identity and community.

Three aspects are particularly important.

First, commitment to community (whether we refer to the Asian Pacific American community broadly defined or to the Judaic-Christian community) involves taking on the history of that community and incorporating oneself into that history. This can take place by way of memory. Israel was continually reminded in Scripture to "remember" and to recite and rehearse the history of God's involvements with her (e.g., Deuteronomy 26:1-11). For contemporary Christians this "memory" is basically learned and nurtured through worship, education, and participation in the life of the church. When one responds in faith to the faith, the church, and God's people one's own history. So too, Asian Pacific Americans who feel distant from the Asian Pacific American experience can, by learned memory, recover or reclaim their history. As communities can incorporate individuals into their life stream, so individuals can incorporate communities into their being.

Second, most of us belong not just to one community, but to several—for example, to the Samoan, Pilipino, or Taiwanese American community, to our church community, to our neighborhood community, and perhaps to our work community. We also belong to a global community. These different communities have varying degrees of importance in our lives and affect us in different ways. The issue of *which* community is more important to an individual is, like identity, to a large degree, a matter of choice. Christian choice, symbolized in the sacraments of baptism and Communion, incorporate Christians into the body of Christ as their primary community. Yet this choice need not necessarily be in opposition to significant participation in other communities—for example, one's racial ethnic community.

Third, our commitments to community must always be subject to broadening. A mark of maturity is the ability to incorporate, and to be incorporated, into larger communities, as well as into more communities. Such involvement means broadening our concerns to a greater common good. Bishop Sano gives us an example of what this means when he talks about how certain of his experiences in Asia led him to new arenas of participation in Asian human rights matters—matters that he formerly thought were beyond the scope of Asian Pacific American concerns.[21] For another example and from an Asian American women's perspective, Naomi Southard and Rita Nakashima Brock, a United Methodist minister and a Christian Church theologian respectively, state that a primary concern of Asian American women in ministry, given their marginaliza-tion from church and community, is for "full acceptance and participation in community for all . . . . We begin with other Asian American women, and extend this as our hope to all of Creation." The "community of all creation" and "the interconnectedness of all life experienced in ethnic community, in local churches, and in national struggles for justic and international concerns is a fundamental theological assumption for Asian American women."[22]

For Asian Pacific Americans, then, participation in community, particularly the Asian Pacific American community, can be critical for shaping ethnic identity. For Asian Pacific American Christians, this can also be a challenge of faith. Lloyd Wake found this to be the challenge of the book of Esther.[23] Esther is a Jewish woman who has "made it." She has won a "beauty contest" and has become the queen of a non-Jewish country. But in order to succeed, she has to hide her Jewishness (Esther 2:10, 20). Later on, when the regime decides to annihilate all the Jews in the land, Esther is faced with a dilemma. Her uncle Mordecai, who had earlier advised Esther to hide her Jewishness, now confronts her with the need to speak out and intercede, saying, "Think not that in the king's palace you will escape any more than all the other Jews" (4:13). As to her need to act, Mordecai says, "And who knows whether you have not come to the kingdom for such a time as this?" (4:14). Esther's response is positive: "Then I will go to the king, though it is against the law; and if I perish, I perish" (4:16).

Compare the Esther story with the story of Ruth, mentioned earlier. Rather than leave her own people as Ruth did, it was time for Esther to reclaim her identity, to return to her people and save them. So too, Asian Pacific Americans may need to recover their identities and respond to the cries of their communities. We hear this same message in the story of Moses' response to his people's suffering. We read in Hebrews 11:24-25: "By faith Moses, when he was grown up, refused to be called the son of Pharaoh's daughter, choosing rather to share ill-treatment with the people of God than to enjoy the fleeting pleasures of sin."

Vocation

In one sense, Moses was faced with a vocational decision, for our identities and our vocations are related. "Who we are" is tied to "what we do." Of course, all young persons must deal with the issue of vocation. With respect to contemporary Asian Pacific American young persons, recent observations suggest that they are choosing occupations like engineering, business, the hard sciences, and law.[24] Like the general American youth population, pragmatic concerns for actually securing a job, prestigious positions, and good salaries seem to be the overriding factors in these choices. For Asian Pacific American youth these choices are generally consonant with what their parents would hope for their offspring as well. While these are not necessarily wrong choices, there ought to be theological and faith considerations in Asian Pacific American youth vocational decisions.

The word "vocation" comes from the Latin *vocatio* and refers to "call" or "calling." Biblically, it refers to God's call to people to become instruments of divine purpose at work in history and to be recipients of grace and salvation. In the Old Testament this involves calling Israel to be the people of God. But Israel is also called to a servant role. For example, we read in Isaiah 49:1-3:

> Listen to me, O coastlands,
>   and hearken, you peoples from afar.
> The Lord called me from the womb,
>   from the body of my mother he named my name.
> He made my mouth like a sharp sword,
>   in the shadow of his hand he hid me;
> he made me a polished arrow,
>   in his quiver he hid me away.
> And he said to me, "You are my servant,
>   Israel, in whom I will be glorified."

God also calls individuals to particular service—for example, Moses (Exodus 3), Isaiah (Isaiah 6), Jeremiah (Jeremiah 1:4–10), and Amos (Amos 7:14-15). In the New Testament "vocation" refers to calling people to follow Christ, to be incorporated into the church, and to share in Christian hope. We read about Jesus' personal call to Peter and Andrew (Matthew 4:18-22) and God's broader call to all Christians (Romans 8:28-30).[25] Our identity as children of God, then, not only defines our being, but shapes our vocation.

Vocation can be understood as responsible, committed, and faithful response to God's grace. In making decisions about our vocation we need first to discern God's call. Factors to be considered include our talents and the gifts God bestows upon us, the life situations in which we are located, and the needs of the community (including the global one) at this time in history. This latter factor reminds us that our vocations, like our identities, are influenced by our sense of community. Does this or that particular occupation serve a common good? Does it respond to the needs of a particular community? Or does it mainly satisfy individual self-interests? Vocational decisions must also take into account the vision of the kingdom of God. Does this or that particular occupation further the upbuilding of God's kingdom? Does it work toward peace, justice, and righteousness? As we have gained a vision of the kingdom of God, do our vocational activities help others to gain this same vision?

These questions do not imply that everyone must be a minister, social worker, schoolteacher, or human services worker. One of the central teachings of the Reformation was that vocation can be manifested in a variety of occupations. Prior to this, the medieval church believed that only special religious occupations could be considered vocations ("callings"). But Martin Luther taught that people were called to serve God in whatever situation they found themselves. Everyday work was as much a calling as the work of clergy. Luther said that while it looks like a great thing for a monk to renounce the world and pursue a life of asceticism, fasting, and prayer, "it looks like a small thing when a maid cooks and cleans and does other housework. But because God's command is there, even such small work must be praised as a service of God far surpassing the holiness and asceticism of all monks and nuns."[26] Reformer John Calvin, who was more "activist" than Luther in his understanding, said that Christians had a duty to glorify God by way of their occupations. To Calvin, vocation was a way to express obedience to God—obedience which was motivated by gratitude. Whereas, in Luther's thought, one could almost assume that one's occupation serves God and the common good, Calvin would say that one has to make sure it does.[27] Nevertheless, whatever the occupation, the doctrine of "the priesthood of all believers" teaches that there are no hierarchies with respect to vocations. There are also no value differences between "religious" and "secular" work. There are only differences of function.

It is not possible here to discuss which occupations, given our time and circumstances, best serve the demands of vocation as described. The critical issue is that occupational choices must be made in the light of our faith and theological commitments. We need not only to be faithful to God in whatever occupations we find ourselves, but we must also try, as best we can, to seek out occupations which lend themselves to vocational commitments. In making a choice we must seek ways to glorify God and express God's love for all of creation. This requirement involves intentionality and responsibility. Only then are occupation (a specific job) and vocation (God's calling) properly linked. In light of our overall discussion, for many Asian Pacific American Christian youth this may mean taking a good look also at the needs of the Asian Pacific American community. It may also mean considering occupations that require them and allow them, vocationally speaking, to work towards wholeness for all.

There is a necessary caveat to this course of action. Some jobs defy affirmation. There are economic and political conditions under which choices are not possible. Some jobs are, in fact, oppressive and involve "toiling under Pharaoh" in slave-like conditions. For example, we can think of the way Asian laborers were exploited in the past or of the present condition of Asian women garment workers. So, as one pastor, Robert G. Middleton, comments, assembly-line workers, for example, will find it difficult to find anything about their jobs to affirm. "The detestation felt by workers for the conditions under which they labor is fierce and widespread; if their complaints are listened to with sympathy, it is possible to hear in them a cry for elemental rights."[28] This insight helps us to avoid a status quo view of work and reminds us that work conditions and the quality of the workplace for many people need to be improved. We need also to change the conditions that create such working conditions.

Conclusion

In a study of Hebrews 11:23-28 Paul Nagano suggests that Moses was faced with the questions of identity, belongingness, and direction.[29] Nagano poses these same questions for Asian Pacific Americans. We have considered some theological responses to these questions with respect to their impact on Asian Pacific American youth ministries. In the end, theologically speaking, Asian Pacific American youth ministries must challenge, encourage, nurture, and sustain young people as they discover and create identities that:

—are faithful to God's desires for humanity as envisioned in images of the kingdom of God;

—are shaped in the context of community and corporate commitments;

and

—are expressed in vocations that are aimed at a greater common good.

Notes

1. See the lead article by Virstan Choy, Nicholas Iyoya, Warren Lee, and Wesley Woo in *Choosing Sides: The Book of Judges from an Asian American Perspective* (a graded Christian education curriculum published in 1986 by the Asian American Christian Education Curriculum Project, c/o San Francisco Presbytery, 545 Ashbury Avenue, El Cerrito, CA 94530.

2. Arthur Schlesinger, Jr., "The Missionary Enterprise and Theories of Imperialism," in *The Missionary Enterprise in China and America,* ed. John K. Fairbank (Cambridge: Harvard University Press, 1974), p. 363.

3. Roy I. Sano, "Transforming Suffering: Struggling with Life as an Asian American," in *Changing Contexts of Our Faith,* ed. Letty M. Russell (Philadelphia: Fortress Press, 1985), pp. 74–77.

4. Nicholas Wolterstorff, *Until Peace and Justice Embrace* (Grand Rapids: William B. Eerdmans, 1983). p. 69.

5. Walter Brueggemann, "The Earth: A Theology of Earth and Land," *Sojourners* (October 1986):32.

6. Leonardo and Clodovis Boff, *Salvation and Liberation, in Search of a Balance Between Faith and Politics* (Maryknoll, N.Y.: Orbis Books, 1984), pp. 56–57.

7. Allan Boesak, *Black and Reformed: Apartheid, Liberation and the Calvinist Tradition* (Maryknoll, N.Y.: Orbis Books, 1984), p. 24.

8. Wolterstorff, *op. cit.,* p. 11.

9. Violet Masuda, "Amazing Grace," *Radical Religion* 1 (Spring 1974): 45–47.

10. Rose Hum Lee, *The Chinese in the U.S.A.,* (Hong Kong: University Press, 1960), p. 294.

11. Leonard D. Cain, Jr., "Japanese-American Protestants: Acculturation and Assimilation," *Review of Religious Research* 3 (Winter 1982): 115, 119.

12. Jesse M. Vazquez, "The Ethnic Matrix: Implications for Human Service Practitioners," *Explorations in Ethnic Studies* 9 (July 1986):8.

13. Michael Omi and Howard Winant, *Racial Formation in the United States from the 1960s to the 1980s* (New York: Routledge & Kegan Paul, 1986). pp.90–91.

14. *One in Christ: The Letter to the Galatians from an Asian American Perspective* (a graded Christian education curriculum published in 1986 by the Asian American Christian Education Curriculum Project, c/o San Francisco Presbytery, 545 Ashbury Avenue, El Cerrito, CA 94530.

15. Sang Hyun Lee, "Called to Be Pilgrim: Toward a Theology Within a Korean Immigrant Context," in *The Korean Immigrant in America,* ed. Byong-suh Kim and Sang Hyun Lee (Montclair, N.J.: Association of Korean Christian Scholars in North America, Inc., 1980), p. 37.

16. Roy I. Sano, *Outside the Gate: A Study of the Letter to the Hebrews* (New York: General Board of Global Ministries, United Methodist Church, 1982).

17. Vazquez, *op. cit.,* p. 11.

18. Bok-Lim C. Kim is quoted in Stanley Sue and James K. Morishima, *The Mental Health of Asian Americans* (San Francisco: Jossey-Bass, 1982), pp. 122–24.

19. For example, see Antonio J.A. Pido, *The Pilipinos in America* (New York: Center for Migration Studies, 1986), pp. 19, 34–35.

20. Joseph M. Kitagawa, *Religions of the East* (Philadelphia: The Westminster Press, 1976), pp. 43, 80.

21. Sano, "Transforming Suffering," pp. 63–64.

22. Naomi Southard and Rita Nakashima Brock, "The Other Half of the Basket: Asian American Women and the Search for a Theological Home," forthcoming in *Journal of Feminist Studies in Religion,* pp. 7–8 of draft.

23. Roy I. Sano, "Ethnic Liberation Theology: Neo-Orthodoxy Reshaped—or Replaced?" *Christianity and Crisis* (November 10, 1975): 259–60.

24. Young Pai, Deloras Pemberton, and John Worley, "Findings on Korean-American Early Adolescents and Adolescents," School of Education, University of Missouri, January 1987, pp. 46, 55–56.

25. "Vocation," *Interpreter's Dictionary of the Bible,* Vol. 4 (Nashville: Abingdon Press, 1962), pp. 791–92.

26. Robert G. Middleton, "Revising the Concept of Vocation for the Industrial Age," *Christian Century* (October 29, 1986):943.

27. Wolterstorff, *op. cit.,* p. 16; John Dillenberger and Claude Welch, *Protestant Christianity Interpreted Through Its Development* (New York: Charles Scribner's Sons, 1954), p. 234.

28. Middleton, *op. cit.,* p. 944.

29. Paul Nagano, "Identity, Identification, and Initiative: Hebrews 11:23–28," in *The Theologies of Asian American and Pacific Peoples: A Reader,* Roy Sano, compiler (Berkeley: Pacific and Asian American Center for Theology and Strategies, 1976), pp. 220–24.

2

Historical and Cultural Context

by Joan May Cordova

Today's youth live in a world which differs greatly from the one in which their parents were reared. While parents may yearn for the simpler times they have known in the past, youth live in a fast paced, high-tech world of computers, space travel, MTV, designer labels, and more. They're pressured to conform, to achieve, to acquire, and to succeed.

For Asian Pacific Americans, contrasts between the experiences of youth and their parents may be even sharper, particularly if the parents are immigrants. Parental expectations may have been shaped by experiences in cultures where behavior and roles—of parents and children, men and women—were defined more strictly than in their new homeland. Parents held greater authority and commanded a higher degree of respect, while the family remained a primary influence on all areas of youth's life. Today's youth, however, must deal with aspects of American culture which challenge parental control and traditional Asian cultural values.

Consider these glimpses of the world Asian Pacific American youth must face:

> . . . adolescence has never been tougher—with all-time high numbers of teen runaways, pregnancies, imprisonments and suicides . . . . More than 14 million teenagers have driver's licenses, and while 37 states have raised the drinking age, drunk driving is still the leading cause of death in that age group.[1]

> Sedatives are the drug of choice among many Chinese, Japanese, and Vietnamese Americans. According to a recent study initiated by the Asian American Substance Abuse Task Force, Asian teens are experimenting with this drug at such early ages as 11 or 12.[2]

> Stereotypes of Asians in the minds and institutions of the American people are indeed insulting, but for many Asian youth they are also debilitating, separating and isolating. Institutionalized racism in the educational system has denied the history and culture of Asian people in America but for some Asian youth, it has also denied them self-confidence in the validity of their very existence.[3]

> . . . there is something grievously wrong with a culture that values Wall Street sharks above social workers, armament manufacturers above artists . . . more and more young people [are] forced to choose between their ideals and their economic security . . . .[4]

Against this backdrop, Asian Pacific American youth must make tough decisions—not only about what they are to do or become, but about how they are to respond to situations which may involve choices between the values of two cultures.

How will youth respond to parents whose values and experiences differ from theirs? What decisions or compromises may have to be made so that youth and their elders may peacefully live in mutual respect of each other? Which elements of their Asian Pacific American heritage will youth choose to retain and which will they discard? What relationship will youth have to a larger Asian Pacific American community? How will youth respond to issues affecting all Asian Pacific Americans?

There are no easy answers. The thoughts which follow, however, may provide a tool, a mirror to be used in beginning a process of reflecting oneself in relation to the Asian Pacific American experience. We shall seek to identify the various historical themes and elements of Asian Pacific American culture which help to clarify and influence some of the choices and decisions faced by youth. By so doing we hope to enable youth to name and define their own particular Asian Pacific American experiences and to provide them with some background for interpreting current issues affecting Asian Pacific Americans. It is to be hoped that young Asian Pacific Americans will draw upon their understandings of history and culture when faced with decisions relating to their concerns about parents, community, career, or broader Asian Pacific American issues.

Asian Pacific Americans: Who Are They?

Any definition of the umbrella-like term "Asian Pacific American" must emphasize the great diversity among its growing number of distinct national ancestry groups, which include Burmese, Cambodian, Chinese, Pilipino, Hmong, Indian, Indonesian, Japanese, Korean, Laotian, Malaysian, Mien, Pacific Islanders,

Singaporean, Thai, Vietnamese, and others. Although the experiences of some of the groups may overlap at different points in time, each has a distinct culture, language, history.

Even the experiences of persons within a single national ancestry group are likely to vary in relation to the geographic region of their homes, their socioeconomic status, their family background, or their generation of immigration. The first generation includes family members who have emigrated to the United States; the second, American-born children of immigrants; and the third, American-born grandchildren of immigrants. Hence, Asian Pacific Americans—even within the same national ancestry group—perceive and define their experiences differently. Some Asian Pacific Americans may choose to identify themselves as:

Chinese. Chinese American. Japanese American. Issei. Nisei. Sansei. Yonsei. Kibei. Neither. In-between. Pilipino American. Pilipino. Filipino. Pinoy. Korean. Korean American. Vietnamese. Laotian. Hmong. American born. Immigrant. First, second, third, or fourth generation. "Of Asian descent." "Not into labels." "Just a human being." Oriental. Asian American.

And the list continues to grow.

In light of such diversity, many people—including Asian Pacific Americans themselves—find it difficult to use the term "Asian Pacific American." Problems arise when the experiences of one segment of the Asian Pacific American population are inaccurately viewed as representative of all. To avoid this confusion, all generalizations of Asian Pacific Americans must be interpreted with an awareness of the differences in the history, culture, and backgrounds of specific groups.

Given the wide range of experiences within the Asian Pacific American population, why must one consider a collective Asian Pacific American identity at all?

Asian Pacific American youth have been instrumental in forging a collective identity. In response to the civil rights movement and the black and brown identity movements of the late 1960s, Chinese, Japanese, Korean, and Pilipino youth formed alliances on college campuses throughout the United States. Asian American studies courses spawned new research and publication of Asian American history and literature. In one Asian American publication an Asian American student described this self-designated identity as "a rejection of the passive Oriental stereotype and symbol of the birth of a new Asian—one who will recognize and deal with injustices."[5]

The concept of Asian Pacific American identity spread from youth to older adults, from students to workers, from American-born to immigrants. Responding to specific needs of growing Asian Pacific American communities, many rallied around common concerns such as housing, education, the elderly, child care, and employment. Some began to recognize that various Asian national ancestry groups shared a history of struggle against the injustices of racism. Asian American coalitions formed to advocate and work for justice.

Asian Pacific Americans recognize a necessary distinction between their experiences as a racial ethnic minority group in North America, and the experiences of Asians living in Asia. For too long, Asian Pacific Americans—even those whose families have been in American for several generations—have been unjustly regarded as foreigners. In the same way that the history and culture of blacks, Europeans, Mexicans, and others are recognized as part of an indigenous American experience that is influenced by but separate from their country of origin, so Asian Pacific Americans—with their own history and culture—must no longer be viewed as foreigners.

As the experience of Asian Pacific American immigrants evolves into the second or third generation, some persons feel that distinctions between various Asian Pacific American groups seem to diminish. Asian Pacific American young people often find that they have more in common with persons of their own generation than those of their own racial ethnic group. They choose to identify themselves broadly as Asian Pacific American rather than by the narrower terminology of their specific ancestry.

Young people and many others also recognize that there is a distinct Asian Pacific American culture that may have its roots in specific Asian cultures but has developed characteristics that are unique to the total Asian Pacific American experience. Cultural expressions—in literature, music, theater, film, community organizations, and activities—also incorporate memories and visions that Asian Pacific Americans hold collectively.

Some people feel that Asian Pacific Americans should be allied with each other for political reasons. As a coalition of a greater number of people, they form a stronger base of potential political power.

Thus, despite the sometimes problematic "Asian Pacific American" designation, its use will undoubtedly continue.

Why Should Youth Learn Asian Pacific American History?

Why must Asian Pacific American youth know their history? One Pilipino American researcher/writer, Dorothy Cordova, responds this way:

America is made up of many different kinds of people. I want to be part of that whole without having to deny myself and what I am. I want my grandchildren to have a chance to know about the history of our people so that they can be proud of who they are.[6]

Frequently omitted from American textbooks, the history of Asian Pacific Americans must be told to youth. Their history is replete with events which enable them more fully to appreciate and understand the experiences of their elders. Knowledge of history provides youth with not only a framework for interpreting their own experiences but also a tool for analyzing current issues affecting Asian Pacific Americans as a whole.

Underlying the presentation of history is the goal that youth develop a *sense* of history; that youth feel a proud sense of continuity with the past, recognizing that their experiences are linked to those of many generations of Asian Pacific Americans. Youth are personally connected with this history through the experiences of their own families, beginning at a point where one's first family member came to America. Woven together, the family histories of national ancestry groups form the common story of a variety of people. These strands of Chinese, Japanese, Pilipino, Korean, Vietnamese, and other groups' experiences create a broader picture of Asian Pacific American history, a significant piece of the total fabric of American history.

While the history of each national ancestry group may have distinct characteristics within specific time periods, the strands often overlap and intersect. Common themes emerge as each group responds to American and economic interests and to the dynamics of institutional racism.

The historical narrative which follows is not intended to provide a comprehensive view of all Asian Pacific American history. However, the nineteenth-century history of the earliest Asian Pacific American groups—Chinese, Pilipino, Japanese, Korean—will illustrate the cyclical patterns of the United States' efforts at stimulating Asian immigration (often through the bold recruitment of laborers), exploiting Asian Pacific American laborers in the development of the West, restricting Asians' rights through numerous pieces of anti-Asian legislation, and eventually excluding specific Asian groups from immigration. The overlapping strands of history exemplify how, as one Asian group was excluded, another Asian group was recruited to take its place in the demands for labor.

To convey a sense of how history comprises more than mere events and legislation, quotes of individuals who have lived through these years will be interspersed throughout the narrative. It is hoped that youth readers will view history as the active lives of people—people working, feeling, responding, celebrating, envisioning, overcoming—for among them are persons in our own communities, our grandparents, our parents, and our contemporaries.

The following questions will aid in analyzing one's own family history or the history of a specific national ancestry group:

• Why did they come to America? What expectations did they bring?
• What social conditions did they encounter here?
• How did they respond to conditions encountered?
• What types of political and economic discrimination did they face?
• How did their racial differences affect discrimination?
• How did the American public seem to respond to their immigrant group?
• How did the immigrants feel about their treatment by the public?

As youth begin to acquire knowledge of Asian Pacific American history, they are encouraged to reflect on how history influences or contributes to an understanding of their individual experiences. Each might ask:

• How does history relate to me?
• How will knowledge of my family's history enable me to understand their expectations?
• How does an analysis of Asian Pacific American history help me to understand current issues?
• How does an awareness of past and present injustice influence my actions and values in response to current issues?

Asian Pacific American History: Beginnings

The history of Asian Pacific peoples in America begins with dreams that life in a new land will be better than life in the ancestral home. Some hope that life in America will yield resources that will enable them to return home to better their families' lives. Others, especially the young, are led by the spirit of adventure to journey far from home, taking great risks.

Imagine life in the Philippines, still a colony of Spain in the 1700s: Spanish domination and exploitation has invaded every area of Pilipino life. Forced labor, severe taxation, a weak economy, and the sovereignty of the Spanish Catholic church oppresses everyone. Corruption abounds. Nevertheless, the Manila galleon trade flourishes. A few adventurous Pilipinos sail with the Spanish crews. Glimpsing freedom from the harsh treatment of their brutal Spanish masters, they jump ship to build villages in southeastern Louisiana. In 1763 theirs become the first Asian settlements in the United States.[7]

The Chinese American Experience

The Chinese are the first Asian immigrant group to settle in the United States in large numbers. In the mid-1800s China suffers from political unrest (the Opium War and Taiping Rebellion), banditry, the collapse of the agricultural economy, a disastrous flood, and an increase in population. Physical survival is difficult and is a "push factor" motivating many to leave the country, despite the risks of agreeing to work for years in America just to pay the large debts incurred for passage. The California Gold Rush of 1848 and the overall need to develop the West creates a demand for cheap labor. More Chinese arrive, twenty thousand in 1852 alone. Providing Chinese labor becomes a thriving trade. Reports by early Chinese pioneers in the West also spur interest in the possibilities there:

> The glamour of gold outweighed the dangers in the first few years . . . . As lucky miners showed the gold dust to friends and relatives at homecoming banquets, reports of the fabulous *Gum Shan,* the "Mountain of Gold," across the water spread like flames through dry underbrush.[8]

At first the Chinese had not intended to stay. A few students plan to use western knowledge to benefit China. Others—sojourners clinging to dreams of making fortunes in America before returning home as wealthy men—endure intolerable conditions. So that they may send money home to support their families in China, they accept the only jobs available to them—menial labor in cities, farms, fields, and mines. Such employment offers the lowest pay, no security, and harsh working conditions, and sometimes incites violent reactions among those who resent Chinese labor. Many white Americans now feel threatened by the growing presence of Chinese. Some forty thousand Chinese miners are driven out of the country that year. California enacts four separate miners' taxes for Chinese. This legislation is the first of many laws intended to discriminate against the Chinese. In addition to the miners' tax, they must pay a "police tax," fishing and shellfish taxes, and more. The Chinese suffer beatings, burnings, robberies, brutal attacks, lynchings, and murders.

Immigration from China drops off slightly until construction of the transcontinental railroad demands workers, particularly for the most dangerous jobs. It is the Chinese who must endure hard labor with pick and shovel through sun or snow, on cliffs, in caves. Many die. In all, some twelve thousand Chinese work on the railroads, which would not have been completed without their labor. Yet, as crowds celebrate the completion of this first transcontinental railroad, no one acknowledges the sacrifices of the Chinese.

Still, the Chinese continue to work hard, and at one point in the 1880s they comprise almost 75 percent of the agricultural work force in California. The anti-Chinese movement grows, this time formally directed by white labor unions. One San Francisco labor leader, Dennis Kearney, effectively organizes discontented white workers and others. One rallying point is the chant, "The Chinese must go!" Congress passes the Chinese Exclusion Act of 1882, prohibiting further immigration of nearly all Chinese. (This act and the amendments to it remain in effect for sixty-one years.) Thus, Chinese become the first immigrants to be excluded by federal law from entry into the United States on the basis of their nationality.

Anti-Chinese legislation continues. Chinese are ineligible for citizenship, and laborers are not allowed to bring their wives from China. Chinese are also prohibited from owning land and real estate, ineligible to apply for business licenses, and forbidden to testify in court against a white person.

Yet the Chinese survive. Some Chinese hold on to their dreams of returning to China. A few men go back and marry, return to the United States, and eventually send for their wives and families. Others, faced with a disproportionate ratio (18:1) of eligible Chinese men to women in the United States, never marry. They spend their lives as bachelors in America, often in Chinatown communities.

The Japanese American Experience

Because of the Chinese Exclusion Act, the United States looks elsewhere for another labor supply. It turns to Japan, where historically foreign trade was kept to a minimum until 1853, when Commodore Perry in Tokyo Bay pressured Japan to agree to diplomatic and trade relations with the United States. Other conditions are ripe for emigration, including changes in the Japanese feudal system during the Meiji era, which have caused economic disruptions. One immigrant recalls:

> I remember the 'rice riot' best. The wealthier families which had a large crop of rice were all burned out. Some townsmen did it. In those days the price of rice went skyhigh, and the poor had a hard time. The poor took their revenge on the rich and set the fire.[9]

Japanese share the dream of many immigrants—to make a better life for themselves through hard work. Many come to pursue their dreams abroad and then return home with the resources to improve their families' lives. Others are trying to escape the military draft. Still others come to learn about the West so as to build a better Japan.

Some emigrate by way of Hawaii, even while it is still an independent kingdom, signing years of their lives away in contracts binding them to work on American-owned sugar plantations. Little do they know that many will be mistreated, sometimes being made to work as slaves. Some live in better conditions; they choose to stay in Hawaii, working and saving to become self-employed. Others move on to live and work in the continental United States. There many Japanese find work in the railroads, lumber mills, mines, and fish canneries. Some work as houseboys—caring for the homes of English-speaking Americans. They often move to wherever work may be found. They labor on farms until harvest, then move to cities for new jobs in the winter. The Japanese continue to dream of a better life. Some find that they cannot save the fortune which they need in order to return to Japan. Many choose to stay in America.

As skilled, experienced farmers, many of the Japanese look for ways to start their own farms and businesses. They begin by sharecropping a farm with a landowner's help. Some lease land until they are able to buy their own. Despite the fact that they can only afford to buy land which many other farmers find unsuitable for farming, the Japanese achieve success through hard work and skill.

> At one point the Japanese provided 80% of the celery labor, 70% of the asparagus, and 90% of the garden labor. The Japanese in California introduced the lucrative rice culture into the Sacramento Valley and also turned the vast marsh land in the Stockton area into one of the state's richest agricultural regions.[10]

Now the Japanese become unfortunate victims of the hostility and resentment once directed at the Chinese. In 1905, after Japan has defeated Russia in the Russo-Japanese war, the *San Francisco Chronicle* headlines read: "The Yellow Peril—How the Japanese Crowd Out the White Race." Other articles in this series continue to stir up anti-Japanese feelings which are not limited to California. Many forces opposed to Japanese immigration organize the Asiatic Exclusion League with this objective: "The preservation of the Caucasian race upon American soil . . . necessitates the adoption of all possible measures to prevent or minimize the immigration of Asiatics to America."[11]

The San Francisco Board of Education suddenly calls for the segregation of Japanese, Chinese, and Korean children into a separate school. This ordinance, however, is never enforced. In 1907 President Roosevelt negotiates the Gentlemen's Agreement, a pledge by the government of Japan to restrict emigration of laborers to the United States. Immigration drops from ten thousand to twenty-five hundred a year. One provision of the Gentlemen's Agreement, however, benefits the Japanese. Although women comprise only 4 percent of the resident Japanese population in the United States at the time, the Gentlemen's Agreement allows additional women to enter the states as "picture brides." This enables the sex ratio to become gradually more balanced, reaching 34 percent by 1920 and increasing the number of native-born Japanese American children.

Anti-Japanese sentiments grow as California adopts the Alien Land Act in 1913, forbidding all aliens, or noncitizens, to own land. Eleven other states pass similar laws. Like other Asian immigrants, the Japanese are now prevented by law from becoming American citizens or buying land. Yet some find a way: they simply purchase land in the names of corporations of whites who act as trustees, or in the names of their children who are American citizens by birth. Another law, passed in 1920, closes the door to this strategy by prohibiting corporations or trustees to own land for others. Such legislation has an adverse effect on Japanese farms.

Organized labor groups and politicians continue to raise anti-Japanese feelings. The Ku Klux Klan is on the rise as well. Finally, in 1924 the federal government passes the Immigration Quota Act, which, among other provisions, completely stops all immigration from Japan. This act also worsens international relations between the United States and Japan. Ineligible for citizenship and not allowed to own land, the Japanese in America raise their families in isolated communities. Refused service in beauty parlors, barbershops, hotels, and restaurants run by white Americans, the Japanese develop their own businesses to serve their community.

> "Do you cut Japanese hair?"
> "Can we come swim in the pool? We're Japanese."
> "Will you rent us a house? Will the neighbors object?"
> These were the kinds of questions we asked in order to avoid embarrassment and humiliation. We avoided the better shops and restaurants where we knew we would not be welcome.[12]

It is in this climate that the United States and Japan enter World War II. Certain pressure groups in California see this as a time to diminish competition from Japanese American farmers. A number of organized growers begin petitioning their congressmen for the evacuation of the Japanese.

Shocked by the bombing of Pearl Harbor, other organizations such as veterans' groups and Native Sons of the Golden West also demand that the Japanese be interned. The media are reporting fantastic rumors of Japanese sabotage, even though no evidence of disloyalty or sabotage is documented. (Not a single incident has ever been proved.)

President Roosevelt issues Executive Order 9066, which authorizes military commanders to prescribe areas from which persons may be excluded. Directed solely at people of Japanese ancestry, the order results in the forced relocation of more than 120,000 men, women, and children—most of whom are American citizens. Although the United States is also at war with Germany and Italy, no efforts are made to relocate Germans or Italians in this country. As Casey McWilliams observes, "Mass evacuation was not the product of war-time hysteria; it was the logical end-product, the goal of a strategy of dominance which began forty years earlier. . . ."[13]

Not allowed to prove their innocence, the Japanese follow orders to leave their homes on the West Coast. A few successfully manage to move voluntarily outside the restricted zones, but the majority must hastily sell or dispose of all household belongings that cannot be carried in the two suitcases allowed per person.

> Many tears were shed as people sadly left their homes behind . . . . When they arrived at these [relocation] centers, they found the grounds enclosed by barbed wire fences. Soldiers were on duty at the entrances, and sentries with guns and bayonets were posted in the guard towers around the camp. It was a frightening sight.[14]

For most of the war, the Japanese endure life behind barbed wire. They cope with little privacy, long lines for food, the disruption of normal family life, and the knowledge that their constitutional rights of liberty and justice as American citizens are being violated. They suffer staggering economic losses of homes, property, businesses, and crops.

Despite all this hardship, many Japanese still prove their loyalty to the United States. Young men volunteer as soldiers in the 442nd Regional Combat Team, fighting for their country in Italy and France with the motto "Go for Broke!" Winning more than eighteen thousand individual decorations for valor, they become the most decorated group of soldiers in World War II. After the war, the Japanese Americans return to rebuild their lives once more, often beginning with much less than they had previously earned.

Things are different in Hawaii. Throughout the war, despite Hawaii's strategic geographic position in the Pacific, not a single Japanese American in Hawaii is interned. As a powerful agricultural labor force, Japanese Americans are crucial to Hawaii's economy. However, there is also a Korean factor in Hawaii.

The Korean American Experience

Earlier, in the years 1900–1905, Japanese agricultural workers had conducted thirty-four strikes in Hawaii. At this point the Hawaiian Sugar Planters Association (HSPA) has begun to explore alternate possibilities for recruiting labor. They turn to Korea, where the United States has signed the Treaty of Amity and Commerce (also called the Chemulpo Treaty) of 1882, establishing diplomatic and trade relationships between the United States and Korea.

Although the first Korean immigrants—mostly diplomats, political refugees, students and merchants—have arrived in America much earlier, Koreans do not emigrate in significant numbers until after 1903 as a result of recruitment by the Hawaiian sugar planters, the encouragement of Christian missionaries in Korea, the drought in Pyongyang province, and a history of regional factionalism. Some seven thousand Koreans settle in the Hawaiian Islands as plantation laborers between 1902 and 1905—Korea's principal emigration period. Most of these are peasants and laborers who have lost their means of livelihood in Korea as a result of bad crops or government exploitation. Unlike those who will emigrate from Korea later, this group is motivated by Korea's impoverished economy, and arrives with few professional skills.

The influence of Christian missionaries in Korea must not be taken lightly. In 1904 about 174 Western missionaries of fourteen denominations are found in Korea. The number rises to 205 in 1909, and of the 77 percent who are Protestant, nearly all are Americans.

In Korea's semiofficial period of emigration, between 1905 (when the nation passed into Japanese control) and 1940, a few hundred political refugees arrive in the United States, along with students coming for advanced studies. Many leaders of the Korean community in America emerge from these groups and become the core of the Korean independence movement outside Korea. They form community organizations, build churches, begin Korean language schools, start businesses, and raise funds.

The uniqueness of the Korean American experience is related to the Korean independence movement, which is strongly supported by most Korean immigrants in America. Many feel that they should work together to achieve a common goal. For many years (1905–1945) this goal is independence for Korea.

"Picture brides" also arrive during this period. Recall that for Koreans, as for other Asian groups, the first immigrants were male plantation workers. Seeking companionship and family life, many of these men mail photographs of themselves (sometimes deceptively posing as younger than they really are) home to Korea. Women pledge to marry men they know only through their photographs, and embark on long journeys to meet their husbands. Though many young women are shocked to discover that their husbands are old men, nevertheless families and communities grow out of these marriages.

Koreans in America, unfortunately, will be subjected to the same hostile sentiments experienced by the Japanese. Both the 1907 Gentlemen's Agreement Act and the 1924 Exclusion Act will restrict immigration for Koreans also. One Korean American historian, Bong-youn Choy, describes the plight of Korean Americans this way:

> However, the Korean population in America was very small compared with that of the Japanese or Chinese. The total number of Koreans in the United States never exceeded ten thousand, including students, until the end of the Second World War. Koreans were sometimes called "invisible Americans." Often they were regarded as being either Chinese or Japanese because their family names were the same as the Chinese and their physical appearance resembled both. Koreans in America were a forgotten people indeed until the Korean War.[15]

The Philippine American Experience

Another Asian immigrant group recruited to fill the void in the labor market first caused by the Gentlemen's Agreement with Japan in 1907 are the Filipinos. Like other Asian immigrants, Pilipinos long to improve their lives through hard work and education which will be the basis for the fulfillment of dreams: to send money home to improve family life, and to instill family pride in the son who had done well. Unlike other Asian immigrants, however, Pilipinos do not emigrate from a foreign country. Following the end of the Spanish-American War in 1898, the Philippine Islands have become an American colony, remaining under control of the United States until independence comes in 1946. To many people this is the controversial American doctrine of Manifest Destiny at work. During these years American teachers in the Philippines reinforce American ideals of freedom, equality, and opportunity. In the process, Americans educate a generation of Pilipinos away from the islands. A few Pilipinos from the wealthy class travel to the United States from 1907 to 1919. These government-sponsored Philippine students return with favorable reports of their life in American universities.

In 1907 HSPA brings two hundred Pilipino laborers to work in Hawaiian sugar plantations. Large-scale recruitment follows as HSPA entices many with the promises of "good job opportunities" described in lectures and movies which actually misrepresent plantation life. When the Immigration Act of 1924 excludes Japanese and Chinese from immigration, no restrictions are placed on Pilipinos because they are classified as American "nationals," neither aliens nor citizens. In all, about 150,000 Pilipinos leave the Philippines for Hawaii or the mainland United States from 1907 to 1930.[16] Growers find single, Pilipino immigrant men to be "desirable laborers" who adapt to the demand for "stoop labor" on the West Coast. Pilipino labor becomes a key factor in the development of lettuce, asparagus, celery, and table grape industries.

> When they were first recruited, they were paid the lowest rate which migratory labor received. Like the other racial groups, their isolation was exploited to beat down wage rates. In certain lines, as for example in the asparagus fields, the growers were enabled to use, when Pilipino labor was introduced, more men per acre. . . ." As might have been expected, the use of more men per acre had the effect of decreasing the average daily earnings of the men employed while it increased the return per acre, to the grower.[17]

Soon, anti-Pilipino incidents mark the beginning of a larger anti-Pilipino movement. As early as 1928, Congressman Richard Welch of California introduces a bill in the House of Representatives prohibiting further immigration from the Philippines by reclassifying Filipinos as "aliens." Americans are divided on this issue: some advocate Philippine independence so that Filipinos can be legally excluded as aliens; others want the United States to retain possession of the Philippines to protect American commercial interests.

The Tydings–McDuffie Act (also referred to as the Philippine Independence Act) of 1934 solves this dilemma. Under this law the Philippines will become a commonwealth of the United States for a specified ten years, after which it may become an independent nation. At the same time, this act limits Filipino immigration to only fifty per year. Soon anti-Filipino factions also want the deportation of Filipinos and sponsor the Repatriation Act which allows Filipinos to return to their islands with transportation expenses paid by the United States government. Those taking advantage of this will not be allowed to return to the United States. Only 2,190 Filipinos return to the Philippines under this act.

Though initially recruited to work as farm laborers, many Pilipinos find work in canneries, in homes, or on the sea; a few work in barbershops, restaurants, dance halls, and other small businesses. One Philippine American pioneer recalls:

> I noticed that all the low class jobs were filled by foreigners, mostly Filipinos or Chinese. I didn't feel any job discrimination. But it seems that even college graduates you know, could never get a good job like the others. Even if you were a college graduate you could still be a dishwasher during those times.[18]

Despite a high ratio of men to women—fourteen to one—some Filipinos manage to marry and raise families. Many others grow old in America, spending their twilight years alone.

World War II creates new alternatives for Filipinos. At first those who volunteer for military service are barred from registration for lack of citizenship status.

On January 3, 1942, however, the national headquarters of the Selective Service System issues the following instructions to all local boards: "All registrants who are citizens of the Philippine Commonwealth are deemed nationals of the United States and shall be reclassified in the same manner as citizens of the United States." By February 1942 the Secretary of War announces the formation of the First Filipino Infantry Battalion, United States Army, stationed at San Luis Obispo, California.

During World War II—with China and the Philippines allied against Japan—the United States government repeals its Chinese Exclusion Act in 1943, allowing a little over one hundred Chinese immigrants to enter each year. In 1946, foreign-born Filipinos who entered the country before the Tydings–McDuffie Act can become naturalized citizens. Finally, in 1952, the Immigration and Nationality Act, which provides that all races are eligible for citizenship, is passed.

Asian Pacific American History Since World War II

Since world War II the United States' cycle of stimulating immigration, exploiting labor, and limiting the rights of immigrants has not been so clearly defined as in the nineteenth century. In recent years the political and economic dynamics of international relations have become more complex. Yet, in the same way that Asian labor was recruited to develop the growing industrial economy of the 1800s, new sources of Asian labor are still sought as the American economy moves from a manufacturing to a service and information society. American intervention in Asia, often resulting in the political and economic instability of Asian nations, serves to stimulate the flow of Asian labor into the United States.

The Immigration and Naturalization Act of 1965 abolished quotas based on national origins and allowed a maximum of twenty thousand persons per year from each Asian country. Immediate relatives of American citizens, including minor children, spouses, and parents, could enter without numerical limitations. Within the immigration limits, preference is given to other relatives and to workers with skills deemed necessary to the American economy.

"Physicians, nurses, dentists, and pharmacists from the Philippines and Korea were actively recruited during the 1960s and early 1970s, when there was a severe shortage of U.S. health professionals."[19] Once these professionals arrived in the United States, however, many found that they could not pass state licensing exams because of differences in language and medical practices. Lobbying efforts of American professional societies succeeded in toughening licensing requirements. As a result of these efforts, many Asian immigrant professionals find themselves underemployed.

> On the whole, those Korean scientists who were educated in American institutions are well established. . . . Among the Korean professionals, Korean-educated medical doctors, pharmacists, and nurses who failed to pass State Board Examinations. . . are forced to find jobs as clerks, technicians, or nurse's aides. . . in order to support their families. . . . Most find themselves in jobs that are inconsistent with their qualfications and experience and that pay low wages.[20]

Changes in immigration laws have led to dramatic alterations in the Asian Pacific American population. Asian immigration jumped to 34 percent of the total immigrant population in 1979, and reached 48 percent of all entering immigrants by 1984. Groups such as Koreans and Pilipinos, which had historically been outnumbered, are now among the fastest growing. Backgrounds and expectations of recent immigrants are more varied than those of earlier generations. Many are able to come with their families and intend to stay. A higher percentage of immigrants are educated professionals, responding to the professional and technical preferences established by American immigration and naturalization quotas. Although there are relatively more Asian immigrants of professional backgrounds than in earlier times, there are still high numbers of unskilled workers.

> Examination of the immigration of the sixties reveals that the ease of entrance into American society is still strongly affected by the social background of the immigrant. The relatively painless assimilation of recent, upper-class Chinese immigrants, thus, has not been duplicated by an equally large portion (nearly half) of Chinese who enter the United States in the status of service workers, machine operatives, craftsmen, and household workers.[21]

Many recent Asian immigrants, not only Chinese, still struggle for survival in the United States. They work long hours for low pay, struggle to learn English, live in ghetto communities (where growing populations strain the facilities of existing service institutions), and find it difficult to obtain adequate health care and social services. Still, many immigrant families make sacrifices and work hard, with hope that their children will fulfill their dreams through the benefits of an American education.

American involvement in Vietnam, Cambodia, and Laos, with the resulting political and economic instability of these countries created a mass exodus of refugees to the United States. In April 1975 a massive evacuation occurred during the fall of Saigon. Generals and high government officials, businessmen, and landowners fled in the initial panic. Other farmers, fishermen, shopkeepers, soldiers, students—some

131,000—also left. Many of those who fled from Vietnam lost family members or had to leave them behind.

> The evacuation procedure was itself an extremely stressful experience and resulted in what was described as a general state of shock for many. . . . [They] consistently portrayed a picture of fear, trauma, low morale and chronic stress as a result of personal hardships and the witnessing of many deaths by enemy gunfire, boarding accidents, thirst, starvation and other causes.[22]

While in resettlement camps, most refugees waited for sponsorship by individuals or organizations. In general, sponsors furnished refugees with free housing, financial assistance, assistance in job seeking, and moral support. Although there are some examples of success among Vietnamese in the United States, many are still struggling with daily adjustment and survival.

As of 1985, the Asian American population—excluding Pacific Islanders—exceeded 5.1 million,[23] and it continues to grow. America must now expand its definition of Asian Pacific Americans to include our most recent immigrants:

> In place of doctors and lawyers looking for higher salaries, the newest Asian-Americans include Amerasian youth and their single mothers, 150,000 highly traumatised Cambodian refugees, Vietnamese boat people, Hmong tribespeople from the mountains of Laos, and others who had little or no schooling in their native lands and limited exposure to Western ways.[24]

As the presence of these most recent Asian immigrants enriches the diversity of the Asian Pacific American population, their special needs in education, housing, health care, and other services also pose new challenges to American institutions. It is unfortunate, however, that as heightened immigration creates a population with greater needs, the media inaccurately portray an image of Asian Pacific Americans as "the model minority," a group which achieves unprecedented gains in economic and educational status. Research proves that this "model minority" myth is false. Although a few Asian Pacific Americans have made significant economic gains, the majority have not. Statistics indicating that Asian Pacific Americans have a high median family income often do not take into account the number of persons working in each household, or the number of hours worked by family members. Considering these facts, Asian Pacific Americans may very well be working longer hours for less pay. In regard to educational achievement, while there are those Asian Pacific American students gaining access to top American universities, there are others being denied essential English-language instruction, as well as those who are dropping out of school at alarming rates.

In the late 1980s anti-Asian violence has occurred in more than just isolated incidents. A white unemployed auto worker blamed Vincent Chin, a Detroit Chinese American, for causing unemployment (thinking Chin was a Japanese) and bludgeoned him to death. In Davis, California, on a high school campus where the White Students' Union distributed white supremacy literature, classmates stabbed Thong Hy Hung, a Vietnamese student.

Legislation which threatens the existence of bilingual voting rights, bilingual education, and other bilingual services was recently passed (1986) in several states. Immigration reform is again a current issue, because the American economy is in transition; this time from a manufacturing to a service and information society.

Recall now the early history of Asian Pacific Americans: a cycle of recruitment, exploitation, violent acts directed at the most recent immigrants, and the limiting of immigrants' rights. Recall, too, how the anti-Chinese violence of the late 1800s was a result of a shifting economy.

What conclusions may be drawn about the political and economic forces that shape current issues today?

How then must we respond?

Asian Pacific American Culture

Many people perceive Asian Pacific American culture to be comprised of New Year's celebrations with dragons and fireworks, dances using bamboo sticks or fans, martial arts, curious artifacts, exotic costumes, and delicious food. Indeed, "cultural theme weeks" in many schools and communities do highlight these activities. Although all of these cultural expressions are necessary—for group visibility, for celebration, for nurturing pride in heritage, and for keeping traditions alive—youth need to know that their own Asian Pacific American culture encompasses much, much more.

History teaches us that past and present-day Asian immigrants have often faced unusually difficult circumstances in the United States, including poverty, violence against Asians, inadequate housing, alienation, and strains on family life (or sometimes the absence of family life). To survive, many Asian immigrants have drawn upon elements of their culture—family and community relationships, language, religion, values, traditions, recreation, art—to sustain them.

Rooted in the individual and collective memories of a people, culture evolves through the interaction of memory with daily experience. For Asian Pacific Americans, culture often varies according to one's generation of immigration as well as one's national ancestry group. Culture, for Asian immigrants, involves a unique dynamic of having one's cultural memories rooted in a homeland abroad—in Asia—while facing realities of life in the United States. For successive Asian Pacific American generations, cultural expressions may develop out of memories of growing up amidst two cultures. Some persons who strongly identify with a collective Asian Pacific American experience are now shaping an Asian Pacific American culture that incorporates elements of the collective memories and future visions of all Asian Pacific Americans.

Before continuing to describe Asian Pacific American culture, one must first clarify the distinction between "traditional culture" and "Asian Pacific American culture." For our purposes, elements of a culture that each national ancestry group has experienced overseas—for example, the Chinese culture in China, Vietnamese culture in Vietnam, and so forth— will be defined as traditional culture. Asian Pacific American culture, distinct and separate from Asia, is lived and experienced on American soil. Validated by generations of Asian Pacific American experience, this authentic Asian Pacific American culture incorporates elements of traditional Asian culture with the dynamics of living as racial ethnic minorities in America.

Aspects of traditional Asian culture, Asian Pacific American culture, and the dominant (white) American culture influence the lives of today's youth. Youth need to be aware of the differences among these cultures in order to understand the perspectives of their elders, and to identify appropriate responses to cross-cultural situations. Differences in cultures need not be perceived only as a source of dissonance; knowledge of cultural differences can provide a wider range of possibilities for situational responses.

Cultural Memories

To understand the Asian Pacific American culture more fully, one must begin by understanding its people, for the values and assumptions of a people determine the significance of cultural activities in their lives. Youth need to know more than just descriptions of cultural activities; they need to know what these cultural activities and expressions mean, and have meant, to generations of Asian Pacific American people. One student researcher reflects on what might be learned about the meaning of culture through an interview with Asian Pacific American pioneers now in their seventies and eighties:

> My questions elicit selected memories, those deemed most important after a lifetime. Some memories are of a homeland and people which they may never see again. Eyes, glazed with tears at times, are bright—reflecting strong spirits, determination, visions, humor, pain. Their voices are rising and falling with emotion; they remember the attitudes, expectations, and values with which they've confronted American life. Their words— sometimes in their first language—describe obligations, commitments, responsibilities, feelings, and struggles which shaped relationships with parents, family, community, and friends here and abroad. Deeply moved by all that they've shared with me, I feel that their eyes, voices, presence, and words convey the spirit with which they've lived.[25]

Here, in the memories which reveal the sensibilities of a people, lies the essence of Asian Pacific American culture. Memories of a people hold the values, attitudes, relationships with family and community, languages, definitions and categories, and the traditions that comprise their culture. Asian Pacific American people have actively drawn upon these memories to create new responses to life in America. By remembering elements of traditional Asian culture, then by expressing these in new forms in the United States, Asian Pacific Americans have created—and still continue to create—a vital culture of their own.

The importance of a people's memories increases when one considers the degree of separation from one's home which characterizes the Asian Pacific American experience. Through history and in recent years, Asian immigrants to the United States have faced periods of separation from homelands some would never see again and from family—recently married wives and husbands, picture brides, children born abroad, parents, and others. Experiences of separation may have been abrupt, the consequences of war or of tragedy, or they may have been well-planned migrations, intended to only be temporary. No matter what the circumstances, all separations were filled with uncertainty. For many Asian Pacific American immigrants, their memories would become all that remained of the lives they once led. The cultural activities and expressions they eventually create in America become acts of remembering valued elements of traditional Asian cultures.

Asian Pacific Americans' cultural memories often focus on differences in the dynamics of relationships between people: the obligations, expectations, responsibilities, and respect that individuals hold toward one another; the social structures that define relationships; the traditions and rituals that nurture relationships; and the many activities that create and affirm bonds between people.

The Asian Family

In traditional Asian cultures, the family is the primary unit of social structure. Although some of the more general themes related to most traditional Asian families will be described here, one must remember that specific roles and family characteristics will vary according to one's national ancestry group, generation of immigration, and individual family background. Care must therefore be taken to avoid stereotyping when ascribing traditional cultural values of Asians in general to specific people or situations. Youth should be encouraged to learn about the attitudes, values, and traditions of their own families and national ancestry groups.

One's family is of primary importance in most traditional Asian cultures. Roles, relationships, values, and traditions often stem from the family structure. Through family relationships, parents model and interpret cultural values for youth. Among these values is a collective rather than individual orientation. Family members often have a sense of collective responsibility for each other, and for the extended family. Having interdependent roles, they feel that what happens to one member affects the rest of the family.

In light of this collective orientation, individual actions of family members reflect on the image of the whole. Hence, family members are obligated not to "bring shame" upon the family through negative actions or failure. There are tendencies to be motivated by shame or by the avoidance of it, and to refrain from expressing feelings that might reflect badly on the family name or image. Instead, all members are encouraged to achieve success which will be a source of great pride and honor for the entire family. To fulfill these expectations, many Asian parents encourage hard work and emphasize the value of education. Parents' words are not to be taken lightly, because filial piety (respect for one's parents and elders) is one of the most important traditional Asian values. Sons and daughters show respect for their elders by addressing them with designated words of titles of respect, by being obedient, by deferring to their wishes, and by working hard to fulfill roles and expectations of the family. It is often expected that children will serve and care for their parents as they grow older.

Asian Culture in the American Environment

Given these traditional expectations and values of Asian families, how then do Asian immigrants interpret these in the context of (white) American culture in the United States? And how do youth respond?

For some Asian Pacific Americans, the values from traditional Asian culture are clearly shared with youth through the words and examples of their elders. One second-generation Philippine American describes how her children were reared with traditional Asian values:

From the time the children were little they heard their father voicing his dream for them: to go to college. . . . He was willing to work as hard as he could for them, to try to put some money away for their education. . . .

Another thing we stressed in our family was the importance of family. . . . The children had good examples as they were being raised.[26]

Yet for some youth, parental pressure to succeed becomes overwhelming. The fear of failure immobilizes some or leads them to tragic ends. Incidents of suicide have been documented among those unable to cope with the pressure to achieve. One Chinese American student describes his frustration of never feeling good enough for his father: "If I got a B+ my father's response was, 'Why not an A?' When I got an A, he didn't say anything about it. I still feel frustrated—like I'm on a treadmill running as fast as I can, but the treadmill will never stop."[27]

For other Asian Pacific American youth and parents, particularly first-generation immigrants, aspects of American culture may clash with traditional Asian values. Professor Bongyoun Choy writes, "The family centered, traditional Korean immigrant finds the freestyle, aggressive, individualistic American way of life incompatible with what he (or she) was accustomed to in his homeland."[28]

Some Asian Pacific American young people have learned to live in the balance between two cultures. Moving fluidly from aggressive behavior in a competitive workplace, they can defer to and be supportive of family elders at home. Some grow up feeling that such chameleon-like behavior fits into the order of the world. Often, their parents, too, have learned to compromise some traditional expectations and adapt their own behaviors to achieve success in the United States. They recognize the strength that often comes from being capable of negotiating through more than one cultural setting. Other Asian Pacific American young people are pulled far away from Asian traditional values. As they lose respect for parents who may still be struggling to survive, the gap between them widens:

Vietnamese parents reported that their children were losing respect for them because of their continued difficulties with learning the English language, making an adequate living, and adapting to American life. Parents were found to have maintained many of the traditional expectations. . . . Children, however, were found to be increasingly reluctant to abide by many of these traditional expectations, and in a number of cases wanted greater independence from the family.[29]

Even when one chooses to adhere to traditional values, difficulties arise when (white) American institutions and culture do not support— and sometimes undermine—one's actions.

In my unpublished journals I find these lines:

Hearing news that my elderly uncle has only a short time to live, I drop professional commitments and deadlines to take the first plane out. An "illness in the family" justifies a week's absence from work, but does not begin to convey the commitment an only child—the favorite niece—has to her only surviving, closest relative. My once invincible uncle wants to "die at home," but neither doctors, insurance companies, social workers, nor my employers will support our efforts. After helping him move to a dreaded convalescent care hospital, I must fly home. Guilt intensifies pain and grief as I plan my next visit with him.

As today's youth—encouraged to strive for professional mobility—begin to face decisions about care for their aging parents, similar scenarios may occur in the future.

One Japanese American researcher reflects on the tension he experienced when having to choose between two cultural styles of dealing with his anger at the injustices endured in wartime by interned Japanese. For him, and for many of us, examples of strong lives that have resolved cultural conflicts, are within our past.

> The Asian in us tells us to feel shame and bear it and the American in us tells us to feel anger and to fight it. The dissonance can be emotionally painful, but fortunately most Asian Americans have learned from those who have preceded us to alternate bearing indignities with fighting back in the constant struggle to live in America.[30]

We can find in Asian Pacific American history an example of how aspects of culture enabled Asian Pacific Americans to survive years of being denied full participation in American life. Recall the history of Chinese Americans: racist legislation limited immigration, creating communities with bachelor populations. Writer Elaine Kim describes how the absence of women and traditional family life led to the development of an organizational network which became a substitute for family life.

> . . . Bound together by their social status as a despised minority, tied by tradition and common beliefs and interests, the Chinese immigrants constructed a world based on social solidarity between families and clans to protect themselves in a cold or hostile environment. This social network provided them with a sense of belonging that they could derive nowhere else.[31]

Like the Chinese, other Asian Pacific Americans faced difficult social conditions. To survive, many of them drew on their memories of cultural values to create new social structures which, in turn, became early expressions of Asian Pacific American culture. In the same way, other national ancestry groups also created community organizations and events to respond to needs unmet by American society at the time:

> We organized the group called Daughters of the Philippines with about 25 or 30 of us girls who took an active part in the Filipino Community. We did all kinds of things like put on celebrations. . . . These social events

were important to the Filipino Community, a necessity. Imagine a life where you are more or less kept to yourselves. We weren't welcome in many public places. So all the social affairs that you could go to were those that you'd have to plan yourselves. These were even more important for all these single men who were alone because there were hardly any women that came with them from the Philippines.[32]

In these early expressions of Asian Pacific American culture the cultural festivals, community events, and various ethnic organizations of today have their roots. With each successive generation, the needs and memories of a people change, and new expressions of Asian Pacific American culture evolve.

In her book *Desert Exile,* Yoshiko Uchida describes how her mother regularly observed certain Japanese customs and took great pains to display dolls for Dolls Festival Day. After her mother's death, Yoshiko carries on the tradition, but she remembers this custom for new reasons: ". . . it is not so much in remembrance of Dolls Festival Day that I display them [the dolls] as in remembrance of my mother and her Japanese ways." This cycle of remembering, and thus transforming, traditional Asian culture to create new expressions of Asian Pacific American culture in the United States becomes part of youth's legacy of Asian Pacific American culture. Today, aspects of Asian Pacific American culture are expressed in the form of traditional and modern dance, art, music, community organizations, movies, theater, and literature.

Not only do individual national ancestry groups seek expression through these cultural forms; coalitions of Asian Pacific American groups now work to promote specific cultural expressions. Although these expressions are rooted in memories, they also reflect visions that Asian Pacific Americans have of the future of their communities. We can find in the most current Asian Pacific American cultural expressions—film, theater, literature—powerful expressions with the potential to change stereotypical images of Asians. Unlike previous generations of Asian Pacific American youth, today's youth will have access to artistic expressions by and for Asian Pacific Americans.

Asian Pacific American Identity

> On identity, an 88-year-old *Issei* woman says, "You are a homeless dog without your identity. Though we are U.S. citizens, we are Japanese. The color of our faces and so on . . . . Losing identity is the same as losing money: you lose your way of life."[33]

Theories and research on Asian American identity and personality development have been published, refuted, revised, and debated. To discuss these theories now is outside the scope of this writing. Instead, from Asian Pacific American youths' own unique perspectives on their experiences and their individually defined identities, we will try to draw some tentative conclusions about Asian Pacific American identity.

Here, in their own words, Asian Pacific American youth present a collage of perceptions of what it means to be Asian Pacific American. They speak as members of various national ancestry groups. (Although some perceptions are identified according to a youth's national ancestry group, such perceptions are not necessarily exclusive to that group.) Furthermore, they speak as persons of various generations of immigration; as urban, rural, or suburban; as growing up middle class, growing up in Chinatown, growing up in poverty; as American born, or born overseas. There are perspectives of youth speaking as youth; there are perspectives of older persons reflecting on their youth and childhood.

Youths' voices have many tones: angry, determined, reticent, soul-searching, spirited, and boldly speaking out for many. Their perceptions are not static, but fluid, in a continuous process of changing self-definitions. Diverse perspectives are presented here to expose youth and adult readers to new experiences, to other ways of being and feeling, to the varying ways Asian Pacific American youth see themselves and the world. It is hoped that some voices will affirm the experiences of others—evoking the response "Aha! I've felt that way, too!"—and that others, perhaps new voices, might challenge youth and adults to beome more sensitive to the broader range of experiences which shape one's individual perspectives.

Voices of the Asian Pacific American Culture

Imagine how it must feel to be expected to succeed in an American school when you are young, overwhelmed by a foreign culture and surroundings, and feeling lonely, remembering a recent separation from all that was once familiar. One Chinese American university student describes the alienation and self-doubt which characterized her life when she first arrived in the United States:

> I remember the first day I went to school in America, I was scared. I did not know anybody or any English. I was 14 years old and in eighth grade. I did not even want to go to school. The school put me in a special class for those who came from other countries. . . . In high school I had to take all the regular classes instead of the special classes. Sometimes I felt bad that I was not born here because then I would not have any language problem, and I would have done better in classes.[34]

Immigrant students with perceptions similar to these need to feel that they are not alone; they need support from others who may share similar experiences. Some may benefit from dialog with parents or elders to clarify expectations of both generations.

For some Asian Pacific American youth, the feeling of having failed to meet previously attainable expectations is accompanied by the tendency to blame oneself. Remembering the years of being silent, of having little confidence, filmmaker Christine Choy describes her feelings as an immigrant college student in New York: "I believed that my problems were caused by my own stupidity and lack of ability. I never thought to consider the situation I was facing." It took many years for Christine to understand the dynamics of being an immigrant minority woman in the United States. She now realizes: "My feelings of inferiority were the result of my situation as an immigrant, a woman, and a minority, and not the result of my own stupidity or inadequacy."[35]

With the support of peers of their own language, cultural, and class background, some Asian Pacific American immigrant youth make strong, positive statements about their national ancestry group's experience. College student Anna Rhee describes the minimal degree of assimilation that Korean young adults experience:

> Contrary to their parents' beliefs, we Korean young adults do not forget our Korean roots. Social assimilation is not accompanied by dissociation from the Korean culture. Somewhat of a distance also exists between Korean young adults and Korean-American young adults. Korean-Americans are mainly those persons born in the United States or others who have spent most of their lives in the United States. One could argue that someone born in the United States is an American, but we do not see it that way. The fact is that we don't look or feel "American." Our identification with being Korean is so strong that interracial dating and marriage, including other Asians are not well accepted. It appears that the strong attachment to our native culture and society is largely unaffected by our length of stay in the United States, socioeconomic status and degree of assimilation/acculturation.[36]

Anna's confidence is bolstered by knowledge of traditional Korean culture as well as by frequent opportunities to interact with other Korean Americans. Implied here is her assumption that "American" is equated with "assimilation." Such an assumption is not shared by everyone.

Maxine Hong Kingston—novelist, educator, mother—recognizes how throughout history Asian Pacific Americans have often been denied full rights and privileges as Americans. For her, "claiming America" refers to Asians claiming their rightful place in American history and in society.

> Does "claiming America" mean assimilation of American values? No. I mean it as a response to the legislation and racism that says we of Chinese origin do not belong here in America. It's a response to the assumption that I

come from Vietnam or another Asian country. When I say that I am a native American with all the rights of an American, I am saying, "No, we're not outsiders; we Chinese belong here. This is our country, this is our history, we are a part of America. If it weren't for us, America would be a different place.[37]

Asian Pacific American history is still not included in current American history texts or courses in school. This omission plus the absence of role models from their own cultures in many communities cause some Asian Pacific American youth to believe that white American values and people are superior to their own. Some young people attempt to forget, to deny who they are. This second-generation Pilipino American chooses to "pretend to be white" at the cost of denying her Pilipino American background:

> Most of the Filipinos we knew were farm workers or busboys who didn't have much of a future. No Filipino teachers taught me . . . . This is partly the reason I grew up looking down on the Filipino . . . . My father ran a bar in Chinatown, which is Delano's oriental ghetto, and this is where the Filipinos congregated. Mostly oldtimers went to this bar. I never wanted to identify with this image of my father. Education was another reason I belittled my own people. I was brainwashed into thinking Filipinos were lower. I actually used to wish I was white. If you didn't at least pretend that you were a white American, you were totally outcast. So, you just tried to forget that you were Filipino.[38]

Some Asian Pacific Americans need years of reflection before they grow beyond feeling ashamed of their Asian background toward an appreciation of family and culture. For this older professional woman, an understanding of her family's experiences in the context of their history, enabled her to recognize the struggles and sacrifices of her elders:

> It wasn't until my mid-twenties that I even began to really appreciate my Filipino father and mother. It hasn't been until the last ten years that I've learned to. . . . Sometimes, as I grew up, I was ashamed that my parents were Filipino with their accents and our home smelling "funny" with the aroma of our ethnic food.[39]

For a number of Asian Pacific Americans living in communities which afford little or no contact with other Asian Pacific Americans, to perceive oneself as white is often not a conscious choice. Rather, it is a response made out of a lack of awareness of other options. Some, both immigrant and American born, may feel that "there's no reason" to identify as a member of an Asian Pacific national ancestry group.

> In White Suburbia, I led a sheltered life. My experiences were very middle class. Growing up in a white community made self-definition very difficult. With an Anglo norm, the Asian becomes the anomaly. Not quite fitting in makes one feel deviant. Self-hatred occasionally results.[40]

There are even many recent immigrants who sometimes experience a period of trying hard to be "American" when "American" is believed to mean "white."

At other times Asian Pacific American youth may be overwhelmed by the differences between their individual experiences and whatever they perceive the experience of the majority to be. Here, the desire to "be white" expresses a need to belong, to fit into what appears to be the order of the world. For some Asian Pacific American youth, perceptions of white identity and white American values may be affirmed as long as youth feel accepted by white society. Such feelings of acceptance may continue, perhaps, until questions in regard to one's "differences" arise:

> By recognizing prejudice directed at you, you are forced to look at yourself and what you are. You are compelled to see yourself as different, as a member of a minority group. Facing the truth can be a painful experience. You are not quite as White as the White society you wish to identify yourself with. I have finally faced this reality. I am yellow—I cannot change what I am.[41]

For many Asian Pacific American youth, instances of the cruelty of childhood jokes or racial slurs hurled without warning become reference points, times when youth must begin to question, to face what it means to be descended from a particular Asian Pacific American national ancestry group or to be an immigrant oneself.

The poem that follows, written by a first-year Asian Pacific American college student, evokes the tension of an internal dialog between one voice which wishes to deny ethnicity, and another voice which wants to call the youth back—to claim the history/culture/people of which the student is a part. At the point of childhood's derogatory racial chants, the two voices affirm each other, remembering common experiences of pain.[42]

You look like me.

But your hair is black
   your eyes brown
   your skin—

You are like me.

We share a people
   a culture
   a past—

You remember.

I see it. In your eyes.

Little children can be
  so cruel.

I look like myself.

No.

I am like myself.

No.

I remember nothing.

See nothing.

"Ching chong Chinaman,
    Why you havee slantee eyes?
      Hey, Jap! Hey, Jap! Hey—"

                   It hurt.

I know.

             I hated them.
             They made me love them.
               Lick their hand
               Be their fool
         Laugh at myself.
             And love them, always love
               them.
             Until I hated myself.
             Until I hated you.

Come back.

             It's too late.

Come back.

             It's too hard.

Come back.

             Yes.

From the point where one chooses, like this student, to say "yes" in an affirmation of ethnicity, there is a new acceptance of one's culture, people, and history. Recognizing how the cultural influences in her life set her apart from white America, this young woman finds her experiences affirmed by others who share similar experiences. She sees herself not only as an individual, but as part of a community whose collective experiences are the history of a people.

Some Asian Pacific American youth probe more deeply into history to find out more about who they are. After hearing about her Asian Pacific American heritage and family history for the first time, one young person confronts her mother, wanting to know why the stories of their past have never been shared: 'But you never asked about it before!' my mother cried. Coming from a position of total ignorance, how was I to know where to begin to ask questions?"[43]

Knowledge of history will provide this young woman with a context for her own experiences. She can begin to formulate questions, to continue the search to define her own experience. She realizes that her feelings and experiences no longer exist in isolation, but that they are influenced by larger forces of racism.

Another dimension of Asian Pacific American identity involves one's relationships with other people, especially how one perceives of members of one's national ancestry group and the larger Asian Pacific American community and how one is linked to them. A young person categorized communities in this way:

I began to mentally divide my world in two. There was the white world made up of my white school friends and neighbors, and encompassing the strangers "out there." There was also a Japanese American world to which I belonged. In this world was my family, cousins, Sunday School and Japanese school friends and the people who my mother said "hello" to in the store. I felt natural in both worlds and thought that this was the order of things.[44]

Other Asian Pacific American youth describe how interaction with others in the Asian American community affirms and strengthens their concept of identity:

Meeting other Asian Americans was in a sense, a relief—the warmth, the elatedness, the understanding that comes from sharing common experiences such that a lot need not be explained or said. I remember . . . the wonderful flashes of self recognition I had, and my identification with something that I could call my own. It was a feeling of power. I was not alone.

I learned to appreciate my past, my community, my family, and me. I felt that I had found my place. I realized that my link with other Asian Americans was through our experiences. I am a part of a living heritage. From my grandmother, to my mother, to me, there is a continuity. . . .[45]

One Asian Pacific American youth incorporates an awareness of history into this description of individual and collective identity:

My feelings and image of what it means to be Asian American have undergone immense change. . . . I recognized the racism I experienced being Chinese. . . . I realized those [derogatory] chants were a part of a great structure of racism in this country. . . . Trying to understand what being Asian American means, there's been joy and pain in my process of self definition. . . . Just recently, however, I have come to the understanding that China and Mandarin are not the places to be putting my energy if I am to understand who I am as an Asian American. It's with other Asian Americans, people at school, in my family and in the community that I reach towards for my individual and collective identity.[46]

There are many more Asian Pacific American voices, from different points in the process of self-definition. Some youth seldom, if ever, felt they had to question the meaning of their ethnic identity:

I'm proud to be a Filipino. . . . I just can't say how much. Even if I've adopted and practiced American customs, I still have my Filipino attitudes. I'm proud of them.

I'm not Korean or American, but a blend of both.

I always knew I was Chinese. My family has lived in the City since my grandparents were born here. Most of my friends at school are Chinese, and we all grew up together. But once when I traveled out of state, people asked me, "How did you learn to speak such good English?"[47]

Some Asian Pacific American youth base their responses to choices about their life's work and values on concepts of identity which integrate an awareness of history, sensitivity to culture, and commitment to community with visions of a more just world:

I never want to forget the feelings of what it means to be an immigrant worker in America. I want to do what I can so that other people will not have to go through what my father went through. . . .

But I want to serve the people who can't afford the health care they need. I believe that health care is the right of every human being . . ., I studied medicine so that I could provide health care to the community that I come from. That community is gone now, and the [old-timers] who pinned their hopes on me have passed away, but I can see them in the faces of the retired farmworkers and the new immigrants who visit our clinic. My work is my way of paying back the family and community that gave me life and nurtured me.[48]

Notes

1 Claudia Glenn Dowling, "A Special Report on Teens," *Life,* March 1986, p. 28.

2 Keith Choy, "Voices . . . Give Teens a Chance," *Asian Week,* August 15, 1986, Sec. 1, p. 26.

3 Linda Wing, "Asian American Studies at Berkeley High," in *Counterpoint Perspectives on Asian America,* ed. Emma Gee (Los Angeles: Asian American Studies Center, UCLA, 1976), p. 227.

4 Barbara Ehrenreich, "Premature Pragmatism: Preliminary Findings on a Campus Epidemic," *Ms,* October 1986, p. 39.

5 Amy Uyematsu, "The Emergence of Yellow Power in America," in *Roots: An Asian American Reader,* ed. Amy Tachiki (Los Angeles: UCLA Asian American Studies Center, 1971), p. 11.

6 Elaine Kim, ed., *With Silk Wings: Asian American Women at Work* (San Francisco: Asian Women United, 1983), p. 62.

7 Fred Cordova, *Filipinos: Forgotten Asian Americans* (Seattle: Demonstration Project for Asian American, 1983), p. 1. Cordova credits Marina Espina for this research.

8 Corinne K. Hoexter, *From Canton to California: The Epic of Chinese Immigration* (New York: Four Winds Press, 1976), p. 9.

9 Minejiro Shibata in *The Issei Portrait of a Pioneer: A Japanese Oral History,* ed. Eileen Sunada Sarasohn (Palo Alto: Pacific Books, 1983), p. 20.

10 *Contacts and Conflicts: The Asian Immigration Experience* (Los Angeles: Asian American Studies Center Resource Development and Publications, UCLA, 1975), p. 14.

11 Paul Jacobs and Saul Landau with Eve Pell, *To Serve the Devil* (vol. 2) *Colonials and Sojourners* (New York: Vintage Books, 1971), p. 174.

12 Yoshiko Uchida, *Desert Exile* (Seattle: University of Washington Press, 1982), p. 42.

13 Carey McWilliams, *Brothers Under the Skin* (Boston: Little Brown and Company, 1946), p. 164.

14 *Japanese American Journey* (San Mateo: Japanese Curriculum Project, Inc., 1985), p. 9.

15 Bong-youn Choy, *Koreans in America* (Chicago: Nelson Hill, 1979), p. 108.

16 Alexis Canillo and Joan May Cordova, *Voices: A Filipino American Oral History* (Stockton: Filipino Oral History Project, Inc., 1984).

17 Carey McWilliams, *Factories in the Field* (Santa Barbara: Peregrine Publications, Inc., 1971).

18 Canillo and Cordova, *op. cit.*

19 Beverly McLeod, "The Oriental Express" *Psychology Today,* April 1986, p. 50.

20 Bong-youn Choy, *op. cit.,* p. 221.

21 Victor G. and Brett de Bary Nee, "The Emergence of a New Working Class," in *Counterpoint Perspectives on Asian America,* ed. Emma Gee (Los Angeles: Asian American Studies Center, UCLA, 1976), p. 378.

22 Laurence Saigo Aylesworth, Peter G. Ossorio, and Larry T. Osaki, "Stress and Mental Health Among Vietnamese in the United States," in *The Mental Health of Asian Americans,* ed. Stanley Sue and James K. Morishima (San Francisco: Jossey-Bass, 1982).

23 Robert W. Gardner, Bryant Robey, and Peter C. Smith, "Asian Americans: Growth, Change, and Diversity," *Population Bulletin,* Vol. 40, No. 4 (Washington: Population Reference Bureau, Inc., 1985).

24 Mark Thompson, "The Elusive Promise," *Far Eastern Economic Review,* October 16, 1986, p. 46.

25 These are excerpts from my own notes on the process of working with oral history by taping personal recollections to retrieve historical information.

26 Canillo and Cordova, *op. cit.*

27 Asian American Student Alliance, *Unity of Three* (Santa Cruz: UCSC Asian American Student Alliance, 1977).

28 Bong-youn Choy, *op. cit.,* p. 258.

29 Aylesworth, Ossorio, and Osaki, *op. cit.*

30 Nelson Nagai, *The Other Side of Infamy* (Stockton: Association of Asian American Educators, 1983).

31 Elaine H. Kim, *Asian American Literature* (Philadelphia: Temple University Press, 1982), p. 102.

32 Canillo and Cordova, *op. cit.*

33 Sarasohn, *op. cit.,* p. 275.

34 Asian American Student Alliance, *op. cit.*

35 Kim, *op. cit.,* p. 70.

36 Anna Rhee, "We Do Not Forget Our Korean Roots" (April 1983).

37 Marilyn Yalom, ed., *Women Writers of the West Coast* (Santa Barbara: Capra Press, 1983), p. 16.

38 Linda Escalona, quoted in "Filipino Immigration: The Creation of a New Social Problem," Tachiki, *op. cit,* p. 197.

39 Marya Castillano Sharer, quoted in Fred Cordova, *Filipinos: Forgotten Asian Americans* (Seattle: Demonstration Project for Asian Americans, 1983), p. 165.

40 Asian American Student Alliance, *op. cit.,* p. 133.

41 "Autobiography of a Sansei Female," Tachiki, *op. cit.,* p. 113.

42 Susan Mukai, "Dialogue," in *Rising Voices,* ed. Lori Higa (Santa Cruz: Asian American Studies Planning Group, 1975).

43 Asian American Student Alliance, *op. cit.,* p. 65.

44 *Ibid.,* p. 65.

45 *Ibid.*

46 *Ibid.*

47 Alex Canillo et al., *Pinoy, Know Yourself: An Introduction to the Filipino American Experience* (Santa Cruz: UCSC Third World Teaching Resource Center, 1975), p. 19.

48 Kim, *op. cit.,* pp. 10, 25.

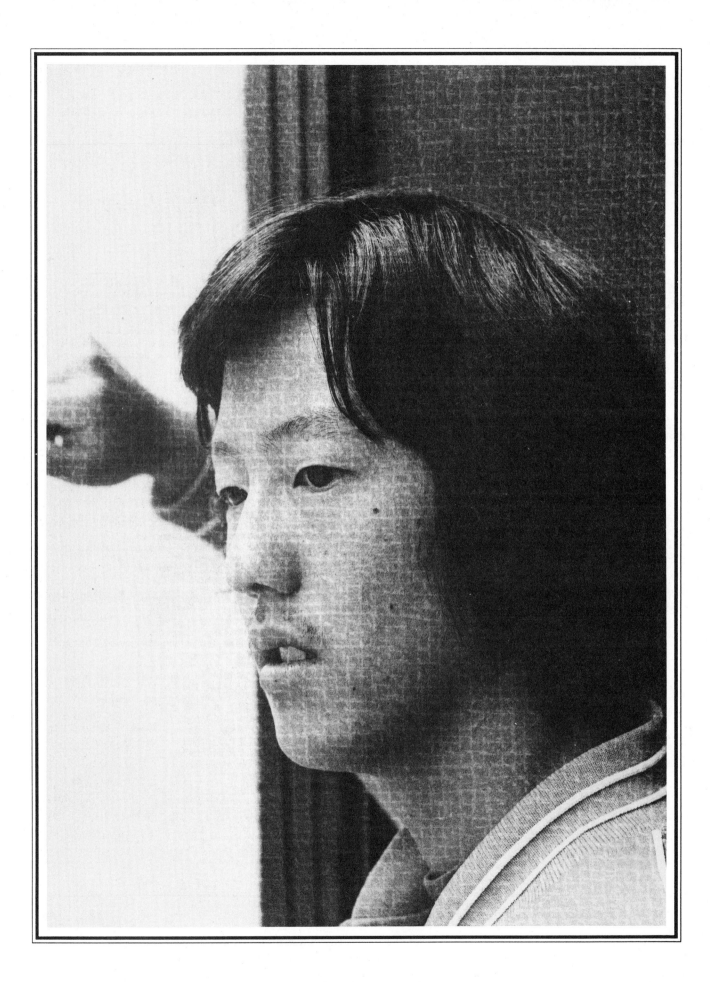

3

Developmental Characteristics of Youth

by Rodger Y. Nishioka

Recently, a poll by a youth-serving agency asked adults what words they would use to describe young people today. With few exceptions, most of the words were negative and included such descriptions as: reckless, rude, lazy, spoiled, and self-centered. American society has been reluctant to recognize and cope with young people who have moved beyond childhood and stand on the verge of adulthood. New parents tend to adopt the attitude that the teen years for their children will be the most difficult. One will often hear parents wish that they could "ship their teenagers off somewhere" and have them return when "they're adults."

The perception of a young person's place in society can best be described as "maintenance." The most popular myth about how to deal with teenagers is simply to hang on for dear life until they grow up and can actually contribute something. The tragedy here is that the church has not only followed this myth, but at times been one of its key leaders.

Only recently have some churches recognized ministry with youth as a separate program from ministry with children, and only recently have churches begun to provide opportunities for young people to become involved in the total life and mission of the congregation. The struggle is to recognize that young people are at a unique point in their lives and to challenge them while still providing a safe, secure place where they are accepted and loved. To do so effectively, those who minister with young people must become acquainted with them.

In this chapter, therefore, we shall examine the many physical, emotional, social, intellectual, and spiritual changes which most early adolescents (ages 12–15) and adolescents (ages 15–19) experience and the implications of these changes. Continuing, we shall look at some major trends in society which affect young people in general today. Then we shall focus more directly on Asian Pacific American youth—the confusing aspects of their identity, the special pressures they face, and the unique aspects of their developmental tasks.

Youth—A Period of Transition

There is no question that the adolescent years are difficult. Furthermore, they are not made any easier by our cultural biases, which too often apply the cliché "children should be seen and not heard" to youth as well. Conflict thus develops, because adolescence is a time when youth are looking for answers, need open discussion and dialogue.

Young people are complex. At no other time in their lives will they face more physical, emotional, social, intellectual, and spiritual changes than during adolescence. What is worse, in any individual any or all of those changes may happen rapidly or slowly, early or late, all at once or over a period of years. For those who work with these amazing individuals, beware! The person you are dealing with today is not the same as yesterday or tomorrow, and certainly not the same as next year. As a leader of young people, how do you cope? The first step is to know and understand the kinds of changes that are taking place and what they imply for your ministry with them.

Physical Changes

Because young people and society in general are so conscious about their physical appearance, the area that causes the most interest and anxiety is this one.

Physical Changes in Early Adolescents

Early adolescents experience the onset of puberty. For girls, this major change happens significantly earlier than for boys. Growth tends to occur in spurts rather than gradually, creating a tendency toward awkwardness and uncoordination. There is great concern for appearance and often embarassment about such matters as weight, height, foot size, skin disorders, sexual development, and voice changes. With the onset of puberty, most teenagers experience the beginnings of genital maturation with their first menstruation or first ejaculation. Sexual interests are developing.

Physical Changes in Adolescents

For most adolescents, growth patterns ease after the early spurts of development. For many young men, however, this may be the "catching up" period. Concern about appearance is even greater here than earlier. Both men and women of this age group are notorious for spending long periods of time dressing and primping to achieve that "right look." Coordination, strength, and physical agility become more manageable and reliable. Sexual maturity is reached, and experimentation tends to increase.

Implications for Ministry with Youth

Education concerning their physical changes is critical for both early adolescents and adolescents. Leaders cannot assume that young people will learn about physical changes and sexual interests at home. In fact, few first-generation Asian immigrant parents understand it to be their responsibility to explain anything about physical changes and sexuality to their children. The church setting, therefore, is the ideal place not only to help youth understand what is happening to their bodies but how they can cope with these changes in healthy ways.

Because of the high attention to physical appearance, programs with youth, especially early adolescents, should never single individuals out for attention. Those working with early adolescents should avoid activities and games which require high-level coordination and agility. All ages, however, need opportunities for physical movement, early adolescents more frequently than older adolescents.

Emotional Changes

There have been numerous studies in recent years about the emotional health of young people. All have discovered that stress and anxiety are on the rise. Some have characterized it as an epidemic in worry.

Emotional Changes in Early Adolescents

Mood swings are especially common among early adolescents. One moment you may be working with an excited, enthusiastic person, and a little later the same individual is negative and lethargic. There is a struggle between childhood and adulthood. Many early teens are easily depressed. Most are trying to cope with basic feelings of low self-esteem, insecurity, and inadequacy.

Emotional Changes in Adolescents

As youth advance further into adolescence, there is movement toward better emotional control, but the range of their emotions includes anger, defiance, rebellion, cooperation, and assuming responsibility. Most are asserting themselves towards independence and will resist and resent prying adult questioning. Issues of integrity and honesty in self and others are important. Self-image is often tenuous and fragile.

Implications for Ministry with Youth

Acceptance is the key word here. As young people (both early adolescents and especially adolescents) experience a whole variety of mood swings and emotions, being accepted by others will ultimately let them know they are loved and cared for. Particular attention must be given to enabling each individual to develop a healthy self-esteem and self-image. Asian Pacific American youth, for a variety of long-standing cultural reasons, tend to have particular difficulty in seeing themselves in a positive way. Programs and discussions that help them see themselves as God's creations with purpose, meaning, and beauty are badly needed. The church must also be careful to avoid contributing to the already high stress levels in many teenagers' lives. If acceptance is real, church can be a place where youth can truly let down their guards and risk being themselves.

Social Changes

Peer group and peer approval emerge as more important than family relationships. Belonging to a peer group and being accepted is critical for some young people as tension develops between themselves and parents and siblings.

Social Changes in Early Adolescents

Many early adolescents are searching for positive adult role models. There is inconsistency however, between dependence on adults and independence from them. Much of the low self-esteem and insecurity is rooted in their relationships with peer groups and family members. The need to belong is so critical that self is often shunted.

Social Changes in Adolescents

As they move further into the adolescent years, the peer group becomes even more important. Social patterns in relating to peers and adults have long been established. Leadership qualities in some begin to mature as opportunities to lead are provided. Many develop strong same-sex and opposite-sex friendships. Relationships to adults vary from conflict to friendship. Authority becomes personified in adults, and (for many) authority becomes a personal threat to freedom. Adult role models and heroes remain important. Often Asian Pacific American youth develop skills in relating differently to non-Asian friends and to Asian Pacific

American friends. Some see this duality as contradictory and are uncomfortable. Others are not concerned.

Implications for Ministry with Youth

As peer relationships become critical for many young people and tensions begin to rise in families, leaders can play an important role in keeping communication lines open. Programs that involve groups of parents and youth together in dealing openly with conflict will be helpful. Youth will also require time to build healthy relationships with friends. Leaders will be wise in providing a variety of activities that allow young people to get to know each other.

As youth look for positive adult role models, adult advisers are in a perfect position to develop adult-youth friendships. In many youth groups, because young people are likely to be scattered throughout the area and therefore attending different schools, the weekly meetings at church are probably the only times they will see each other on a regular basis. Providing time during meetings for them to talk with each other and develop as a community will be helpful. Also, providing special weekend retreats and social events will continue to build those peer relationships which are so important at this time in their lives.

Intellectual Changes

Significant intellectual changes in youth create a marked difference between the two classifications we have been considering.

Intellectual Changes in Early Adolescents

Most are still thinking in the concrete stage, while a few are able to think abstractly and in symbolic ways. The reading level of early adolescents varies greatly. Many learn more easily through electronic media than print media. Most have very short attention spans.

Intellectual Changes in Adolescents

Later teens are more able to think abstractly and globally. Most are able to concentrate for slightly longer periods of time. The electronic media continue to be important in education.

Implications for Ministry with Youth

Because most early adolescents are unable to focus on abstract images, references to faith issues must be as concrete as possible. For more mature adolescents who are able and often eager to be challenged, open and real discussions are often the most exciting and interesting. For all age levels, use of audiovisual teaching program aids will insure higher levels of attention and participation. For early adolescents, plan for short attention spans and provide frequent and drastic changes in activities.

Spiritual Changes

Contrary to popular belief, most youth are seeking or wanting personal meaning through involvement and faith in the church and what the church stands for.

Spiritual Changes in Early Adolescents

Most early adolescents are beginning to question the literal faith of childhood while still looking for something to take its place. Some are moving into the development of a more personal faith based on reflection. There is still a strong need for information in a clear format that demonstrates how faith can be applied to everyday life. Some are struggling as they look for specific, clear answers and discover that faith is not easy.

Spiritual Changes in Adolescents

Many adolescents of the middle teens are beginning to put faith together for themselves. There is a tendency not only to reject the simple faith of childhood but to ask hard questions. Often there is extreme questioning and testing of concepts and doctrines as they seek to develop their own faith. Often there is a reorganizing of religious concepts and faith. Many are developing their own personal life philosophy.

Implications for Ministry with Youth

As youth move from a faith that is simple to a faith that is deeply personal, opportunities for youth to ask questions and to explore their own answers must be provided. For those who are just beginning to question some of their own faith beliefs, leaders must provide some "solid ground" upon which they may stand as they begin to struggle and balance themselves. For those who are reaching some conclusions and answers, leaders must push for articulation, asking them what they believe, why they believe it, and how it will impact the way they live. In many churches, membership programs (such as communicant classes, confirmation, commissioning, and discipleship classes) take place during these ages. Young people must be challenged to know what it means to be members of the covenant community.

Throughout each of these various developmental categories, it is important to remember that young people are very different from each other and from adults. The descriptions you have just read are generalities. Only you know the specifics about the youth with whom you are in ministry. Be wary of lumping a group of young people together based upon their age or behavior. Effective leaders of young people recognize each individual for who that person is and who he or she is becoming.

Current Youth Trends

One of the most influential developmental changes that occur in the lives of young people is the need or desire to "fit in" and to be one of the group. This need is so overriding that they often succumb to fads and trends more readily than persons of other age groups, so that they will be more like their friends and not appear "different." It is just as important for youth leaders to be aware of these trends among young people as it is to know their developmental patterns. What follows is a series of general trends that most young people share.

A Multiplicity of Choices

The first major trend is simply that today's young people have more choices available to them than those of past generations. It used to be that when a local church planned a special event, virtually all the youth attended simply because there was little else to do. Today's young people are as busy and overcommitted as their parents. They are working at part-time jobs in record numbers in most cases not because they have to work, but to keep up insurance on their cars and purchase the clothes they desire. School activities include everything from sports to drama to music to special clubs and organizations. Teenagers make up a disproportionate percentage of the moviegoing audience. Others are busy at home choosing which of the thirty-plus cable channels to watch on television. For these and many other reasons, the church is competing for youths' attention and time.

An Altered Worldview

In this information age, an incident can happen half a world away and almost instantly be reported on the television screens in our living rooms that same evening. This generation of youth, more than any other, is living and benefiting from the sending and receiving of information. Daily they are inundated by news and information from local communities, the nation, and the world.

Many youth are experiencing the phenomenon of information overload. For this reason, many of them choose simply to focus on their immediate surroundings and to ignore what is happening in the world around them. This narrowing of the worldview shuts out the global community and focuses on self. "All that matters is what can immediately and tangibly affect me." That view is popular not just with youth but with many adults as well. The end result is a young person who not only is ignorant about the global community

but truly does not possess the ability to care.

Disintegration of the Family

Steadily increasing divorce rates and the practice of both parents working full-time outside the home have badly shaken the stability of the family and reduced its influence among young people. While many parents care about their children, fewer and fewer of them can find the time and energy to be involved in their sons' and daughters' nurture and upbringing. Thousands of children and youth return after school to empty homes. Many suffer from little or no adult supervision. Teenagers are often being called upon to take on a "co-parenting" role for younger sisters and brothers. While the responsibility and trust displayed in this relationship may be helpful in many ways, nevertheless teenagers are often robbed of the opportunity to be young themselves.

Without a consistent parental role model in their lives, young people are more and more turning to other adults to fill that void. Consequently, church youth leaders, schoolteachers, scout leaders, and others are having to do more parenting than ever before.

Electronic Media

Electronic media have always had an important influence on young people, but this influence is increasing because of its availability. Surveys indicate that the average teenager spends between two and four hours a day watching the television. Youth continue to be the primary target of advertisements, since they have a disposable income which (when totaled as a whole group) is estimated to annually run into billions of dollars.

Young people also continue to be the primary audience for the broadcast and recording industries. With the creation of personal stereos, youth no longer need to interact, but may simply put on their headphones, select their favorite cassette tape or radio station, and tune out their surroundings. While many dispute whether the influence of the media is good or bad, none dispute that the influence is extraordinarily powerful.

Fast Foods

One final major trend which is dramatically affecting youth is the movement towards a "fast-food society" or instant gratification mentality. It is hard for many of today's youth to imagine spending hours in the kitchen preparing a meal. Microwave cooking and prepackaged foods have revolutionized and speeded mealtimes in our society. They are also changing our expectations. Today, youth tend to expect immediate results. If something is going to take a long time to get results, most will probably think the work is not worth doing. The work ethic has not died. Youth are willing to work. What has vanished is the belief that work in and of itself has value. Most believe that the value of the work relates only to the pay received for doing it. Therefore, jobs that may help other people but afford only a meager lifestyle will be shunted, while jobs that may benefit society less directly, but pay well, will be the first chosen. This trend has not occurred overnight, and parents are largely responsible for it. Asian Pacific American parents in particular are notorious for challenging their children to make a better life for themselves. The unfortunate problem is that "making a better life" means to most young people that they will exceed their parents' income and have a more comfortable lifestyle.

Who Are Asian Pacific American Youth?

Jin lives with his family in suburban Maryland just outside the Beltway of Washington, D.C. Born in Seoul, he moved eight years ago to the United States with his father, mother, and two sisters. He is now 16 years old. He remembers bits and pieces of his life in Korea, but most of his memories are of America. At home his parents speak to him in Korean, and he answers in English. He is uncomfortable speaking Korean because he has been criticized for his poor pronunciation. He attends a large high school, where he is one of a handful of Asian Pacific Americans. The only contact he has with other Korean Americans is through helping his parents run their grocery store in Washington and through the local Korean Presbyterian church he attends with his family. Jin says he considers himself to be more American than Korean, and he is sometimes surprised when he glances at himself in the mirror and sees how different he looks from his friends at school.

Ruby is a sophomore student at the University of California in Berkeley. She is a second-generation Chinese American. Born and raised in San Francisco's Chinatown, she grew up speaking Cantonese before she learned English. Her parents stressed retaining the Cantonese language and culture and would get angry with her if she tried to talk with them in English. She still recalls being embarrassed in kindergarten and frustrated that she couldn't understand what the teacher was saying. Her English is fine now, although she speaks with a thick accent. Often her other second-generation Chinese American friends think she is an F.O.B. (fresh off the boat) rather than an A.B.C. (American-born-Chinese) because of the way she speaks. That doesn't bother her. She believes that it is important to retain her language and culture. Ruby says that she is Chinese first and American second. She is quick to point out that she doesn't mean she isn't glad to be an American and living in this country; just that she is proud of her heritage and appreciative of her ancestry. She tries to hide her annoyance with other second- and third-generation Chinese Americans who have completely lost their language and culture. That bothers her.

Brandon is thirteen and lives with his family in Seattle. Brandon's last name is Stevens, because his father is Caucasian, but his middle name is Tsuruichi, after his grandfather on his mother's side. His mother is a sansei, or third generation Japanese American, whose maiden name was Nagayama. Brandon is tall, athletic, and handsome. His features are a combination of Asian and European. Recently, he told his mom that to his white friends he looks Japanese and to his Japanese American friends he looks more white. He can't speak any Japanese, and neither can his mother. Once in a while his grandparents try to teach him some Japanese words, but he forgets them quickly. The family worships at the Japanese Baptist church downtown, which is his only contact with Japanese Americans. He enjoys eating Japanese food and handles chopsticks well. Aside from the food and his middle name, Brandon says he doesn't feel very Japanese. A few weeks ago, though, he got into a fight at school when some older kids were picking on a younger, smaller Japanese American boy. Brandon explained to the vice principal that he didn't like the boys calling the kid a "Jap."

These three profiles demonstrate the complexity and diversity of Asian Pacific American youth. Asian Pacific American young people include those who were born in a Pacific or Asian country and have emigrated to the United States as well as those born here whose ancestors emigrated to this country one, two, three, four, and even five generations ago. Asian Pacific American youth also include many who were born overseas and have been adopted by non-Asian families here, as well as some of mixed ancestry with perhaps one parent being an Asian Pacific American and the other non-Asian. Asian Pacific American youth include a first generation Korean American like Jin, a second generation Chinese American like Ruby, and a person like Brandon, of mixed ancestry with a fourth-generation Japanese American mother and a Caucasian father.

Among Asian Pacific Americans themselves, there are distinct cultures and national heritages. Vast differences exist between Filipinos, Indonesians, Vietnamese, Taiwanese, and Koreans. Yet, because there also are marked similarities in cultural attitudes and immigration experiences, it is helpful to think of the groups together under one category.

Young people often move on a continuum with regard to their identities as Asian, American, or as Asian Pacific American. In a paper on how best to conceptualize Asian American personality, authors Sue and Sue[1] identified three types of Asian Americans.

The first type, the *traditionalist,* strongly internalizes Asian values. Traditionalists identify with their particular culture and conform to parental wishes concerning filial piety and high achievement in order to bring a good name to the family. They tend to prefer socializing with members of their own ethnic group.

The second type according to Sue and Sue is the *marginal,* who desires total assimilation, rejects ethnic values, and sometimes exhibits racial self-hatred. A less judgmental name for this type may be *assimilationist.* Assimilating individuals tend to associate with white Americans and are at the opposite end of the acculturation/assimilation dimension from traditionalists.

The Sues' third type, the *Asian American,* cannot be easily placed on the acculturation/assimilation continuum. These persons attempt to formulate a new identity by integrating ethnic cultural values, Western influences, and minority-group experiences. Alliances are made with other Asian Pacific Americans and oppressed minority groups.

As is often the case, the purpose of providing three types or labels is not to say that everyone fits neatly into one of them. Rather, given a continuum with traditionalists and assimilationists at opposite ends and Asian Pacific Americans somewhere in the middle, we recognize that each of us, depending upon where we are, who we are with, and what we are doing, will slide back and forth. Asian Pacific American youth, then, because they are in the midst of great identity struggles, are likely to move the most across that continuum. Because many of them have to live, go to school, and go to worship in three totally different settings, they may be forced to develop skills of extreme flexibility and adaptability.

As each of us looks back on his or her journey, we can identify particular experiences and people who have profoundly helped to shape who we are. Likewise, as young people strive to discover a place on the continuum where they can be comfortable, the role of the youth leader is critical.

Who are Asian Pacific American youth? They are a collection of young people who, at least partly, draw their heritage and ancestry from the Pacific Rim and Asia and at the same time find themselves growing up in the United States. Some struggle with a new language and totally new culture. Others struggle with learning the language of their parents, grandparents, or great-grandparents and beg to have explained to them again and again why they have to attend a cultural language school when their friends have to do no such thing. Some are thrilled by the opportunity for education and work hard to uphold the family name and make their parents proud. Others take school for granted and become distracted. Still others are attracted to liberal arts and humanities while their teachers assume them to be most interested in sciences and mathhematics. Some view themselves as Americans who happen to be of Asian heritage; others see themselves as Asians who happen to be living in America. To add to the complexities, all of them will have to confront an American society and dominant white Anglo culture which ultimately seeks to remind them that they do not truly belong here but rather are lucky to have been "let in." All must confront racism, prejudice, and sterotypes.

These are the Asian Pacific American youth.

Unique Pressures and Challenges

- Asian Pacific American youth struggle in particular with being part of a minority racial culture which in many ways shares the same values held by the predominant white culture. They struggle with what it means to be an Asian Pacific American versus simply buying into the white culture completely.

- Academic pressure and motivation to succeed are high. Asian Pacific American youth are known for their hard work habits and tendency to excel. Too often, they are labeled "model" students and more is expected from them by schoolteachers, administrators, and other adult leaders than from others. Their heritage creates this situation.

- "Never do anything that will shame the family name" is heard, in one form or another, by many Asian Pacific American youth throughout all of their childhood and adolescent years. Family pressure not to bring shame and to make ancestors proud is strong and sometimes overbearing. Asian Pacific American parents expect as much from their children as was expected from them by their parents. Young people tell stories about taking home an *A* on a difficult test and being scolded for not getting an *A* +.

- Asian Pacific American youth, like other racial/ethnic minority youth, experience some form of racism and prejudice. Whether it is in the form of "slant-eyes" jokes, name calling (Chink, Jap, etc.) or in a rejection letter from a major university because there are already "too many" Asian Pacific American students, they must cope with racism. Because of their physical characteristics, they will be easily identifiable as racial/ethnic minorities. And because much of the white culture still does not accept the reality of second- and third-generation Americans of Asian ancestry, many will be complimented about their "good English" and asked "where they come from." When the reply is California, or New York, or Georgia, the asker will be puzzled and repeat, "No, where do you come FROM?"

All of this is further complicated by the white culture's tendency to hold up the Asian Pacific American as the model of assimilation for other minorities, thus breeding resentment and further division. What is more, Asian Pacific Americans themselves will deal with racism among the many ethnic groups in the Asian Pacific category. These pressures will be different for each youth, but they are pressures, and they will have an impact.

Basic Developmental Tasks of Youth

Now that we have a better understanding of the kinds of changes, trends, and pressures young people are experiencing through their adolescent years, it is important to look at the critical developmental tasks they are confronting. Though these tasks continue throughout life, they are particularly critical during adolescence. They can be called "life tasks." They have been categorized, following a model by Ludwig[2], as the five I's of youth: identity, independence, intimacy, inspiration, and investment.

Identity

The life task of identity enables young persons to understand who they are, how their history has influenced who they are, and how their history and present actions will influence who they will become.

Understanding Their History

A critical part of identity is knowing and appreciating the past. Traditionally, Asian cultures have placed a high value on familial and societal history. Often the presence of grandparents and great-grandparents living in the home has reinforced the value of knowing one's family history. Asian Pacific American young people, however, have tended to adopt the predominant American impatience with learning history; they often fail to see how their own history impacts their lives today. The value of knowing one's background, however, cannot be discounted.

Issues of cultural identity come not only from present-day culture but from the past. Traditions and ritual celebrations have always been a critical part of historical and cultural identity. Those Asian Pacific American cultures which choose to celebrate New Year's Day based on the lunar calendar need not only to know that they have always done so but *why* they have always done so.

Japanese American youth, for whom 1942 seems like ancient history, need to know that their parents and grandparents were interned in concentration camps and to understand the impact of that experience upon their lives. They must also learn about the heroic efforts of an all-volunteer Japanese American fighting regiment which endured more casualties and earned more medals than any other in that war while their families and friends were behind barbed wire in the very country for which they were fighting.

Understanding history not only means knowing what happened in the past but also how it impacts lives today. Knowing one's history enables young persons to get a better understanding of their identity.

Who Am I Now?

For many young people, their identity is marked with struggle and conflict. That struggle is enhanced by the fact that identity is not passed on from generation to generation but must be carefully gathered and owned by each person. It is not enough to know and understand one's history. The heart of the matter lies in being able to connect the past to the present and the present to the future. This struggle is further enhanced by the many physical, emotional, social, spiritual, and intellectual changes the adolescent is experiencing.

Gaining a personal identity focuses on developing a personal sense of self-worth, meaning, and purpose in life. My identity means understanding who I am and how others see me. A personal identity forms the basis for how an individual will interact with others.

For this particular life task, the role of young persons is to gain a healthy understanding of who they are. It means understanding how they are changing and how these changes impact them. It means understanding their history. It means recognizing their personal interests and skills. This journey of identity is not done alone, for family and friends play a critical role. Often in the struggle for identity, young people will try on different roles to see how they feel. If they find themselves enjoying a particular role, they may explore it more deeply. After a time, they may become bored and seek out another role to play. This role experimentation is natural. What is most important is that they do this within the context of a community of people who understand what is happening and continually communicate the message that the young people are loved and cared for.

Some Asian Pacific American youth will fall into the

trap of racial self-hatred (i.e., become "marginal"), wishing they were white or of some other race beside their own. Such total rejection of family, culture, and history is an extreme but not uncommon role experimentation. In their search for identity, Asian Pacific American youth will battle with what it means to be an American of Asian ancestry versus an Asian who happens to live in America. In families where the parents are first-generation immigrants and the children are first-generation American-born, the conflict and struggle is likely to be greater. Such families are experiencing not only a generation gap but also a culture gap. This conflict often makes it even more difficult for young people to explore their identity roles.

All Asian Pacific American youth, regardless of their generation status, will have to explore the many stereotypes which are attributed to particular ethnic groups. Ultimately, the goal of each young person is to gain a healthy identity which allows him or her to survive in a white Anglo-dominated society as an Asian Pacific American.

Who Will I Be in the Future?

The last component of identity concerns the future. Once young people can grasp a sense of their history and develop a healthy self-worth and a sense of meaning in life, they are then confronted with issues of the future. What are their goals? What must they accomplish to be fulfilled? One of the key elements of maturity is the ability to set realistic goals and to plan ways to achieve them.

Just as American society tends to downplay the past, it tends to focus a great deal on the future. The life task of identity allows individuals to be constantly determining who they are, yet at the same time understanding that they cannot always be looking inward. The ability of youth to move beyond their self-identity enables them to move to the next life task: independence.

Independence

The task of independence challenges young persons to move from their dependence upon others, primarily family and parents, to independence. They are gaining the ability to make decisions for themselves, to see the consequences of such decisions, and to endure them. Independence is a transition from dependency to relying on one's resources.

Achieving Emotional Independence

The critical task of gaining emotional independence applies for the most part to family relationships. As youth develop and mature, they must move beyond the constant need for their parents' approval. This reordering of family relationships is often done in the midst of great struggle and conflict. Often, because parents seem to epitomize the essence of the Asian culture, youth will reject both the culture and their parents. Unless the young person is eventually able to separate the two, this total rejection of culture is likely to cause even greater struggles in the area of personal identity.

Keep in mind, however, that the struggle for independence is not a *rejection,* but rather a *reordering* of family relationships. Youth who are successful in striving for independence will discover themselves developing a new and more mature relationship with their parents. Although some parents may never acknowledge this change, it is enough that young people reorder their view from their own perspectives. Emotional independence means that young people are able to stand on their own without needing validation from others.

Achieving Economic Independence

Economic independence, like emotional independence, relates primarily to family. It is simply the ability of youth to take steps to depend upon their own fiscal resources rather than those of their parents. This transition is lived out in seeking and securing part-time jobs, moving away from home to school or sharing an apartment with friends, and ultimately securing their own full-time career. These rites of passage are common among young people as they strive to become more independent.

Yet at the same time there is a great struggle within many Asian Pacific American youth because of the cultural issues involved in independence. For some, issues of their primary and secondary languages will hinder or help their ability to be independent. Youth who immigrated to the United States as young children are likely to have developed English-speaking skills more quickly than their parents. Consequently, parents often rely upon them to translate and sometimes take the lead in dealing with finances and business issues.

Some cultural traditions hold that young women will live in the family home until the day they are married. With more and more women entering careers before marriage, this tradition is no longer practicable for many Asian Pacific American women. In a similar kind of conflict, particular Asian ethnic groups have demonstrated a history of working in certain professions. Their vocational and career choices, therefore, which are the primary basis for economic independence, may be severely restricted.

These factors, unique to Asian Pacific American

youth, greatly impact a young person's movement in the life task of gaining independence. Whether the factors hinder or help young people, however, their overriding need for independence remains the same.

Intimacy

Gaining a strong personal identity and moving toward independence are coupled with the life task of achieving intimacy. Intimacy enables young persons to sort out their sexual identities and to develop relationships with other people that are meaningful and genuine.

Developing Relationships

Developing the ability to relate to others is critical. As youth strive for greater independence from family, they begin to depend more on relationships with friends and peers. Eventually in their development, youth begin to discriminate between relationships that are light and superficial, and "best friends," relationships that are deep, meaningful, and genuine.

It is the "best friend" relationships that give young people a sense of what intimacy is about. Intimacy depends upon trust, honesty, vulnerability, and integrity. For youth, intimate relationships are not necessarily physical and are not restricted to the opposite sex. Intimate relationships may be developed with brothers and sisters and other adults. Ultimately, intimacy means a young person has matured enough to be able to share his or her most private thoughts and to bare heart and soul with another person.

Sexual Intimacy

Issues of sexual identity are a struggle in any adolescent's development. Amid all of the physical changes that are occurring, feelings and emotions of sexual attraction are awakening also. A significant part of achieving sexual intimacy depends upon how individuals perceive themselves and relate to others.

Culturally, Asian Pacific Americans tend to have clearly defined roles for males and females. The tradition of most Asian cultures places the male in charge of the family and relegates the female to subservient and submissive roles. While this model is slowly disappearing in the American society as a whole, Asian Pacific American families, especially recent immigrants, are influenced by thousands of years of cultural history. What is confusing for most Asian Pacific American youth, is to acquire one view in the home and then to confront a completely different view, that of equality between men and women, in American culture. This conflict in roles of men and women leads to a further conflict in masculine and feminine personality traits.

The possibility of the wife's working outside the home and the husband's providing primary care for the children and home is even more in conflict with traditional Asian views of the husband-wife relationship.

As Asian Pacific American youth strive for intimacy, then, they must resolve the issues of male and female roles. In a similar way, as youth strive to understand sex roles sociologically between their cultural heritage and American society, they must also strive to understand themselves personally as sexual human beings. Youth who are slower in developing secondary sexual characteristics and sexual drive may be confused as their peers express more sexual interest. The quest for sexual intimacy is often hampered within the Asian Pacific American family by a hesitancy to talk openly about issues of sexuality.

Another issue which confronts Asian Pacific American young people in their search for intimacy focuses on marriage. Statistically, Asian Pacific Americans have the highest "out marriage rate" (marriage to someone from another racial or ethnic group) among racial/ethnic minorities. Many Asian Pacific Americans are choosing to marry white Caucasians. Among Japanese Americans, out marriage exceeds 50 percent. Among Chinese Americans, the rate is not far behind. Interracial marriages, while increasing in number, bring up a whole new set of issues of identity, independence, and intimacy. In all cases, the role of the family and community continues to be that of providing an opportunity for young people to deal with these issues honestly and openly, without judgment or condemnation.

Inspiration

The fourth developmental task of youth is inspiration. This task focuses on moving beyond a selfish preoccupation with one's own needs to being concerned about the needs of others. Young people are often best known for their idealism and their ability to hope and dream. Inspiration enables youth to go beyond the present and look to the future with creativity and vitality. Issues that become of great concern often focus on justice and injustice. It is critical that youth develop the ability to care about others outside of their immediate community. This task stands against the trend of a narrowing worldview mentioned in the earlier section of this chapter about trends among youth.

For us as Christians, an important basis for inspiration can be God's call to ministry, to be disciples of Jesus Christ.

A second basis is the international ties many Asian Pacific American youth experience. For instance, recent conflicts in South Korea and the Philippines may have direct impact for recent immigrants from those areas, since many family members may still be living there. Likewise, when the United States destroyed the cities of Hiroshima and Nagasaki in World War II, many Japanese American families lost relatives. This "internationalism" provides Asian Pacific American youth with a tangible inspiration to move out beyond themselves and their isolated local communities to become members of the global community.

In the midst of fears that today's generation of young people have lost their idealism and desire to challenge the status quo, the need for youth to regain and renew their inspiration is stronger than ever.

Investment

The final developmental task of youth is investment. Once young persons begin to establish for themselves their identity, independence, intimacy, and inspiration, they begin to select those places and causes in which they will invest themselves. They are moving toward commitment. The task of investment relates directly to the youth's developing a personal faith commitment to God and to living that faith commitment in the context of a believing community.

The issue here is purpose and meaning. Young people are searching for purpose in life and true meaning. The question most often asked is "What really counts?" "What really matters?" Enabling youth to invest themselves in areas of their choice provides answers.

In our earlier discussion of spiritual development among early adolescents and adolescents, the characteristic of questioning was prominent. In order to enable investment to occur, effective programs must provide an environment where it is permissible and even encouraged to ask questions and where help is available in the search for answers. Youth who feel it is unsafe or inappropriate to ask serious questions about their faith will eventually leave the community.

At the same time, once young people have begun to formulate their own faith, they must be challenged to apply it through a variety of commitments. When the congregation takes young people seriously, the youth respond. But youth will only invest their lives when they are given the opportunity to do so. Leaders must be ready to give young people chances to live out their faith through tangible, practical commitments which use their various gifts and skills in ways that enhance their faith and strengthen the level of investment.

Further, when investment happens and is used in dynamic ways, all other developmental tasks benefit.

Conclusion

We began this chapter looking at the physical, emotional, social, intellectual, and spiritual changes in adolescence and the implications of those changes for ministry with youth. We next focused on five major trends among young people today. Then we examined Asian Pacific American youth in particular, and finally, we discussed five major developmental or life tasks for youth.

* So what does it all mean?

It means that developmentally, as youth continue to struggle through this period in their lives, the only really consistent factor they may depend on is that they are changing. In light of this, adults who are in ministry with these young people, must be flexible and understanding. Change is not easy for anyone, let alone a thirteen-year-old. Nevertheless, change can be handled better when that thirteen-year-old knows there is a caring community that accepts him/her in the midst of these great changes. That is the role of the church. The church ministers at its best when it responds to youth in such a way that it challenges them to be disciples of Jesus Christ living out that call to their friends, their families, their congregations, and ultimately to themselves.

---

[1]Stanley and Devald W. Sue, "Chinese American Personality and Mental Health," *Amerasia Journal,* Vol. 1, no. 2.

[2]Glenn E. Ludwig, *Building an Effective Youth Ministry* (Nashville: Abingdon Press, 1979), pp. 46-47.

4

Educational Approaches

How Youth Learn

by David Ng

From Concrete to Abstract Thinking

As an adult who relates with young people you know from experience that adolescents are in a fascinating stage in life marked by rapid or sudden changes and great growth in body, mind, and spirit. Asian Pacific American young people are no exception.

Persons of junior high age, for instance, are likely to impress you with their youthful appearance and concrete thinking. Many of them are still asking simple, direct questions in a concrete fashion, gathering pieces of informaton to put together in various combinations. For example, a seventh grader in an Asian Pacific American family may ask when Mother and Father came to Chicago, which overseas village they came from, who comprised their families, and what they all did back in the home country. This seventh grader will put all this information together into a coherent and logical story.

Older adolescents often go beyond such concrete thinking to more abstract concerns. An eleventh grader, for instance, may ask how Mother felt, compared with how Father felt, about leaving home and journeying to a strange new land. Further, how did the relatives back home feel? What were Mother and Father hoping to accomplish? Did the relatives support or oppose this move? How have Mother and Father adjusted their hopes? What if they had settled in a suburb like Glenview rather than Chicago? What if there were no church to provide social and moral support? What if . . .?

One of the exciting factors in relating with adolescents and teaching them is to be sensitive to their increasing capacity for abstract thinking, for asking the "what if . . ." questions. Adolescents are exploring the possibilities. As they mature, they can see not only present reality and even past history; they can imagine future possibilities as well. They can think about current situations and imagine the consequences of a number of possible decisions or actions. "If my friends and I all graduate with honors and attend Ivy League colleges, then we may get influential positions and even high salaries, so that we can come back to our communities with enough power to change things. On the other hand. . . ." Adolescents are in a time of reviewing previous learning, questioning much of that, exploring possibilities, and making personal judgments and commitments.

Much adolescent thinking is experimental or tentative in nature. These young people are trying out potential answers. They are drawing tentative conclusions on the basis of the information available—and most of this thinking and decision making is done with very little experience! Some adolescents may experiment just a little, but others may think up outlandish scenarios for living which boggle our more experienced and cautious adult minds!

A young person can make big strides in understanding her or his faith and commitments. With the growing ability to think abstractly comes the ability to think theologically, relating personally to God and relating God's will to all of life. In thinking about vocation or family relationships or ethical behavior, young persons can understand these topics in terms of God's creation and God's creative presence in their lives. The Christian faith can be more than a series of facts, it can truly be a faith—a way of living based on a spiritual relationship with God.

How Adults Can Help

As an adult leader working with young persons you have opportunities to help these adolescents in their thinking and learning, and in their ability to be faithful. You can help by leading them to the basic information they need for their personal decision making. As they decide about personal values, faith, relationships, work, and mission, they need to make choices on the basis of correct information properly organized. Do they have the facts they need? For example, do they know enough about Jesus Christ and the people whom Jesus confronted to make intelligent decisions concerning their own attitudes and commitments about Christ? Do they know enough about the church to make informed commitments about church membership and mission? One of your tasks as an adult leader is to see that young people have the essential information they need for their decisions.

As adolescents move from concrete to abstract thinking, you can help them develop their cognitive tools: the ability to ask good questions, to hypothesize (that is, to pose tentative conclusions to "what if" questions), to gather and analyze data, and to draw conclusions. As you design teaching plans and lead discussions, you can be a mentor who helps young persons to raise questions, to organize thoughts, and to draw logical conclusions.

As an adult leader and mentor you can also help young persons overcome stereotypical information and thinking that they may have picked up in the past. Particularly among persons of ethnic and cultural minority background, stereotypical ideas may abound which limit their self-esteem and their ability to make free choices. If, for example, a young person somehow grows up with the idea that his racial background is inferior, or that his national origin classifies him as "backwards," then he or she is greatly handicapped in developing a positive identity. Adults can be extremely supportive as adolescents gain new perspectives, seeing themselves and their people as culturally rich contributors to the mosaic of human society.

During the half-dozen years when adolescents are changing, learning, growing, and making crucial decisions about life, you and your colleagues can be significant mentors and guarantors—role models—who share their journey toward faith and misson. You can help in many ways, including:

- Using "open" approaches and settings for learning by young persons
- Encouraging young persons to raise questions, to explore possibilities, and to discover for themselves
- Being facilitators, who set up opportunities for young persons to learn for themselves
- Being yourself—sharing with young persons your own thoughts and questions and your own faith journey

How Asian Pacific American Youth Learn

The developmental factors just described suggest that virtually all young persons experience a time of questioning, doubting, searching, and, it is hoped, self-discovery. Teaching adolescents is more a challenge of setting up opportunities for them to learn for themselves than for an adult authority to impose his or her own experience and knowledge on them. This general approach to education holds for Asian Pacific American youth too. If growing up in an ethnic minor-

ity setting rather than a majority setting creates differences, these may be differences of degree more than of specific developmental tasks. Asian Pacific American young people, like other youth, are in the natural process of reviewing the customs, values, and beliefs which were taught to them as children. In this complex process, they use their newly developed skills of abstract thinking to arrive at their own personally-held values and beliefs. To do so, however, may require some approaches for an Asian Pacific American young person which differ from those of the majority culture.

In Asian Pacific American cultures the authority of elders often is much more dominant and prominent than in other cultures. Norms and values such as respect for elders, participation in close-knit communities, and acceptance of traditional social roles are enforced by elders. Parents try to pass these cultural values on to their children and are often quite anxious when the children, upon reaching adolescence, show signs of resisting or rebelling. Often Asian Pacific American adults and elders try harder or use more pressure, right at the time when adolescents are wanting to think things through and to decide for themselves.

Moratorium Experiences

Experts who have studied adolescent development suggest that it is often useful to provide adolescents with a "moratorium." What they mean is to recognize how much pressure adolescents must endure in sorting through the various value systems and social demands placed upon them and to accept the implications of this pressure by "easing up." Often it is the home and the church which place the greatest pressures upon adolescents to conform to traditional values and beliefs. However, the chances of adolescents being able to think through these matters and to come to wholesome and independent decisions may be jeopardized when home and church push the young people too hard just when they are seeking to think and decide for themselves. Often it is more helpful to "back off" a bit, and to allow the young people the room they need to explore, experiment, and discover for themselves the values and beliefs which they will claim as their own. In a sense, young persons need some "moratorium experiences" in which they can get away from the usual pressures and have freedom to try things out, to make mistakes, to learn from the mistakes as well as the successes, and to arrive at their own conclusions. In fact, many young persons would actually benefit from a time away from home or church, to think things out for themselves. Some parents even, with a sense of humor, wish they *could* send their teenager away for a couple of years!

There are, however, methods short of a complete break. Asian Pacific American families and churches may find value in providing numerous short-term moratorium-type experiences for their youth. A weekend retreat, when the young people are away from home and parents and from the usual surroundings, may be such an experience. Traveling to another city and visiting another church group, or participating in an exchange program, or spending time with adults and siblings other than those of one's own family, would be brief and often effective experiences of moratorium. In effect the church is saying to the young people: "We know that you are doing some searching and deciding; we will support your search and provide opportunities for you to experience different settings, to make comparisons, and to experiment with various ideas and ways of doing things. We want you to find an identity and a faith which is just right for you."

The idea of moratorium experiences may not find ready acceptance in Asian Pacific American churches. Often the church elders and parents want just the opposite—they want more pressure on the young people. They want to push the young people into affirming their cultural values, making lifelong commitments, and professing their Christian faith before the young people drop out and are lost to the church. Actually, a moratorium experience may prove to be a wiser approach, as it recognizes where the young people are and gives them the space and freedom they need to come to their own faith and commitments. Rather than forcing a young person to be a dentist like himself, a father using a moratorium approach shows what dentistry can be, and also what other lines of work can be. He trusts that his son or daughter will choose on the basis of wide knowledge and accurate comparisons rather than being forced to accept unwillingly something he or she will cast off at the first opportunity.

Caught in the Middle

Asian Pacific American young people often find themselves caught in a bind between their own racial, ethnic, and cultural values and those of the majority "American values." Young men and women may be torn between differing ways of self-expression and identity formation. Such ambivalence or even role confusion is especially difficult for individual adolescents who are going through a self-conscious or shy period.

Language may also be a problem. Some Asian Pacific American young persons have not gained fluency in English, thus creating problems at school and among friends. Others speak only English, with ensuing problems of communication with those who use the language of the mother country at home and in the church. The church may experience problems of deciding which language to use in youth groups and classes or in obtaining printed resources which can be understood by leaders and learners alike. A young person who knows the basic native language such as Japanese, Tagalog, or Korean, may still be helpless in trying to communicate with her or his parents—how do you explain that you are on the evangelism committee and must attend a retreat at Wesley Woods—when you do not know the Korean words for evangelism, committee, retreat and Wesley?

Although cultural differences can create difficulties, there are also cultural strengths and values. Most Asian Pacific American groups value and encourage education and academic achievement. Therefore, they usually provide nurture and learning in communal settings which exemplify the corporate nature of our selfhood and identity. They also value tradition, continuity, and accountability to the community. Such values can be seen as advantages which may enhance a person's understanding of Christian faith and practice, when these values are correlated with the Christian faith.

Adult leaders need to be aware of the cultural differences which place greater demands on Asian Pacific American young people than on many of their non-Asian counterparts. They may have a double load to carry on their journey toward self-understanding and personal faith. Adults who walk with these youth need to be patient and understanding, and to be gentle mentors and guarantors who help them identify these pressures and who can assure them that these pressures can be dealt with successfully. One important insight the adults can share is that they, the adults, have gone through similar challenges and have come out of the experiences with integrity and mature selfhood. Adults can help in other ways too, as will be seen in this next section.

Learning About the Christian Faith

A Context for Thinking About Faith

As a leader you earnestly desire that the Asian Pacific American youth in your charge will become disciples of our Lord Jesus Christ and be committed to Christ's church and its ministry. It is quite possible that their immigrant or minority status can be a stimulating context for them in their choices. The Christian faith calls for commitment, sacrifice, faithfulness to a gathered community, willingness to serve others, appreciation for tradition, and spiritual communion with those who have been faithful in earlier centuries. These are virtues with which they are familiar. Many Asian Pacific American youth (but not all of them) have already experienced what it means to be committed to a special group, to make sacrifices, to serve the needs of the community, and to be a part of a larger tradition. The demands of the gospel and the culture of the church are not totally strange to such youth. They may therefore be especially open to considerations of discipleship, commitment, service, and communion with brothers and sisters in the faith.

Nevertheless, particular ethnic churches may not necessarily be models of discipleship, commitment, and Christian community. They may be models of social gatherings and cultural fellowship, or of narrow racial or ethnic pride, or even of ancient and irrelevant cultural myths. Here is where you as an adult leader of Asian Pacific American youth may have a dual ministry to the youth and to the church! You may be in the opportune situation of helping youth and church together to discover key Christian concerns such as discipleship, sacrifice, ministry to others, and communal support for each other. What is more, you may be helping youth and church to draw on their unique cultural experiences and values to understand and act on these as Christians. For example, in the Gospels we learn that Jesus calls us to be his disciples by giving up or losing our lives for his sake and the sake of the gospel. As Asian Pacific Americans we have a pretty good idea of what giving up our self-interests for the sake of others might mean. As an adult leader you may be able to help youth and church alike to make these connections between faith and life.

Racial and ethnic minority experiences may provide the backdrop for dealing with broad social issues such as racism, conflicts in values, materialism, and family conflicts, as well as more personal problems like immigrant status, identity confusion, lack of educational and economic opportunity, and so forth. The study topics presented later in this book are examples of themes which are real and relevant to Asian Pacific American youth. In many cases, to have really experienced a social problem such as racism opens a person to the comfort or challenge which is found in the Bible and other Christian sources for dealing with it. You can help the young people to say, "This is our story—this Bible event tells about us," when you lead them in a study of Abraham and Sarah sojourning in a foreign land, or the Galatians struggling to be Christians without first having to adopt Jewish religious and cultural practices. In a similar manner you may be able to point out the challenge of being workers for social and racial justice and being leaders in the church, when they who have been victims of injustice now have an opportunity to do something about it.

Opportunities also exist for studying the church's mission in an Asian Pacific American church context. Young people can be spurred to mission and service for the sake of the fathers and mothers and brothers and sisters in the ethnic minority church. There is a challenge to be examples of love and acceptance as brothers and sisters in Christ. There is a challenge to help other Christians to accept and affirm a multicultural and multiracial church. The Asian Pacific American church and its members have gifts to contribute to the greater fellowship of Christians.

An Asian Pacific American Perspective

Asian Pacific American youth, indeed all Asian American church members, can be encouraged to read the Bible through the perspective of ethnic and racial experiences and values. Such a perspective gives our reading of the Bible a special poignancy and power. As minority persons who have known the pain of suffering as well as the joy of mutual support, we can appreciate the true realism of many biblical stories. We can apply many of the lessons of the Bible to daily life and to our interpersonal relationships and corporate experiences. Our way of interpreting, from the perspective of our own lives, can be valuable for the rest of the church. Our understandings of what the Bible says about peace, justice, community, service, spirituality, and mutual love can be shared with non-Asians whose personal lives and church life have not been enriched by the realities that racial- and ethnic-minority churches have experienced. In leading young people, you can be asking them, as they study the biblical story of the Passover and the deliverance from bondage in Egypt, what does this biblical passage say to us? What can we, through our unique understanding of this passage, say to the rest of the church? Or you might find yourself working with young people on the question of how to choose a career. In that process it may be important to ask: "Does being an Asian Pacific American make any difference in choosing a career? Does being a Christian make any difference? And does being a combination of Asian Pacific American *and* Christian make any difference?"

In this book some theological assumptions are made. It is assumed that it *does* make a difference for young persons to be acutely aware that they are Asian Pacific American. They carry certain problems as well as possibilities with that identity. Also, being Christian (whether of Asian descent or not) has its problems and possibilities. These dimensions of a young person's identity affect the way he or she thinks about and acts upon the usual adolescent issues such as identity formation, fulfillment of vocation and mission, and participation in community. These are topics that are natural for adolescents to deal with. They are at the age of asking: "Who am I?" "What will I do with my life?" "How shall I relate with others?" Your job as an adult leader is to help these young people to work on these questions in the light of being both Asian Pacific American and Christian.

In this "Foundation for Ministry" section of this book you have been challenged to consider the theological, historical, cultural, psychological, and educational underpinnings for your ministry with Asian Pacific American youth. These foundational understandings offer you a basis for sharing your faith with the young persons in your church. In the next section some practical suggestions will be given to help you to plan appropriately and to teach young persons in your own particular setting. Then follows a section with actual program topics and ideas for group study.

PART *2*

Ministry with
Asian Pacific American Youth

Planning to Meet Specific Needs, *by David Ng*
Effective Methods in Youth Ministry, *by David Ng and*
John Stevens Kerr

5

Planning to Meet Specific Needs

by David Ng

This chapter offers some help with planning for your youth group, especially with using the discussion programs provided in Part 3 of this book. Some simple procedures are shown for gaining an overview of what is happening in your congregation and with the young persons. Chapter 6 will offer some practical suggestions for conducting discussions—led by adults or by the young persons themselves.

This book is not intended to be a full description of how to organize and conduct a complete youth ministry program. There are a number of useful youth ministry manuals which provide concise and easy-to-understand guidance for developing a full program. Several such resources and some teaching and learning resources are listed at the end of this chapter. You can consult these materials for the help you and your colleagues need.

Getting an Overall Picture

A Checklist of Your Congregation's Educational Ministry

Use the questions listed below to get a general picture of how your congregation conducts its educational ministry and the general climate for youth ministry in the church. What does this general picture tell you and your colleagues about the place of young people in the church, and about the attitudes the members of the church have about youth?

1. Our church offers educational activities for the following groups:

Group	Major Activities	Well Supported	Poorly Supported
Children			
Youth			
Young Adults			
Middle Adults			
Older Adults			

2. Our church fosters growth in these areas:

Area	We do this well	We do this poorly
Personal faith		
Relationship with others		
Biblical and theological knowledge		
Mission and witness		
Personal ethical behavior		

3. The strongest part of our educational ministry is . . .

4. The weakest part of our educational ministry is . . .

5. The adults believe the youth in the church should be . . .

6. The youth look upon church activities as . . .

A checklist of your congregation's youth ministry

The checklist below can help provide a general picture of the situation in your church regarding youth ministry.

1. Write your estimates or general ideas of the following:

   Number of young persons in the church _____

   Number of boys, ages 12–15 _____

   Number of girls, ages 12–15 _____

   Number of boys, ages 16–18 _____

   Number of girls, ages 16–18 _____

   Percentage of youth who speak English _____

   Percentage of youth who speak a native Asian language _____

Percentage of youth born in Asia _____

Percentage of youth born in the
United States or Canada _____

Percentage of youth living in the
neighborhood of the church _____

Percentage of youth living within thirty minutes
traveling time of the church _____

Percentage of youth living more than
thirty minutes away _____

Percentage of youth, ages 12–15, who need
family or other transportation to
come to the church _____

Percentage of youth, ages 16–18, who need
family or other transportation to
come to the church _____

2. How the youth of the church spend their time.
Briefly describe some typical activities of the
youth and the number of hours each week spent
on these activities.

Category	Typical Activities	Hours Per Week
School		
Work		
Leisure		
Church		
Home		

3. Where do the young people in the church find
their friends?

Neighborhood ___ School ___
Asian community ___ Church ___

4. What seems to be the economic status of the
youth?

High income ___ Middle income ___
Low income ___

5. What seems to be the possible future for the
youth?

Work ___ Higher education ___
Moving away ___

6. What leadership skills do the youth show?

Leading peer group discussions ___

Planning meetings ___

Leading social and recreation programs ___

Planning and leading worship ___

Other leadership skills ___

7. What types of planned activities are provided for
the youth of the church? (Write some examples of
each type.)

Worship ___

Study ___

Social and relational ___

Mission and service ___

8. The adult leaders of the youth programs
seem to be:

experienced ___   inexperienced ___
trained ___   in need of training ___
enthusiastic ___   discouraged ___

9. The parents of the young people are:
English-speaking ___   non-English
                          speaking ___

comfortable about   anxious about youth ___
youth ___
active in the church ___   not active in
                              the church ___

10. What two or three changes would improve the
youth ministry in your congregation?

11. What are some major goals for youth ministry
for your congregation this year?

Goals for identity formation:

Goals for a sense of vocation (such as purpose of
life, career, mission):

Goals for discipleship and mission:

Goals for faith development:

Goals for participation in the church:

Settings for Youth Ministry

Youth ministry can take place in a wide variety of
times and places, as well as organizational structures.

These settings can be chosen according to the types of activities which are planned and the availability of the youth. Although many Asian Pacific American churches gather on Sundays (often spending the entire morning and afternoon in worship, education, and social activities), there may be other times and places when the young people can meet. Here are some typical settings:

Fellowship groups. Young people often are organized by age group, such as junior high and senior high, for peer group meetings which combine recreation, education, and service.

Church school. Most churches have church school classes, usually on Sundays. Adult leaders teach or help young persons to lead part or all of the discussion.

Elective studies. Some churches offer special courses or programs, often on a seasonal basis, such as a Lenten series or summer course of perhaps four to six sessions. Often a choice of courses is offered.

Retreats. Occasionally a youth group will go away for a retreat which combines study, worship, and recreation, and sometimes includes a service project. Going to an outdoor setting or to another church for a weekend can provide ten to fifteen hours of study, discussion, and reflection in a single concentrated weekend.

Interchurch meetings. Young people often benefit from meetings with youth of other churches. Small groups can combine to study certain topics together and to share leadership.

Intergenerational groups. When persons from two or more generations meet together, they can help each other by sharing personal experiences and perspectives. In youth ministry an important opportunity exists for bringing parents and young persons together to foster increased understanding and mutual support.

Independent studies. Adults can provide study materials for young persons such as carefully selected books or audiocassette tapes. After independent study and reflection there can be conversations and small-group discussion to share and reinforce the learning.

Leaders' groups. It is important to provide opportunities for leaders in youth ministry—youth and adults—to learn. Adults who work with youth can form teams which meet for prayer, support, training, and planning.

Involving Young Persons in Leadership

One of the purposes of youth ministry is to help young persons grow in their ability to serve others in the name of Christ. When young people assume leadership, they learn as they serve. While they may not have much experience as adolescents, there are nevertheless many ways they can lead. Probably they should not be burdened with leading an entire meeting at first, but they can lead specific parts, such as a prayer, or a game, or part of a discussion. As they gain experience, their leadership roles and responsibilities can increase, until they assume most if not all of the responsibilities for their meetings.

Any church would be concerned about developing young leaders, persons who will accept the mantle of leadership and decision-making in the church today and in years to come. If a church is to survive and grow, it must be renewed by fresh leadership continually. Young people can supply much of this leadership.

In Asian Pacific American churches it is crucial to develop young leadership. If such churches are to avoid stagnation and to enter into new fields of mission and witness, then the young people of the churches must be given many opportunities to become leaders. The youth ministry program of the church is one place where youth can learn by doing, as leaders.

The diagram below shows the gradual increase in responsibilities taken by the young people. At the beginning the adults need to assume much of the leadership; but, as time progresses, they can do less public leading and the young person can do more. All through this transferring of leadership, one of the roles of the adults is to help young people evaluate what they've done and to learn both from their successes and from their failures as leaders.

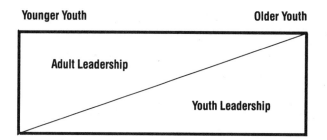

Planning

Much can be said about planning for youth ministry. Some of the resource books listed at the end of this chapter are reliable guides to planning, and they ought to be consulted as you plan. Here, a simple list of planning steps is given, to provide an overview of what you and the leaders among the youth need to do to conduct an effective youth ministry. By using the two checklists which appear earlier in this chapter and discussing them with other leaders, you have already taken the first step in planning! Here are some further steps:

1. Determine the situations and the needs of the youth, along with the situation and the mission of the church.
2. Set goals for youth ministry.
3. Decide on the general approach your church will take in youth ministry. For example, one approach is to emphasize youth involvement in planning and leading their own programs.
4. Decide on the structures and settings for youth ministry.
5. Plan the youth ministry programs.
6. Conduct the programs.
7. Evaluate the programs in the light of the goals you have set.

As for planning for the use of the materials in this book, remember that this is not a complete guide to youth ministry but a special resource focusing on the unique qualities of youth ministry in Asian Pacific American churches. You and your colleagues on the youth ministry team can read and discuss the section entitled "Foundations for Ministry" to develop your own perspectives on the theological, historical, cultural, psychological, and educational bases of the work. These discussions can take place at a leaders' retreat, during regular leaders' meetings, or in other settings.

The latter part of this book contains suggested program plans. Before these are shown to the young people for their consideration and their use in planning meetings, the leaders should become familiar with the topics and have a general idea of the educational methods suggested. These topics are intended to help Asian Pacific American young people develop a sense of identity as Christians and as persons and groups with rich ethnic and cultural gifts. Identity, community, vocation, and mission—these are themes of deep significance for the young people and for the church.

The program plans can be presented to the young people for them to choose which topics to deal with in which settings and at which times. Especially for older youth, the planning and conducting of the meetings can be a partnership between the adult leaders and the youth, with the youth taking on more and more responsibilities as their skills and experience increase. Teams of three or four youth could work with an adult leader to select, plan, and lead the discussion of a topic.

Resources

There are many fine resources to help leaders in youth ministry. The following short list of resources can give a start in ministry with youth, including planning, teaching, and relating with youth.

Effective Methods in Youth Ministry

by David Ng and John Stevens Kerr

Whoever said that variety is the spice of life understood one of the first principles of youth ministry. The various methods for teaching and learning that are available to youth groups are without number, and one of the keys to holding young people's attention is a mix-and-match of these methods. To get us started in our thinking, here is a brainstorming list of possible things to do in an effective study session:

List of Methods

Starting a study session

Descriptive name tags
Paired conversations
Triad interviews
Responding to reaction statements
Unfinished sentences
Values continuum
Circle response
Interviewing your neighbor
Survey or opinion poll

Obtaining information

Reading
Word study
Interview
Brainstorming
Field trip
Lecture
Panel discussion
Listening teams
Questionnaire
Using audiovisual resources
Guest speaker
Looking at art or pictures
Map study
Demonstration
Role play or fishbowl
Play reading
Viewing television
Listening to tape recordings
Simulation games
Service projects
Listening to music

Analyzing information

Problem solving
Debate
Outline
Test, quiz
Film talk-back
Identifying types or organizing by categories
Alternative endings to stories
Various forms of writing such as poems, hymns, paraphrases
Rank ordering or setting priorities
Asking who, what, where, when, how, and why
Conducting an experiment
Interpreting a picture
Developing a chart or time line
Fantasizing
Devising a plan such as a five-year plan
Making a list
Writing a log, journal, or diary
Writing a newspaper

Reporting information

Artwork such as posters, murals, maps, drawings, graphs
Oral reports
Newsprint notes
Dramatization such as play reading, skits, puppets, choral reading, mock TV
Each one teach one
Storytelling
Mock newscasts
Book reports
Symposia
Montages or collages

Using forms of art

Banners

Cartoon strips
Bumper stickers and badges
Creating symbols
Coats of arms
Graffiti boards or boxes
Mobiles
Film slides
Stained-glass pictures
Photography
Relief maps
Tee-shirt designs
Models and mock-ups
Flip charts
Pantomime
Sociodrama
Making films, slide shows, or movies
Paraphrasing songs and hymns, or writing
    new lyrics to old tunes
Writing new songs
Singing
Reading or writing various forms of poetry
    such as haiku or cinquain
Using a videotape recorder
Making and using overhead projector
    transparencies

The preceding list is, of course, just to get our juices flowing. We need to have a fuller understanding of some of the principal methods, their strengths and weaknesses. The List of Methods[2], page 63, will help at this point.

How to Lead Good Discussions[3]

Discussions gain their strength from the way they use the fundamental principle that students learn best when they are involved with learning.

Through discussion, students share feelings and opinions and test out ideas with their peers. In effect, they bear witness to their faith. Small wonder that group discussion has become a staple in the religious educator's pantry of methods.

Ability to discuss develops with one's ability to do abstract thinking. It also requires a certain self-confidence to expose one's opinions and thinking to a group. Consequently, Twelves will not generate a lengthy discussion, probe an issue very deeply, or expose too much of their personal feelings. On the other hand, Fifteens, given a stimulating issue, can spend the large part of a session in creative, active discussion.

Even though the quality and style of discussion vary from age to age, it seems equally effective for all the ages as a learning method. However, you will not apply to Twelves the same standards you would apply to Fifteens.

Ask discussable questions.

Good questions fuel discussion. Poor questions stifle discussion, because they are not really discussable. Questions which review fact offer slim discussion potential. But questions of opinion and feeling spark vigorous discussion. What makes for a good question? Many teachers use these criteria:

Good discussion questions focus on the person.

A good discussion question asks something of a person. A simple way to do this is to use the word *you* in your questions:
    "What do *you* think about . . ."
    "Have *you* ever experienced . . ."
    "What in *your* life does this remind *you* of . . ."
    "Will *you* share what *you* . . ."

Good discussion questions cannot be answered yes or no.

To the question, "Do you think Moses was right in taking the people out of Egypt?" students can answer: "Sure." Such queries have little discussion potential. A better question form: "How do you think Moses felt as he took his people from Egypt?" Questions beginning with "Do," "When," "Who," and "Where" deal with facts. Questions that start with "Why," "How," and "Have" generally call for feelings and opinions which reach beyond simple yes-no responses or statements of fact.

Much frustration stems from confusing discussion with reviewing facts. Confused students play the "guess what's on the teacher's mind" game. Asked, "When Abraham went up Mount Moriah, what did he take with him?" students wonder if the teacher wants to hear about the wood, the two young men, the fire pot, the donkeys, Isaac, or the whole lot of them. Discussion questions, after questions which review the facts of the story, would be, "When in your life have you had to give up something very precious to you?" "How did you feel about it?" "How did it affect your relations with God?"

Good discussion questions probe beyond pat answers.

Students, especially from the middle of Grade 8 and beyond, should be nudged beyond the pat answer to accept God's challenging questions. Younger students have not yet formed their ideas or developed their abstract thinking abilities to the point where they can endure contradictions and "devil's advocate" questions. But older students enjoy pushing and testing ideas; in fact, if the teacher doesn't do so, they will do it themselves.

Good discussion questions require slow answers.

Many discussions die because the leader does not give enough time for participants to develop responses to the questions. Give time for reflection; don't be afraid of silence. Give time, too, for all students to offer answers to such questions as, "What does your baptism mean to you now?" This is the type of question for which each participant may have a different answer.

Good discussion questions don't require evaluation of the answers.

Evaluating answers by responding "That's right" is a bad habit. Discussion reaches beyond simple right and wrong answers. Respond by affirming the person or asking if anyone has something to add.

Good discussion questions don't introduce new information.

A persistent myth, presumably started by the venerable Socrates, asserts that people gain information by answering questions. Teachers do better concentrating information gathering on reading, lectures, and investigations. Focus discussion on what everyone has studied and knows something about. Don't leap to a new, less familiar subject in the middle of a discussion. A big conceptual leap will confuse the participants. Keep within the experience of your group. Discussion can help generalize and apply information already learned, as well as helping to reveal gaps in understanding and to motivate persons toward further information gathering.

Good discussion questions follow the "onion principle."

Discussion leaders unfold the topic in a manner much like peeling away the layers of an onion. They go step-by-step from the factual and concrete to the feelings, then to the generalizations. This is the sequence in which most people think, and to skip or jump a step causes confusion and stifles discussion. Younger ages cannot handle as many steps as older students. The steps are as follows:

—What are the *facts?* This reviews the information at hand. Twelves can do this well.

—What do the facts mean to *me?* Twelves can explore this area, but not much more.

—What do the facts mean to *others?* When others are people they know, Thirteens can go into this level of discussion.

—What do the facts mean to the *world in general?* This level of generalization requires a concept of the "whole world" and would challenge most Fourteens and many Fifteens.

—How do these facts *relate to other facts?* This kind of generalization, which requires bringing together discrete ideas into a new formation, becomes possible, in a tentative way, for Fourteens and Fifteens. However, even Fifteens have trouble synthesizing ideas that are conceptually quite different.

Use techniques that stimulate discussion.

Recognize age-level limitations.

In an ideal discussion, the lines of conversation weave among the participants without connecting very often with the leader. Fourteens and Fifteens can approach this ideal under good leadership. Younger students require more direction and prodding by the leader. Early Twelves mostly respond to the leader's questions, with an occasional spurt of conversation among participants. These differences stem from differences in development and should be expected. Twelves and Thirteens should be encouraged to discuss, but the leader should accept a realistic level of participation.

Since younger adolescents are still experimenting with their new reasoning abilities, they often come to conclusions or combine ideas that seem irrational to adults. Attribute this to lack of skill in reasoning, and lend warm support to every effort they make toward reasoning. If a Twelve gets criticized for "stupid ideas," he or she will learn that church is not a safe place to think. When that same person reaches fifteen and is able to think in more complex, complete ways, he or she will have stopped talking in church.

Affirm all attempts to think theologically and be constantly aware of the marked differences in reasoning abilities over these years.

Encourage the nontalkers.

A few verbal young people who love to talk can dominate any discussion. Shy nontalkers gladly let the vocal ones burn up the discussion time, so that they don't have to talk themselves. A good leader tries to give air time to everyone. Questions specifically directed to the silent ones may help: "Bill, you seem quiet. What's your reaction to what Janet said?"

Keep groups small.

Many experts in small-group work contend that when a group goes above seven participants, people make "presentations" instead of really discussing.

Twelves and Thirteens may find a group of seven rather threatening and might work better in threes or fours. You can form small discussion groups by dividing up the participants into buzz groups of the desired size.

You cannot provide leadership for several small groups at once. You can, however, help increase their effectiveness with a few simple techniques:

—Select the group members yourself. Put the talkers together. If some students have matured socially to the point where they show sensitivity to the feelings of others and want to encourage everyone to participate, intersperse them with hesitant talkers.

—Give very clear discussion questions. Don't give independent groups an assignment as vague as "Discuss the end of the world." Be more specific. For example, "How can the lordship of Christ make us feel more hopeful when we read about the troubles in the world?"

—Relate the discussion to the study. The discussion question should be closely connected to what was studied. Students should only have to give feelings and reactions to what they have learned immediately before. Younger adolescents, especially, cannot deal with broader generalizations without a leader's help.

—Ask for reports. Each discussion group should report a summary conclusion. Expect this, and express disappointment if they don't do it. Establishing a level of expected performance over a period of time will motivate students.

—Keep the discussion brief. For Twelves, two or three minutes may be enough at the start. For Fourteens and Fifteens, five to seven minutes.

Provide for "opening gambits."

Discussion often goes better when each particpant has something to share at the outset. This gives everyone an opening gambit to get started: do this by asking each person to write something before the discussion. The discussion begins when everyone shares what he or she wrote and talks about why he or she wrote it. Here are two effective opening gambits:

Scales. Present the class with a situation or a statement. Ask them to respond on a scale of 1–5 (or 1–10), with the numbers 1 and 10 representing the extreme, opposed positions. Some leaders prefer even-numbered scales (1–4 or 1–10) because they don't have a midpoint number and this discourages fence sitting. Discussion begins as each shares the number chosen and explains why he or she chose it.

Feeling cards. On 3–by–5–inch cards, participants write out some expression of their feelings. These can be words: "Write four words that express your feelings about this Bible passage"; completed sentences: "Write your ending for this sentence—'If I really and

truly believed this, I would . . .' "; or symbols: "Create a coat of arms that expresses your life and show where Christ has his role" or "Draw a symbol or cartoon that tells how you feel about your baptism."

These opening gambits are excellent devices for stimulating discussion in smaller, independent discussion groups!

Maintain an open atmosphere.

We are forgiven children of God. Our task is to help heal broken spirits. In Christ's church, all kinds of people are welcomed here.

The style characteristic of Christianity creates the atmosphere that makes discussion possible. Realizing an atmosphere of acceptance rather than one of judgment and put-downs, poses a great challenge to leaders of young people. It begins when the teacher shows acceptance of and interest in each person. That may not be all you can do but if you don't do this, you can't accomplish anything else.

Talk with the group about the kind of atmosphere you want to establish. Ask them what kind of class spirit they want. Invite them to describe how they would like to be treated and request their help in making the class like that. (Do this at some time other than after a discussion breaks down and you are disgusted.)

In summary, three factors stimulate discussion. Assuming there is a discussable question to begin with, you will need:

—An atmosphere of openness, free of judgment.

—A small group (for some that may be two people).

—A pervasive feeling that "I have something to contribute."

How to Keep Participants Awake[4]

Young adolescents cannot sit still for long with any degree of comfort. As a rule of thumb, ten minutes or so in one location or position is the maximum. In addition, they respond to the change of pace offered by different activities. Variety, movement, stimulating pacing, all contribute to increased interest and alertness on the part of the students.

Mix small– and large–group activities.

Break up the group into discussion or work teams of two to four. Then come back as a whole group to share or compare results. This simple trick provides for movement and exercise. Try to have them move at least two to four feet and rearrange their chairs, instead of simply forming a small group where they been sitting already. Ideally, have one part of the room set up for the whole group and another part reserved for working as small groups.

Use graffiti sheets.

A graffiti sheet is simply a large piece of paper, either newsprint or wrapping paper. Students write on it with felt-tip pens. Since the graffiti sheet is taped to a wall with masking tape, students must walk up to the wall to do the writing.

If students are to complete a sentence, for example, you could write the sentence stem on the graffiti sheet and let everyone mill about as they pen in their own endings.

It is essential to tape a blank sheet of paper underneath the graffiti sheet, to prevent ink from bleeding through to the wall.

Use against-the-wall debates.

Along one wall, tape up pieces of paper, each containing one number from 1–4 or 1–10, depending on the length of the wall. The wall now becomes a kind of rating scale.

Pose a question or statement for discussion. It should be one that allows various shades of opinion or reaction. Let the low number stand for one extreme, the high number for the other extreme. Give the participants a few moments to evaluate their opinions and each to choose a number. At your signal, participants go to the spot on the wall that represents their chosen rating number.

Let each participant explain why he or she chose that particular spot. Then let those toward each extreme try to argue others into joining them. Let those toward the middle do the same with the extremes. As soon as someone changes his or her mind, the person shifts position along the wall.

The activity of physically expressing one's position helps young people learn the importance of taking a stand.

Provide learning areas.

If the area permits, assign different parts of your space to different activities. As participants engage in the various activities, they will be moving around through a variety of learnings.

Use projects and simulations.

Curriculum leader guides often include simulations (a form of game in which participants act out a situation to experience what in actuality it might be like) and projects of various kinds, such as collages, posters, and crafts.

Some leaders ignore these activities, because they consume large blocks of time and the leaders don't understand how they teach anything. If fact they are excellent teaching devices, because they have a high degree of participant involvement; and they provide for physical movement.

How to Provide Experiential Learning

Many authorities argue that everything we learn is a result of experience; that is, we must *do* something in order to learn. But the best learning experiences are the ones that are the most direct. We can read about the danger of going around a curve too fast (and reading is an indirect experience) without learning as much as we would learn from a serious skid while actually speeding around a curve (which is a very direct experience).

Obviously, students would learn more about missions from six months working in a mission in Tanzania than from a book about missions. But such direct experiences aren't always possible. You must compromise and choose an experience more direct than reading, yet realistic and feasible. Three possibilities are: talking with someone who has worked in Tanzania; seeing a film on Tanzania; or having a Tanzanian meal while dressed in Tanzanian costumes.

However, we don't automatically learn from experience. Think of the people who continually cut themselves on the same knife! We need to process the experience, run it thorough some steps so that we can take advantage of all the learning it has to offer us.

Authorities in the field have identified four steps to learning from experience, which are easily remembered by the acronym DRAG:

DO—Do the experience, whether it is a field trip, a speaker, film, or a simulation game. (Reading is also a DO, and can be processed in this manner of DRAG. Reading is simply less direct, less involving of several senses than a field trip, for instance.)

REFLECT—At this point, participants think and talk about the experience. In a sense, they relive it through words.

ANALYZE—Participants now probe the experience: What does it mean? How did I react? What does it say to me? What did I learn?

GENERALIZE—Finally, participants explore how this experience can apply to their own lives. They apply the specific learnings from this one experience to other situations.

Thinking in terms of this simple sequence makes good sense. It describes how we learn most of what we know.

Adolescents accomplish these four steps with different degrees of sophistication, depending upon their age. Few have any trouble with DO and REFLECT. Twelves and Thirteens will not be as penetrating in the ANALYZE stage as Fourteens and Fifteens. Early

Twelves may have trouble doing much at all with the GENERALIZE step, but later Twelves and Thirteens can make simple generalizations related to similar experiences in their own lives. Fifteens can generalize rather broadly, although not with the consistency and profundity adults might demonstrate.

Select good learning experiences (DO).

Be alert to possible experiences in addition to reading, writing, or talking. Use your curriculum suggestions. Besides curriculum suggestions, draw on your imagination to develop good experiences: gathering around the font to view a baptism, going with the pastor on certain pastoral and sick calls, having a seder, sitting in on a church council meeting, or visiting an institution of the church. Films, outside speakers with firsthand expertise, and simulations are also worthwhile experiences.

A good learning experience relates directly to the topic under study. Ask yourself, "Do I see clear and obvious connections between this experience and what we have been discussing and studying in class?" The tighter the connections, the easier it is for them to generalize from the experience to the topic.

Introduce any experience by explaining what they will be doing and how it fits into the program.

Provide some structure for reflection (REFLECT).

Adolescents need help with their thinking, which you provide through structured or organized methods for reflecting.

Reflection has two parts: general reflection and individual reflection.

General reflection means simply going over the experience. What did they observe, do, smell, hear? Five people will perceive the same experience in five different ways. Going over it allows everyone to share their own perceptions and bring the whole group to a commonly shared perception of the experience. Otherwise, the group could end up discussing several experiences—based on their separate perceptions of what happened.

Individual reflection requires that each participant reflect on what the experience has meant to him or her. Simply asking, "What did you learn from this?" seldom works. Adolescents need a structured, step-by-step approach. The structure can be simple. Here are some examples:

—Pass out 3-by-5-inch cards. On each, ask participants to answer an incomplete sentence, such as "When observing the baptism, I felt (*or* learned *or* was amazed by *or* didn't realize before). . . ." With Fourteens and Fifteens you can be more general, such as

"The four things that happened to me in this experience are. . . ."

—Fold sheets of paper once each way to form four sections. Give one sheet to each participant. Ask each to do the following:

    a. Color one part the color of your experience. (Here they choose a color that suggests or symbolizes their reactions, such as yellow for joy, purple for being disturbed, or whatever.)

    b. In another part, write three words to name different feelings you had during the experience. (With Twelves, one or two words will be enough.)

    c. In another part, complete this sentence: "I saw God at work in. . . ." (You may choose another sentence if more appropriate to your experience.)

    d. In the final part, write endings to these sentences: "I learned . . .," "I was surprised . . .," "I wonder. . . ."

—Ask each participant to write three or four questions they have about the experience or as the result of it.

—With Fourteens and Fifteens, imagination exercises may prove interesting. Give these instructions slowly: "Close your eyes and relive the experience in your mind. Think of the beginning of the experience. What happened first? . . . Then what happened? . . . Then what happened? . . . After that, what did you do (or see)? . . . What came next? . . . How did it end? . . . Now open your eyes . . . Write five phrases as a kind of outline of the most significant parts of your experience. Share these with others in the group."

Identify learnings and feelings (ANALYZE).

After doing something and reflecting upon it, it is time to nail down the learnings and feelings, to analyze and explore them.

You could post a graffiti sheet (a large piece of wrapping paper or newsprint) and have each participant write on it what he or she learned or relearned, using a felt-tip pen. Or you could have each complete this sentence: "I am glad we had this experience because . . . ."

When the specific learnings are identified, you have analyzed the experience enough to find out what it teaches.

Twelves and Thirteens will, of course, evidence far less analytical ability than will Fourteens and Fifteens. Younger adolescents may express such simple learnings that you will be tempted to think, "I could have told them that in ten seconds!" Don't let their inexperience with abstraction, analysis, and expression confuse you. They have learned, in important ways, more than they can identify and express. Being inexperienced in abstract thinking, they let things run together into simple wholes, while older youth and adults make more careful distinctions.

Remember age-level abilities when generalizing (GENERALIZE).

Spend some time relating the identified experiential learnings to other learnings. Twelves can relate learnings from experience to similar learnings from earlier reading and discussion. Fifteens can begin to generalize learnings across subjects, such as applying a theological learning to psychology or another secular subject.

All experiences involve feelings, and these may be a large part of the learnings identified by fourteen- and fifteen-year-olds. Feelings from one experience can be generalized into other experiences. For example, Mary

was frightened during a trust walk (where blindfolded participants are led through an obstacle course by partners and must trust their partners with their safety). If Mary were twelve or thirteen years old, she could express her fear and ascribe it to lack of trust in her partner. From this she can make the simple generalization that God is more reliable than Sam (her partner), so when it comes to trusting God, she need not fear. But if Mary is fourteen of fifteen years of age, she can recognize ambivalent feelings on the walk (fear and thrills) and generalize these to the ambivalence of her faith in God—trusting and fearing God at the same time.

Don't expect Twelves to perform as well at this stage as older adolescents. Expect more expression of feelings from mid-Thirteens and beyond than from younger participants.

[1]David Ng, "List of Methods" reprinted from *Youth: A Manual for Christian Education: Shared Approaches.* Copyright © 1977 by the Geneva Press. Used by permission.

[2]David Ng, "Methods Chart and List" reprinted from *Youth: A Manual for Christian Education: Shared Approaches.* Copyright © 1977 by the Geneva Press. Used by permission.

[3]"How to Lead Good Discussions" reprinted from *Teaching Grades Seven Through Ten: A Handbook,* John Stevens Kerr, ed. Copyright © 1980 by Parish Life Press. Used by permission.

[4]*Ibid.*

CHART OF METHODS

METHOD*	DESCRIPTION OF METHOD	ILLUSTRATION
Audio-Visual	This is a method which uses eye- and ear-gates for communicating ideas. It includes sound films, sound filmstrips, and recordings used with pictures.	
Brainstorming	Ideas are expressed in a climate of complete freedom. ANY idea is accepted; NO judgments are expressed about an idea. The subject matter is described, and everyone expresses any and all ideas that come to mind. A time limit is prescribed at the beginning. ALL ideas are recorded by a secretary.	
Buzz Groups	The total group is divided into smaller groups (3 to 6 in each) to provide an opportunity for reaction to a problem, lecture, audio-visual, or other presentation. Buzz groups can be formed by clustering or by counting off. Discussion should be limited to not more than five to six minutes. Reports should be made to total group, reassembled.	
Circular Response	Leader and total group are seated in a circle. After topic of consideration is introduced, leader invites person on right to express views on the subject. Leader is followed by the next person on the right, and so on, around the circle until every person has had an opportunity to speak. A person may speak more than once, but only in turn.	
Colloquy	This is a modified form of a panel. Following a lecture, the audience can be clustered or reassigned to small groups to discuss the subject. Then one representative from each group becomes part of a panel to ask questions of the lecturer and other resource persons who form a second panel. A moderator keeps questions and answers moving.	
Directed Reading	Assignments for simultaneous reading are written on a flip chart or chalkboard. Participants pair off to read together silently or aloud and to discuss the reading in relation to the subject.	
Discussion	Ideas are shared orally in a group. The group should be small (15 maximum, if possible). All participants should be able to make eye contact with one another. Each participant's accepting responsibility for all others to express themselves is important.	

*This chart is not comprehensive, either in the methods listed or in their uses.

VALUES	LIMITATIONS	EXAMPLES	
		WHEN TO USE	WHEN NOT TO USE
Presents facts in a remember-able way; makes the in-accessible accessible.	Easily construed as enter-tainment; must be expertly done or it loses its value. Equipment failure is a hazard.	When a group needs a living experience from outside the life of the group.	If the illustration portrayed is beyond the need of the group; if obtaining the film in time to be useful is difficult.
Creates a climate of free ex-pression by removing the threat of judgment; special-izes on ideas only, so every-one can "think up a storm."	Produces a lot of apparently unusable material, thus mak-ing some people feel it has been a waste of time.	When a group is ready to be extremely creative, daring, and adventuresome; when it is up against a blank wall and needs new ideas.	If a group already has come to a final decision, for this process could very well upset the work that has been done.
Provides time and climate for every person to state ideas, ask questions, and think through the question; gets 100% participation.	Ideas are likely to be shallow and disorganized, due to the shortness of time.	When everyone has the urge to talk; when group members seem to be stymied or re-luctant to express their ideas.	If the group has moved into deep discussion or is dealing in technical matters that do not need opinions.
Provides equal opportunity for each group member to ex-press an opinion; puts brakes on argumentative members and encourages timid ones to speak.	If used too long at a time, may make discussion of a hot issue seem stilted or mechani-cal.	When group is dealing with a controversial issue; when it is difficult to get group parti-cipation.	When group is larger than 12 to 15; when majority of group is inadequately in-formed about subject of dis-cussion.
Permits direct group repre-sentation and participation; lifts the questions of the group to a verbalization level.	A large-group (above 50 peo-ple) method; resource person must be well informed on the subject and able to talk in-formally with the group.	When expert knowledge is needed; when in a large group it is advisable to have com-plete oral participation.	When a group is under 50 in number; when the group is in-formal enough to feel free to ask the expert questions for clarification.
Assures that every participant reads the resource material es-sential to group discussion.	Difficult to time because some people are slow readers, others very fast; difficult for some pairs to stick to subject being covered.	When a group comes together and it is obvious they have not had a chance to read ahead of time.	When the reading material is limited (just a few copies of the book); when it appears that everyone has read the as-signment.
Draws ideas from the experi-ences of all participants and helps develop area of agree-ment.	Limited to small groups (15); more aggressive persons can dominate; discussion cannot be hurried if it is to be fruit-ful.	When personal opinions and illustrations are needed; when differences of opinion and agreements need to be ex-pressed.	If the group is in need of ac-curate, technical, detailed in-formation.

From *Learning About Methods: a Group Development Unit;* by D. Alison Holt; Copyright © 1965. Christian Board of Publication. Used by permission.

METHOD*	DESCRIPTION OF METHOD	ILLUSTRATIONS
Field Trip	A group visits setting(s) other than its normal meeting place, usually to investigate a problem or to confront group with a real situation.	
Lecture	A carefully prepared oral presentation of a subject is made by a qualified person. This is one person presenting a set of ideas, either memorized or read, to a group of listeners.	
Paired Reading Review	Two persons are assigned a body of reading—such as a chapter in a book—which they read separately before the session. During the session they discuss the reading content before the group. A third person (perhaps the leader) interviews them, relating their reading to the subject.	
Panel (Panel Forum)	A group of four to eight persons who have special knowledge of the topic sit at a table in front of the audience and hold an orderly and logical conversation on the assigned subject, guided by a moderator. (It becomes a panel forum if the audience directs questions to panel.) The moderator closes with a summary.	
Resource Person	A person who has extensive knowledge of a subject is called upon to provide knowledge the group needs. Resource person gives the facts and does not seek to mount a pet soapbox or to thwart group creativity.	
Role Play	A group of "players" act out a given situation dealing with a specific problem confronting the group. It includes these steps: select the situation; assign roles; brief the players and the group; enact the situation; cut; interview some of the observing group and the players; summarize the findings; "de-role" the players.	
Symposium	A series of speeches is given by two to five speakers who are experts in the field being studied. A moderator guides and limits the presentations. Each speaker may take a different aspect of the subject under consideration.	
Visual Aid	This includes a chalkboard, cartoon, chart, display, film, filmstrip, flannel board, graph, map, model, opaque projector, photograph, illustration, poster, puppet, slide, and other objects. Each item has its own method of use.	

VALUES	LIMITATIONS	EXAMPLES	
		WHEN TO USE	WHEN NOT TO USE
Provides opportunity for a group to procure firsthand knowledge or confront a real situation related to or stimulating a subject of group study or action.	Requires extra time and energy for planning; may have to be scheduled at a time inconvenient to some group members.	When it provides the group the best means of obtaining accurate information, insights, or feelings about a subject that will help achieve the group goal.	When leader is ill-prepared; when members are not aware of purpose of the trip; when trip is seen only as something to do, and little or no planning for learning is made.
Communicates a body of material in an orderly, logical, and factual fashion; makes listening an art.	Audience cannot complete its participation—can only listen; easy for persons to get lost in their own thoughts.	When a unified message is needed; when one person is an authority on a subject and can be stimulating.	Only if audience participation is needed, in which case it can be used in conjunction with other methods.
Makes possible advance preparation for bringing resource material to the group; helps involve the group through listening.	Persons assigned need to be very stimulating in their conversation. Much depends upon their ability to communicate.	When the resource material is limited or is difficult to read or understand.	When there is no one available who can make a stimulating presentation.
Brings a variety of knowledge—agreements and disagreements—to the group; audience can identify with various panel members.	Easy for panel members to ramble if they are not thoroughly oriented to the subject.	To introduce a new topic; to help a stymied group regain its perspective by considering different views of a subject in an orderly and logical conversation.	If a group is assembling for the first time; if the members have had a thoroughly satisfying discussion of the subject.
Provides the wisdom of someone who "has been there"; helps group test its ideas against real experience.	Possibility of creating dependence on a "headliner" to provide the answers.	When a group is in need of an experienced voice; when a group feels the need to find out what others are doing.	If the group members have not really thought through their own position on the matter.
A nonthreatening way of dealing with emotional situations; authentic because it is spontaneous, never rehearsed.	Tendency to let the role play become entertainment or to feel it is fictitious and so not of value, to forget that the emotions ARE real.	When a group needs to have some real data about its own life, not something from outside itself.	If a group is extremely tired and its emotions seem on edge, a role play could easily get out of hand.
Brings several sides to an issue in an authoritative way.	Needs to be used with a method that involves the audience.	When a group seems to be bogging down because it cannot see several sides to an issue.	If a group still has its creative spirit in struggling for its own solution to the problem.
Uses "eye-gate" to provide better recall of an idea; helps mind establish relationships.	Getting equipment may be a problem.	When the group is in need of the help of the "eye-gate" to unravel an abstraction.	Unacceptable only when its use would be offensive to group members or when accompanying noise might disturb others outside the group.

Key Resources for Youth Ministry

Program Resources

Making Sense of Your Faith Marsha B. Woodard, Editor. (Valley Forge: Judson Press, 1987). $9.95.

An exciting adventure in discipleship for senior high youth! Bible study, group discussion, case studies and coordinated activities encourage youth to dig deep into God's Word as they explore foundations of faith for daily living.

Building a Faith to Live By Byron R. McCane and Preston Van Loon. (Valley Forge: Judson Press, 1987). $9.95.

An action-packed series for senior high youth with a practical, experiential approach to Christian concepts and spiritual disciplines.

Connections Steven L. Edwards. (Valley Forge: Judson Press, 1986). $7.95.

A new youth ministry concept: six mini-retreats in which a small group of senior-high youth focus on faith disciplines, salvation, worship, service, and witness for Christ.

Bible Journeys Dick Orr and David L. Bartlett (Valley Forge: Judson Press, 1980). $4.95.

A unique resource to help youth in their personal search for Christian growth. Through imaginative first person narrative, the Bible comes alive.

The New Games Book, and **More New Games** Andrew Fluegelman. (Garden City, New York: Doubleday/Dolphin, 1976, 1981). $6.95 each.

Many, many games that encourage playing over winning, cooperation, self-competition, and creating your own rules.

Controversial Topics for Youth Groups Edward N. McNulty. (Loveland, CO: Group Books, 1988). $13.95.

Practical programs for dealing with forty tough issues, including abortion, rock music, pornography, premarital sex, drugs and drinking and capital punishment.

My Identity: A Gift From God Rodger Nishioka and Mary Lee Talbot (New York: Youth and Young Adult Program, Presbyterian Church, USA, 1987). $2.00 each (minimum order of 5).

A unique resource to help racial and ethnic senior-high youth look at the forces that shape identity, and to develop those positive values that come from family, ethnic heritage, culture, society and church. Seven sessions in three languages: English, Spanish, and Korean.

Planning Resources

Organizing a Youth Ministry to Fit Your Needs Jeffrey D. Jones and Kenneth C. Potts. (Valley Forge: Judson Press, 1983). $3.95.

A resource that will help churches develop a youth ministry best suited to their needs.

The Group Retreat Book Arlo Reichter and others. (Loveland, CO: Group Books, 1983). $15.95.

Complete retreat planning guide, plus 34 ready-to-use designs for junior- and senior-high youth groups.

Youth Ministries: Thinking Big with Small Groups Carolyn C. Brown. (Nashville: Abingdon Press, 1984). $7.95.

Answering the needs of churches that minister to four or five youth (and sometimes even one!), this resource is packed with useful and proven ideas.

Leadership Training Resources

Developing Leaders for Youth Ministry David Ng, (Valley Forge: Judson Press, 1984). $5.95.

A unique workshop concept specifically designed to give both experienced and potential leaders training in the area of Christian lifestyle, faith values, and the importance of relationships in youth leadership.

Creative Youth Leadership Janice Corbett, (Valley Forge: Judson Press, 1977). $4.25.

A practical book for leaders seeking to understand youth, plan group activities, find and use resources, and develop 'survival' skills.

The Exuberant Years: A Guide for Junior High Leaders Ginny Ward Holderness, (Atlanta: John Knox Press, 1976). $6.50.

A handbook to help workers with junior-highs plan, develop and carry out youth programming in the local church.

Philosophy of Youth Ministry Resources

Youth Ministry: Making and Shaping Disciples Jeffrey D. Jones. (Valley Forge: Judson Press, 1984). $4.95.

A call for adults to rediscover the central purpose of youth ministry, to put aside the crowd-pleasing gimmicks and concentrate on helping young persons to a personal encounter with Jesus Christ.

Youth in the Community of Disciples David Ng. (Valley Forge: Judson Press, 1984). $4.95.

A call for adults to rediscover the central purpose of youth ministry, to put aside the crowd-pleasing gimmicks, and concentrate on helping young persons to a personal encounter with Jesus Christ.

Faith Shaping *(Revised Edition)* Stephen Jones, (Valley Forge: Judson Press, 1987). $7.95.

How parents and the church can nurture teens in their search for a solid foundation of faith that will continue to grow in young adulthood. Jones discusses stages of the faith cycle, evangelism, creating a nurturing environment, how youth can shape their culture, and more.

Reaching Youth Today: Heirs To The Whirlwind Barbara Hargrove and Stephen D. Jones, (Valley Forge: Judson Press, 1983). $7.95.

Helps adults understand the world in which youth live and helps churches see opportunities for effective evangelism with youth.

Youth Ministry: The New Team Approach Ginny Ward Holderness, (Atlanta: John Knox Press, 1981). $9.95.

A model to involve youth in the total life of the church.

Theological Themes of Youth Ministry William Myers, (New York: The Pilgrim Press, 1987). $8.95.

Seven theological themes, based on the lectionary or seasons of the year framework, focus on ministry with youth.

Materials for Youth Reading

I Am Special Marlene Bagnull. (Valley Forge: Judson Press, 1987). $5.95.

Prayer diary for junior-high girls. Opportunities to talk with God about fears, doubts, happy times, down times, and those very personal thoughts you can't share with anyone else.

I've Got Mixed-Up Feelings, God John Brown, (Valley Forge: Judson Press, 1984). $3.95.

Helps in focusing real feelings, and learning more about yourself and what God is doing in your life.

Alive Now!

A contemporary reading and meditation magazine for older youth who want resources for their personal devotions. Published six times a year. Order on Judson Curriculum Order Form. $7.00 per year.

This listing was compiled by the Department of Ministry with Youth, Educational Ministries, ABC, USA.

Prices subject to change. All books listed, unless otherwise indicated, can be ordered from Judson Book Store, P.O. Box 851, Valley Forge, PA 19482-0851.

PART 3

Program Plans for Asian Pacific American Youth Groups

Theme 1: Identity and Culture
Theme 2: Relationships and Community
Theme 3: Beliefs and the Christian Faith
Theme 4: Vocation and the World

THEME 1

Identity and Culture

Answering the question "Who Am I?" is a major task for all youth, but especially those of the Asian Pacific American heritage. Some answers are found by looking at cultural histories and taking time to claim these histories for oneself. Asian Pacific American heritage, traditions, and communities all contribute to who youth are. At the same time, Asian Pacific Americans have the opportunity to affirm and develop what they like about themselves as full members in the family of God.

- What Is a Sojourner? *by Carole Chuck*
- Wah-Kiu, *by Carole Chuck*
- Who Am I? *by Carole Chuck*
- Self-Image and Self-Esteem, *by Kathryn Choy–Wong*
- Naming, *by Kathryn Choy–Wong*

What Is a Sojourner?[1]

by Carole Chuck

Goal:

• Youth will be able to express various meanings for the concept "sojourner" as it is used today.

Introduction:

Although the word "sojourner" seldom appears in the daily newspapers, many stories of sojourners do: people of the underclass forced to find new homes, refugees seeking help after natural disasters, day laborers crossing dangerous borders to make a meager living, migrating tribes in Africa seeking food and water. Behind these stories are forces larger than the people themselves: political change, natural disasters, economic inequalities.

Most youth do not experience the lives of sojourners. They are not living in a place temporarily. Quite the opposite, they are secure, neither displaced nor relocated. Nevertheless, they often feel insecure, out of place, pushed around and unsettled. Therefore they can often attach some meaning to the word "sojourner." A sojourner is one who stays for a time in a place, lives temporarily, travels, but does not reside anywhere permanently. A sojourner has two contrasting sets of emotions: feelings of lostness, loneliness, or anxiety, and feelings of newness, adventure, or freedom. By studying this session, youth will find that "sojourning" is a common daily experience in this weary world.

Preparation:

Clip newspaper headlines and photos of people who have been displaced, and make a collage before your session. Gather additional materials for the youth to put together their own collages on the meaning of "sojourner." You may need magazines, newspapers, colored construction paper, scissors, glue, etc. Have some dictionaries available (including, if possible, one or more rather large ones and some copies of Roget's *Thesaurus*). Make enough copies of the "Family History Survey" for each member of the group.

Procedure:

Opening

Step 1. Create the Setting *(5 minutes)*

Have the word "sojourner" written on the chalkboard or on newsprint for the class to see as they come in. If you have access to songs that speak about travel or journey, have these playing. The songs can stress feelings of separation, longing, homesickness. Such music would add to the classroom atmosphere.

Step 2. Introduce the Topic *(15 minutes)*

When all the students have arrived, have them brainstorm together as many different synonyms for the word "sojourner" as possible. (If they need help, suggest one or two as starters.) Write these synonyms in a column on a chalkboard or newsprint and leave room for two other columns as well. Some possibilities are: wayfarer, alien, traveler, pilgrim, immigrant, emigrant, stranger, foreigner. Discuss nuances and connotations of these. Is a sojourner usually accepted in the place where he or she is living temporarily? Does the sojourner intend to accept this as a place of permanent residence, or does this person plan to return home?

Have the students volunteer examples of times when they felt like sojourners. Jot these down in the second column. Try to stimulate the students by probing or by giving examples. Possibilities are: when they were traveling to an unfamiliar destination; at camp where they were strangers; being lost somewhere; being at a place or in a situation where they did not feel they fully belonged; the first day in a new school, a new church school class, or a new neighborhood. The students will probably be able to come up with additional examples from their own experiences.

In a third column, write down a list of feelings the students associate with being a sojourner. Perhaps they would like to close their eyes for a minute, remembering the experiences they listed in column two, and concentrate on how they felt. Some possibilities are: helplessness, rootlessness, loneliness, strangeness, homesickness, shyness; feeling frightened, out of place, lost. Encourage any positive feelings, also, such as a sense of freedom, adventure, well-being, excitement, exploration, newness, curiosity.

Discovering

Step 3. Look in a Dictionary *(10 minutes)*

Have a number of dictionaries and Roget's *Thesaurus* on hand for a few students to look up the word "sojourner" or "sojourn" and read the definitions or synonyms aloud for the rest of the class. What seem to be the important parts of the definitions? What elements do the definitions have in common? What things are different? What new synonyms did you find? Do the definitions and synonyms contribute any new insight into our own understanding?

Step 4. Highlight Today's Headlines (5 minutes)

Show the students a collage you have made of newspaper headlines and photos you have collected. As you show them each picture, describe the circumstances that engulfed these people and caused them to leave and go to a strange land.

Step 5. Personalize the Meaning of Sojourner (30 minutes)

The students will now work individually on expressions of their current understanding of the "sojourner" concept. Some may wish to write about an experience in which they felt like a sojourner, stressing feelings, how they resolved any tension, coped with loneliness, etc. Encourage the students to be as descriptive as possible. Others may feel more at ease expressing themselves through the medium of a collage. Share with them that a "picture can be worth a thousand words" and that it can be a challenge to their skill to select appropriate pictures and images to express many meanings and associations with the concept "sojourner." Have materials on hand such as old magazines, glue, scissors, construction paper.

Give both groups a reasonable length of time, depending upon the length of the session. It would be encouraging to the group if the leader would also participate in one of these creative expressions and share it at the close of the session.

Closing

Step 6. Sharing Time (10 minutes)

Have each youth share what he/she has expressed in words or collage. Hopefully, through your own interest and through the supportive atmosphere you have been able to establish, the students will feel free to react to one another's work and will encourage and appreciate one another's uniqueness.

Step 7. Sharing a Learning (5 minutes)

Perhaps the students can think of one new thing they have learned or one new insight that never occurred to them before today. Invite them to share this. Offer a sentence prayer of appreciation for their contributions.

Wah-Kiu[1]

by Carole Chuck

Goals:

• Youth will be able to describe the circumstances under which many Chinese first came to America.

• Youth will be able to describe the life of the early Chinese sojourners, especially the kinds of jobs they had, the problems they encountered, and the growing hostility against them.

Introduction:

Wau-Kiu is the name of overseas Chinese people, pronounced in the Cantonese dialect.

Not more than ten miles from San Francisco are three Chinese cemeteries, each of several acres. Thousands of Chinese are buried there, some with dates in the early 1900s. Many of these were sojourners who could not afford the trip back to China. Their lives in California were very difficult, as the following poem attests, carved by a detainee on a wall of Angel Island, a quarantined camp in San Francisco Bay.

America is a strong country but it has no justice;
In this prison we were robbed of our freedom.
Without a chance to explain, it is really horrible;
I bow my head and think in vain,
But there is nothing I can do.

Our ancestors were sojourners when they came to America. Many came in search of gold in California; others were responding to the need for cheap, unskilled labor in the growing western frontier; still others came to escape unstable political and economic conditions in China.

The sojourners' experiences were filled with hard work and little reward, and there was a growing hostility and discrimination against them.

Preparation:

Set up three learning centers. In this session the youth will be able to participate in individualized, self-directed learning. The leader's role will be one of a resource person and guide and as the facilitator for the debriefing at the end. It would be helpful if the leader could have the learning centers set up in three different areas of the room before the students arrive, complete with materials needed and step-by-step instructions written on a piece of paper. Then, after a brief introduction on the contents of each center, each youth can choose the one in which he or she would like to work. Depending upon the length of the session, the number of youth and their interest, they could participate in more than one center.

Provide copies of Daniel and Samuel Chu's book *Passage to the Golden Gate: A History of the Chinese in America to 1910* (Garden City, N.Y.: Doubleday and Company, Inc., Zenith Books, 1967) for one of the learning centers, and make copies of the quiz based on this book. Make copies of the Sojourner Game, including the rules, for the second center. Make copies of "Story of a Young Chinese Girl" (page 80 of this book) for the third center, and if possible secure one or more copies of the book *Number One Son,* by Monfoon Leong (San Francisco: East/West Publishing Company, 1975) for the same center. Also make copies of the directions which appear in Step 2.

Procedure:

Opening
Step 1. Introduce the Centers *(5 minutes)*

After introducing the content of each center, encourage the youth to begin by choosing one to participate in.

Discovering
Step 2. Participate in the Centers *(30 minutes)*

Print the following directions and make copies available at the appropriate learning centers.

• *Passage to the Golden Gate*
This book is a simplified history of the Chinese who first came to America, complete with attractive drawings. If you can, read chapters 1–4 silently. You might want to also read chapter 8. Or you might want to skim the book and then select chapters for yourself to read that have particular interest to you. If there are enough copies, you may want to ask the teacher if you can take the book home. You will find a short quiz that you may want to try, covering the first four chapters. Or you might want to write down questions based on your reading and bring them to the debriefing time with the total group. (Step 3)

• *The "Sojourner Game"*
You will find a board game with playing pieces. The purpose of this game is to familiarize you with some of

the events and experiences that shaped the impressions of the first generations of Chinese in America. If you have questions or disagreements as you play the game, feel free to ask the leader.

• *Story of a Young Chinese Girl*

Read the true life story of a young Chinese girl who came to America on a clipper ship. Reflect on its meaning for your own family history.

In addition to this, or as an alternative, read chapter 3 of the short novel, "Precious Jade" found in the book, *Number One Son* by Monfoon Leong. This is a remarkably sensitive and vivid account of a young girl, Precious Jade, and her journey across the Pacific in a clipper ship to San Francisco to meet her husband-to-be. If you would like to read the entire story, ask the leader about borrowing this book.

Step 3. Share Learnings *(15 minutes)*

Take some time to gather as a whole group to share learnings. What have you learned today? What new discoveries did you make? What questions did you think of that you have never thought of before? What resources do we have where we might do further research?

Closing
Step 4. Close with Prayer *(5 minutes)*

Encourage prayers that could center on thanksgiving for a rich heritage and its meaning for us today.

The Sojourner Game

Instructions to the Leader

The leader needs to prepare for this game carefully. It is a board game in whch the players compete to reach their goal first. Complete rules are printed with the game. Each player needs a playing piece to advance around the board. These pieces may be chess pieces, buttons, beans, coins, checkers, or any other suitable objects. A spinner needs to be constructed, by which the player spins to see how many spaces he/she is to advance at each turn. This might be a simple one made from cardboard. An alternative to this would be a pile of index cards with numbers written on them indicating the number of spaces to advance. In either case, the numbers should probably range from 1–5.

After making a photocopy of the game board, set it up by pasting or taping the two sections together. It may be helpful to mount it on a large piece of cardboard.

STORY OF A YOUNG CHINESE GIRL

(It may be interesting to know that one of the writers collected this information recently from her mother. The writer had heard bits and pieces of the stories as she grew up. She remembered how she lived with her grandmother in the same house: she and her parents in one bedroom, her grandmother in the other bedroom. Her mother never pressed this story on the writer. Only when the writer asked was any part of the story uncovered. This is the kind of story which many of us can uncover for ourselves in our own families.)

I was eighteen years old when the matchmaker came to my village and sought out my mother and father. The look of delight in my mother's glance could not be disguised behind her normally stoic face. She had borne the criticism of the old biddies of the village about her old-maid daughter for too long. And so today, the slow, triumphant smile creased her browned face broadly, her white teeth gleaming, as the matchmaker told of the merits of the young man who wished my hand.

His name was Chin Quong, from the village of Sam Gop, many miles from my home, born of a poor farming family. At the age of twelve he had been converted to something called Christian faith by an American missionary in that area and had left his home and family to travel to America with that missionary, Dr. Hager. After his arrival, the young boy worked at several odd jobs, doing mostly domestic work, such as being a houseboy. He was also able to learn English from Dr. Hager, and thus became one of the few Chinese at the time in San Francisco who could speak English well.

Chin Quong had made several trips back to his homeland and now he was here to seek a strong and able wife. But the matchmaker made it clear that even though there would be a marriage, I would have to stay behind in China with my mother-in-law, separated from my husband, until the strict immigration laws of the United States were lifted. This part of the negotiation was not altogether satisfactory to my mother, but with an unmarried eighteen-year-old daughter still living at home, and with very few eligible men in the village, what could she do but to consent?

Chin Quong was a kind and gentle man, tall and almost distinguished-looking with confident eyes and high cheekbones. When we met formally for the first time, he bowed slightly, and looked up into my face with a reassuring and comforting grin. He told me of his family background, how his mother, father, sisters, brothers, aunts, uncles, and cousins had struggled to keep their small farm alive. He told of his conversion to the Christian faith and of his decision to follow the missionary to America at a young age; also of the opportunity to learn English and to work. The light seemed to flicker on his tanned, smooth face, his strong angular body animated and moving as he related his story. I could not help thinking that this stranger would become my husband, and that one day I would go to America also.

We were married in a simple Christian ceremony by another missionary friend of Chin Quong's. I was more than ready for the day. My mother, overjoyed at the betrothal of her eldest daughter, had given me two bolts of trousseau cloth, even though only one was customary. On the day before the wedding, I had trudged up the old familiar hill with the matchmaker, to take a last look at Lo Po Shan, my village, and thought of my parents, because I sensed in my inmost self, that I would never see my home and my parents again. I never did.

In the ensuing years I lived in my husband's village with his family while he returned to his work in America. I had two male children for my husband, who was able to make trips back to China from America. It was lonely without him, but there was much work to do in the village, cooking, sewing, mending, fetching water, working in the fields, and taking care of my babies.. I was 36 by the time Chin Quong returned on one of his trips and told me to get my things ready, that our family would be traveling to America on the next clipper ship. Joy crept secretly into my heart as I made preparations for the long journey. At last I would be joining my husband and I would see for myself this place called, "Gum San" or "Golden Mountains," the name we Chinese called California.

The trip by clipper ship took two months and I never did get used to the rolling, pitching, swaying, creaking boat. But I was grateful that our family was together, and that soon we would begin our life in America. We moved into a small house in Chinatown, where most Chinese people lived in San Francisco. It was here that my next four children were born, three boys and a girl. Raising them in America was not an easy task. I knew no English, but my children learned, and I could not help feeling that somehow, in some way, they would have a better life here than back in my poor village in China.

I never saw China again. From time to time, when Chin Quong would read to me from the newspapers about famine and war and poverty in China, I would cry and soak my pillow. My heart remembers the view from the hill above Lo Po Shan, the spring breezes, the bird sounds, and the sweet smells. There is nothing quite like this in my new home, America.

Rules for the Sojourner Game

1. The Sojourner Game can be played with two or more players. After the game has started, other players may join in at any time, as long as they start from the clipper ship in the upper left-hand corner and take their turns in order.

2. The object of the game is to advance to the end, that is, to complete the sojourn, first.

3. Before the game begins, each player must say aloud which of the five goals he/she is trying to reach at the end of the game, for example, "Save enough money to send for your wife from China," "Marry and settle down in San Francisco with your family," etc. All players must reach the space marked "Stop! End of Sojourning," and wait there until the next turn when he/she spins or draws the required number to advance to the ending he/she selected before the game began. Not until the player reaches the intended goal has the player won the game. Other players may come in second, third, fourth place, etc.

4. To start the game, each player must have a playing piece which moves about the board. Beginning on the space marked, "Clipper arrives." To leave the clipper, the player must spin or draw a "1" or "2." If the player does not get a "1" or a "2" on his/her turn, he/she does not advance out of the clipper ship, but waits until the next turn to try again.

5. Once out of the clipper ship, the players take turns in spinning or drawing numbers which they advance around the board on each turn. When the player lands on a space through spinning or drawing, he/she must read the instructions in the space and follow them.

6. If a player lands on a space which has been previously occupied by another player, the new player stays on the space, and the other player must return to the clipper ship and start the game again.

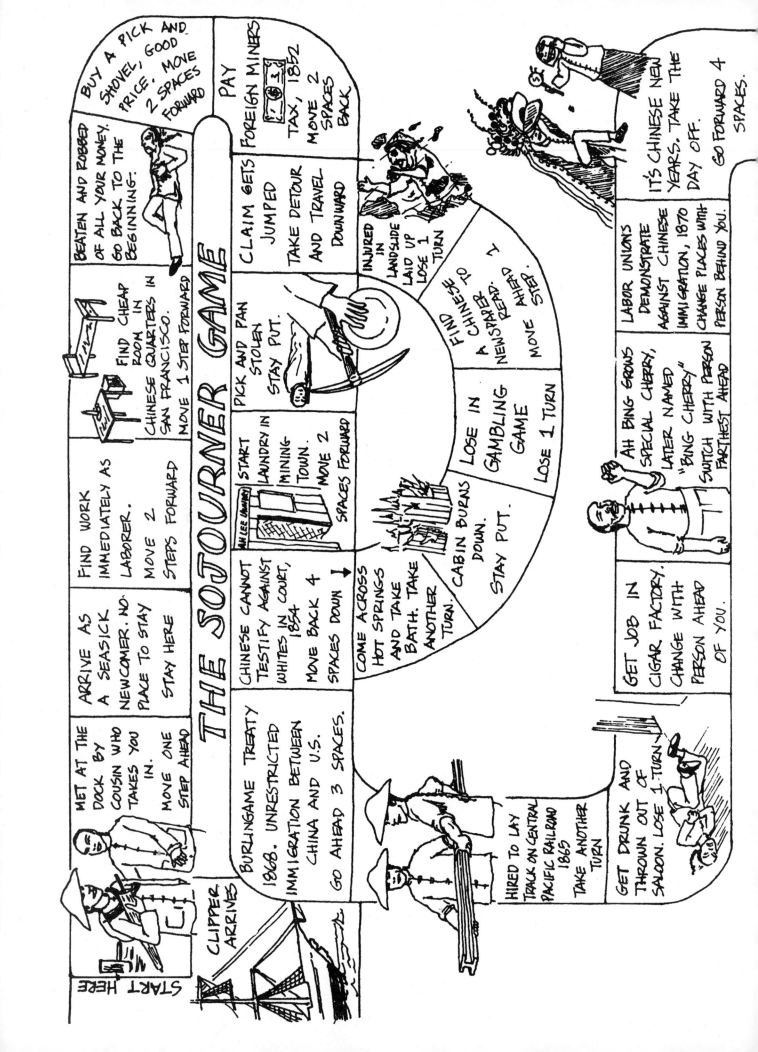

HIRED AS A HOUSEBOY. MOVE AHEAD 1 SPACE

QUEUE ORDINANCE PASSED. CHINESE IN JAIL HAVE QUEUES CUT. GO BACK 2.

HIRED AS A COOK IN CHINESE RESTAURANT. GO FORWARD 2 SPACES

MEET SOMEONE FROM YOUR HOME VILLAGE IN CHINA. GO AHEAD 3

1877, ANTI-CHINESE RALLY HELD IN SAN FRANCISCO, BUILDINGS BURNED. LOSE 1 TURN.

GET JOB IN A SHOE FACTORY. TAKE ANOTHER TURN.

CHINESE EXCLUSION ACT PASSED 1882. BAN ON IMMIGRATION MOVE BACK 5 SPACES

唐人街

OPEN A BARBER SHOP ON "TONG YAN GAI" (CHINESE STREET) MOVE FORWARD 2 SPACES.

GET JOB IN SHRIMP FISHERY MOVE AHEAD 1 SPACE.

BURLINGAME TREATY AMENDED IN 1880. U.S. HAS RIGHT TO REGULATE IMMIGRATION OF CHINESE. GO BACK 3 SPACES.

HIRED AS A FRUIT PICKER. GO AHEAD 1 SPACE.

EARN ENOUGH MONEY TO PAY BACK YOUR PASSAGE TO AMERICA. MOVE 3 SPACES AHEAD

GET JOB IN RECLAMATION WORK IN SACRAMENTO RIVER VALLEY. MOVE 2 AHEAD

GET JOB CONSTRUCTING WINE CELLERS IN NAPA AND SONOMA COUNTIES. MOVE 2 AHEAD.

ROCK SPRINGS MASSACRE OF 1885. 28 CHINESE MINERS KILLED. GO BACK 3 SPACES.

RECEIVE A LETTER FROM YOUR WIFE IN CHINA. MOVE 2 SPACES AHEAD.

INJURED IN TONG WARS OF 1890's LOSE 1 TURN

HIRED AS AN ASSISTANT IN HERB SHOP. GO AHEAD 1

STOP! END OF SOJOURNING. STAY HERE UNTIL YOU GET YOUR NUMBER ******

HAVE A GOLD STRIKE IN ABANDONED CLAIM, KEEP ON MINING.

BECOME PROSPEROUS TEA SHOP OWNER IN SAN FRANCISCO.

RETURN HOME ON NEXT CLIPPER SHIP, A BACHELOR, LITTLE FORTUNE.

MARRY AND SETTLE DOWN IN SAN FRANCISCO WITH YOUR FAMILY

SAVE ENOUGH MONEY TO SEND FOR YOUR WIFE FROM CHINA

GOAL #1   GOAL #2   GOAL #3   GOAL #4   GOAL #5

Passage to the Golden Gate
Short Quiz

Instructions: Write the appropriate letter(s) in the space provided. Then check your answers with those given at the bottom of the page.

1. _____ The main item for which American shipmasters sailed halfway round the world was: (a) molasses, (b) bronze, (c) sea otter furs, (d) tea, (e) furs.

2. _____ In order to reach China from America, the ocean that the clipper ships had to cross was the: (a) Indian, (b) Atlantic, (c) Pacific, (d) Arctic, (e) Antarctic.

3. _____ The significance of the Nanking Treaty of 1842 was as follows: (a) it ended the Opium War, (b) it stimulated trade between China and Britain, (c) it eventually led to American traders, educators, and Christian missionaries coming to see China for themselves, (d) it led to a trickle of Chinese arriving on American shores, (e) it resulted in the building of many more sailing ships called China clippers.

4. _____ The event in 1848 that drew thousands of Chinese to America was: (a) the discovery of gold, (b) the invention of the steam engine, (c) famine in China, (d) the lifting of strict American immigration laws, (e) the beginning of public education in the West.

5. _____ The credit-ticket system was: (a) a method for American traders to motivate Americans to travel to China, (b) a system whereby traders lent passage money to recruited Chinese laborers, who in turn, had to pay back the loan out of their earnings abroad, (c) an arrangement whereby Chinese laborers could buy passage to America and a return ticket at the same time, (d) a discount ticket system when Chinese brought their families to America, (e) a way for poor American laborers to see China on a "go now" pay later basis.

6. _____ The word "coolie": (a) may have come from "kuli," a term used in British India to describe a burden bearer, (b) sounds like Chinese words meaning "bitter strength" or "bitter work," (c) was a good description of the Chinese manual laborer, (d) came to mean Chinese manual laborer, (e) all of the above.

7. _____ Nearly all the Chinese to emigrate to America during the nineteenth century came from: (a) northern China, (b) eastern China, (c) western China, (d) northeastern China, (e) southern China.

8. _____ The three groups of people living in southern China in the nineteenth century were: (a) the Tibetans, (b) Punti, (c) Hakka, (d) Mongolians, (e) Tanka.

9. _____ The sojourner's fondest dream in America was: (a) to become wealthy and buy property in San Francisco, (b) to earn enough to open a shop in San Francisco, (c) to make a great deal of money quickly and return to China to enjoy the fruits of new fortune, (d) after six months, to send for his wife and family from China, (e) to become educated in the U.S.

10. _____ By the late 1850s, when the gold rush had almost run its course, Chinese found other jobs in America, such as: (a) laundering, (b) sewing, (c) household servants, (d) farm workers, (e) work in cigar factories.

ANSWERS: 1. d; 2. c; 3. a,b,c,d,e; 4. a; 5. b; 6. e; 7. e; 8. b,c,e; 9. c; 10. a,b,c,d,e.

[1] Carole Chuck, "Wah-Kiu," revised from *Sojourners in Asian-American and Biblical History, Junior High School.* Copyright © 1979 jointly by the Office of Ethnic and Urban Church Affairs and the Office of Education, Golden Gate Mission Area, San Francisco, Calif. Used by permission.

Who Am I?[1]

by Carole Chuck

Goals:

• Youth will have a better understanding and feeling for the concept "sojourner" through sharing with the class their family stories.

• Youth will be able to recall, remember, and give thanks for those people who are a meaningful part of their histories.

Introduction:

Many second- or third-generation Chinese Americans do not remember much about their grandparents. Today's young people have grown up in America in a time when parents regarded the present and future as more important than the past. Families adopted the new traditions of the society that surrounded them. The "old" traditions of grandparents were only kept up while they were alive. When they died, the traditions slowly waned. While the older generation spoke Chinese to their contemporaries, they spoke English to the young.

Youth today may have a good education, a Christian nurturing community, and positive feelings about themselves. They can stand on their own two feet and get ahead. But two feet may not be enough in this world. A sense of tradition and history of where we have come from provides a fuller answer to the question, "What Am I?"

In our own family histories we can find examples of what it means and how it feels to be a sojourner. When we understand what our forebears experienced to come to America and when we discover the sacrifices that they made to live here, we can have a deeper appreciation of their lives and thankfulness for our heritage.

Although this session is written primarily from a Chinese American perspective, with some minor adaptation it can easily be used in other Asian Pacific American communities.

Preparation:

Advance preparation is needed for this session. Give youth at least two weeks to gather information on their family histories before leading this program session. Ask them to talk to their parents about those ancestors who were the first immigrants to America in the family. The youth should find out as much as they can about these relatives and be prepared to share the stories of their families, particularly the sojourners who came to America. A questionnaire such as the one provided can be used to gather the information. An alternative is to tape on a cassette recorder, or write up, an interview with a parent or other informed relative about the circumstances under which relatives first came to America from China. If a parent or close relative is not available, perhaps a knowledgeable elder in the church would be willing to be interviewed in the same manner. A third possibility is to gather a few old pictures of family members which would form a "mini" photo album and be the basis for a narrative report shared with the rest of the group.

In an earlier session, as preparation, lead the group in a short discussion about the kinds of information they are looking for: stories and interviews. Possibilities are: Who among my ancestors were the first to come to America? When did they come? Where did they settle? Why did they come? What was their life in the old country like? What was their life here like? What jobs did they hold here? Who were their children? What hardships did they endure?

If the youth have any particular problems with this assignment, the leader could make it a point to be available during the week to answer questions.

When the group meets for this session, you will need two maps, one of the world and one of Asia. The value of a map of Asia is that there will be greater detail and information for the youth to look for in finding their ancestors' hometowns or cities. You will also need a large chalkboard or five sheets of newsprint.

Procedure:

Opening
Step 1. Trace the Sojourners' Itineraries
(10 minutes)

Use two maps, one of the world and one of Asia. Post them for the group to see, so that youth can point out where their families are from. The ancestral homes of many of the second- and third-generation Chinese America youth is Guangzhou Province, the most southerly province. The ancestral homes of more recent immigrant youth are more likely to be in Southeast Asia or the Pacific Islands.

Next have them trace on the maps the journeys that the sojourners took in leaving their homes and arriving in the United States.

Discovering

Step 2. Share Reports and Interviews (30 minutes)

Youth are now to share their stories. To get them started, you may wish to share your family history first. Start with the ancestor who first came to this country. Tell what that person did before leaving the old country and what he or she did when living in the United States.

Step 3. Compare Histories (30 minutes)

A large chalkboard (or five newsprint sheets) is necessary for the next steps. Write: "Who was the first in your family tree to come to this country? Name one person only." Record the answers on the following grid on sheet #1.

You	One of Your Great-Grandparents	One of Your Grandparents	One of Your Parents

There are very few fourth- and fifth-generation Chinese Americans. Chinese starting coming in the 1850s, and most Chinese immigrations had stopped by 1882. Those who came in between 1850 and 1880 were men recruited to work on the railroad. Between 1882 and 1965, only students, merchants, refugees, war brides, and sons of United States residents were permitted entry. Beginning in 1965, however, Chinese along with other Asian groups were permitted to emigrate to the United States in large quotas.

Next write: "What kind of work did this person do in the old country?" Tally the number on the board or on sheet #2.

Farmer	Teacher	Shopkeeper	Fisherman
Laborer	Student	Merchant	Other

Many people left China in the early years because they could not make a living at farming. Drought or flood ruined crops. Bandits ruined lives. Government drafted men for war. Local industries were ruined by foreign projects. More recent immigrants, however, represent a broad range of professions, including physicians, lawyers, and engineers.

Next write: "Did this person come alone?" Tally on sheet #3.

Alone	Not Alone

The early sojourners came alone, hoping to make enough money to meet their needs and then return to China. They were not seeking to be millionaires, but they needed enough to help their families back home in times of economic stress. They were recruited for work in the forest and mountains. Married men left their families behind, planning on reunion at a later date. Bachelors expected to return and marry. It was not until World War II ended that Chinese serving in the United States Army could bring wives to America. For a long time, Chinatowns in American cities had a lot of bachelors and very few children. More recent sojourners have come fleeing political persecution and war-torn countries. Others have come searching for a new way of life and to rejoin family members.

Next, write: "What kind of work did this person settle down doing in the new country?" on sheet #4.

Vegetable Farming	Fruit Picking	Teaching	Shopkeeper
Engineer	Cook	Waiter	Cannery Worker

Grocer	Medicine	Laundry	Janitor	Seamstress

The first-generation immigrants usually were not able to go into the same kind of work they had done in their native countries. Language differences, age, lack of opportunity for education, and job discrimination were some problems that the first generation had to cope with. They took any kind of work they could find, because they had to repay the debts they owed for the ship's fare. They also had to send money home to support their families. Recent immigrants face some of the same problems.

Finally, write this grid on the board or newsprint sheet #5.

Became a citizen	Did not become one

Youth who are born in this country take their birthright for granted. A noncitizen wishing to become a citizen must live in the United States for a certain length of time and pass a test on American history given in English. Many of the immigrants did not become citizens—not because they did not want to, but because a law enacted in 1882 prohibited all Chinese from being naturalized as American citizens.

Step 4. Analyze the Stories *(15 minutes)*

What light do these family stories shed on our understanding of what it means to be a sojourner? Did most of our ancestors intend to stay in America, or were they planning to return to their native countries? What were some common hardships they suffered? Common joys?

Closing
Step 5. Share Prayers of Thanksgiving *(5 minutes)*

Deuteronomy 26:10-11 describes the practice of the Jews who took the first of the harvest and offered it in thanks and in remembrance. Read these verses. Close with prayers of thanksgiving for those who have made our lives more secure and meaningful.

WHO AM I?

Questionnaire

1. Who was the first person in your family to come to the United States? For example, grandfather (name is not necessary). In what year did this person come?

2. What work did he/she do before leaving for the United States?

3. Did he/she come alone?

4. What route did he/she take? What stops were made on the way?

5. What was the main job held (held for the longest time) in the United States?

6. Did this person become a citizen? Yes _____ No _____
   Why/why not?

[1]Carole Chuck, "Who Am I?" revised from *Sojourners in Asian–American and Biblical History, Junior High School.* Copyright © 1979 jointly by the Office of Ethnic and Urban Church Affairs and the Office of Education, Golden Gate Mission Area, San Francisco, Calif. Used by permission.

Self-Image and Self-Esteem

by Kathryn Choy-Wong

Goals:
- Youth will begin identifying feelings and attitudes about themselves and learn to share these feelings and attitudes with others.
- Youth will move toward developing positive attitudes and feelings about themselves.

Introduction:

The ability to identify one's positive and negative qualities starts the process of developing a positive self-image. By naming these qualities—the likes and the dislikes—youth can begin the process of sorting them out, changing what they can change and want to change, and accepting or affirming what they can't change. In most Asian Pacific American cultures, however, youth have a difficult time verbalizing their feelings and thoughts. By expressing them outwardly, Asian Pacific American youth may see that they are not alone, and that other youth struggle with similar likes, dislikes, qualities, attitudes, and feelings about themselves. Together they may be able to discover ways of sorting out these self-perceptions in order to begin dealing with them.

Asian Pacific American youth unfortunately are not excluded from the increase in teenage suicide. With parental pressure to do well in school and to succeed, sometimes at the sacrifice of developing social skills and outside relationships, they sometimes are contemplating ways to flee. Generational and cultural gaps, the absence of verbal and physical communication, the little time parents have to spend with their children—all these factors increase the vulnerability of Asian Pacific American adolescents to suicide and depression by contributing to low self-esteem.

Culture also reinforces some of these tendencies for low self-esteem. For example, in traditional Chinese families the emphasis on elders rather than the young and on the family rather than the individual tends to minimize youth self-image. Adolescence is often viewed in these families as a necessary phase of life to be tolerated and not celebrated.

Young people can react in different ways to these pressures. Low self-esteem can lead some to suicide, others to withdrawal, others to join gangs, and still others to commit crimes. On the other hand, many have found support and help from the church, the youth group, or some other community social structure (clubs, sports, etc.).

Asian Pacific American youth are seeking tools to deal with these pressures, to be able to find support from peers and from adults, and to develop a positive self-image and self-esteem. This session will begin to help youth develop these tools.

Preparation:

The session is for a sixty- to ninety-minute time period.

You will need to . . .
- Make copies of the Self-Inventory
- Make copies of the Word List
- Have pencils and pens on hand
- Print the Bible passage on newsprint or chalkboard for all to see (Genesis 1:27)
- Have newsprint and felt-tip markers or chalkboard and chalk available for the closing time in the session
- Arrange the room to allow for movement.

Read over the Bible passage. Think about what it means to be made in "God's own image." Think about your own attitudes and feelings about yourself. What changes would you like to make about yourself? What do you accept or affirm? It may be helpful if you try the Word List and Self-Inventory yourself before the session with the young people.

Procedure:

Opening
Step 1. Getting Acquainted *(10 to 15 minutes)*

Start the session by getting in touch with each other. It is good practice to do this at the beginning of every session. Introduce what the youth will be doing in this session.

Step 2. Word List *(10 to 20 minutes)*

Begin with the Word List, which has a list of descriptive words. Ask youth to circle all the words which they feel describe them as they are today. Say: "If you can't find a word that describes you, add one." Divide the group into pairs or triads. These pairs or triads are to share the descriptive words and briefly explain why one or two of the circled words apply to the participants. Ask: "How did you feel circling a word that suggests you are scared or hateful? Do you like being a son or daughter?"

Discovering

Step 3. Self-Inventory *(10 to 15 minutes)*

Hand out the Self-Inventory forms and have the youth check off appropriate answers as they view them. Clearly indicate that there are no right or wrong answers, only answers which are appropriate to them as individuals.

Step 4. Sharing About Myself *(20 minutes)*

Now have the youth return to their same partners or triads. Ask them to share . . .
1. One thing they like about themselves.
2. One thing they dislike about themselves.
3. One thing they wish to change about themselves.

Closing

Step 5. Read Genesis 1:27 *(10 to 20 minutes)*

Read the Bible passage aloud. Explain that every person was made in God's image and that each has received special blessings from God. The blessings may be different or in varied degrees, but everybody has something special which makes him or her unique. In today's session, it is hoped that each person in the group can identify his or her unique qualities and blessings. There are some things we can change and some things we cannot change about ourselves. Those things we wish to change and can, we may want to commit ourselves to doing. Those things we cannot, we must begin to accept as part of our uniqueness and the beauty of ourselves. On a piece of newsprint have each youth list one word which represents or symbolizes a beauty or blessing he or she has. Ask the young people to pray for one another as each continues to work these things out. Close in prayer.

More Ideas and Activities

1. Drawing a House

Instead of the Word List you might want each young person to draw a house which represents her or him. What would be outside of the house, which everyone can see? What would be inside the house, which very few people can see? What would be in the closets, which perhaps no one can see? Youth can put key words at the appropriate places in and around the house. The can share as much as they want with their partners or triads.

2. Modeling Clay

If you have a two-hour time period, you might want to try having the group work with clay, after the Self-Inventory has been completed. Have the youth make objects from clay which represent themselves as they are right now. The clay symbols can be either abstract or realistic. They can represent the youth's acceptance of himself/herself, or the feelings he or she has right at the moment. These clay symbols can be shared in small groups or in the larger group.

WORD LIST

Circle all the words which best describe you as you are today.

brother	believing	adult	content	follower	scared
sister	doubtful	friend	searching	leader	peaceful
daughter	angry	loner	trusting	rebel	grateful
son	depressed	outgoing	hurting	teacher	hateful
child	joyful	servant	anxious	learner	hopeful

SELF-INVENTORY

About myself	I like this about myself	I dislike this about myself	I want to change this	I accept this about myself
OUTSIDE RELATIONSHIPS				
1. I get along with people.				
2. I like being alone.				
3. I seem to be able to help others.				
4. Other people look up to me.				
5. I can relate to adults.				
6. I can relate to my peers.				
7. I prefer to follow the leadership of others.				
8. I have a difficult time speaking to people.				
9. I usually join many outside activities.				
10. I have very few close friends.				
FAMILY RELATIONSHIPS				
1. I get along with family members.				
2. I have a good relationship with my parents.				
3. I dislike family obligations.				
4. I am proud of my family.				
5. I like the role I play in my family.				
6. I like the family position I was born in (eldest, middle, youngest).				
7. I have a hard time communicating with my family.				
8. I feel family members are my best friends.				
9. I trust my family.				
10. I feel free to tell my family anything.				

About myself	I like this about myself	I dislike this about myself	I want to change this	I accept this about myself
PHYSICAL APPEARANCE				
1. I like the way I look.				
2. I am glad of my ancestry.				
3. I feel I am bicultural.				
4. I feel I have an advantage because of my cultures.				
5. I feel my physical appearance is a disadvantage.				
6. I am proud of my outward appearance.				
7. I feel I can go beyond my physical appearance to be a success.				
8. I am grateful for who I am.				
9. I feel I can enhance my physical appearance.				
10. I am healthy.				
PERSONALITY				
1. I can make my own decisions.				
2. I admit it when I am wrong.				
3. I like to influence others.				
4. I can think out concepts and theories.				
5. I am practical and realistic.				
6. I am good with my hands.				
7. I am flexible.				
8. I am spontaneous.				
9. I take responsibilities seriously.				
10. I worry all the time.				

Naming

by Kathryn Choy-Wong

Goals:
- Youth will discover who they are by examining the names by which they are called.
- Youth will accept their names.

Introduction:

If we look at Genesis and other parts of the Bible we discover that names and naming are important in history. Since the beginning of time, human beings have needed to name things in order to grasp their meanings and talk about them. Thus we see the importance of names when we read the creation story in Genesis, telling how God named the day and then the sky, the earth, and the sea, and then Adam named the birds and the animals.

Names can provide a sense of esteem in a person's identity. At times a new name may mean a new identity. Thus we find "Saul" becoming "Paul" or "Simon" becoming "Peter." Names also denote relationships. Jesus used the term *Abba* (an ancient Chaldean word for "father") in the Lord's Prayer and at other times to denote a special relationship he had with God.

Names to Asian Pacific American youth are just as important as to other people. Many Asian Pacific Americans are given two names at birth—one English and one Asian or Pacific. The Asian or Pacific name often has a meaning which expresses the parents' hopes and dreams for their child. Surnames in the Asian context are listed first, emphasizing the importance of the family connection above that of the individual. Surnames usually carry with them a host of obligations and responsibilities a person has toward the family.

Just as with Hebrew and Greek names, Asian and Pacific names point to relationships. Many parents have special nicknames for their children. Among Pilipinos these are often just as important as their original given names if not more so. In Chinese culture special names are given to aunts and uncles, depending on what side of the family they come from and what position (eldest, middle, youngest) of birth they held within the family structure. Hawaiians call everyone of the same generation as one's parents "mother" or "father," making no distinction in language between one's own parents and the parents of cousins or friends.

For many young people who are recent residents in the United States, English names are given by teachers or others. Sometimes the young people can choose their own English names. Sometimes they choose no English names.

We all know stories of how Asian and Pacific names have been difficult to fit into Western speech patterns. Sometimes, therefore, we may feel it is necessary to change the spelling and pronunciation of our names so Westerners can say them. Therefore, Ng becomes Eng, Dong becomes Don, Jung becomes John. Sometimes the failure of Westerners to pronounce Asian and Pacific names correctly may cause Asian Pacific American young people to be ashamed of their names.

Names, however, are an important part of our personalities. How we view our names reflects on how we view ourselves. A name can label and affect a person for life. Asian Pacific American young people can begin learning about themselves by first examining their own names. Our goal is that they can begin to feel good about some parts, if not all, of their names.

Preparation:

The session is for a sixty- to ninety-minute time period.

You will need to . . .
- Provide index cards
- Provide pencils
- Gather and provide materials for the making of banners, such as:
  - scrap materials
  - yarn of various colors
  - large pieces of felt or burlap for the banner itself
  - dowels and yarn to hang the banners
  - glue
  - scissors
- Provide matches and a large can, or an old metal wastepaper basket
- Provide several colors of markers
- Print the Bible passages on newsprint or chalkboard for all to see (Genesis 1:3-10 and Genesis 1:20)
- Provide tables for banner making
- Arrange the room to allow for movement

Read over the Bible passage. Think about what it means, especially the importance of *naming*. Think about the value of names. How do they affect persons—positively or negatively? By what names are you called? What are your feelings about these names? Has anyone ever abused your name? Do your names have meanings or significant stories behind them? If you could change your name, what "dream" name would you choose?

Procedure:

Opening
Step 1. Getting Acquainted
(5 to 10 minutes)

Start the session by getting in touch with each other using some form of introduction or mixer. It is good practice to begin every session in this way. Introduce the topic of this session to the youth.

Step 2. Name Cards (15 to 20 minutes)

Have each person list on separate index cards all the names by which he or she is called, including nicknames and surnames. When all have finished, have them write on the back of each card any meanings the name on it may have. For example, "Kathryn" means "pure." If a meaning is not known, skip that name. Also on the back, indicate which names were given by whom—parents, friends, etc.

Now have them arrange the cards in priority, starting with those which are most important. On a separate blank index card write the most important names.

Next, have them rearrange the cards in order of preference—which name is the one he/she likes the most. Write the preferred name on the separate index card along with the most important name.

Finally, have them select the name or names which have given them the most problems and write these on the separate index card with the other names.

Discovering
Step 3. Name Sharing (10 to 20 minutes)

Have each person pick from the cards one or two names which he or she would like to share with the rest of the group—for any reason at all. Someone might want to share the meaning of a name, or a horror story of how it was used. Another might share how a nickname was given. Allow enough time for everyone in the group to share.

Step 4. Banner Making (20 to 30 minutes)

Ask each person to choose one name he or she really likes and make a banner about it. A banner might express the meaning of the name, or the story of the name. Be creative!

Step 5. Banner Sharing (10 minutes)

Have the group share their banners with each other. Hang these up around the room. After each banner is shared, have the whole group give a cheer for the work they have done.

Step 6. Bible Reflection (5 minutes)

Look at the Bible passage. Discuss briefly the importance of names and naming. Point out that in the Bible many persons changed their names in order to represent new identities. Simon the fisherman became Peter the disciple. Saul the persecutor became Paul the apostle.

Step 7. Trashing Unwanted Names (5 minutes)

Get into a circle. In the middle of the circle place a large can or an old wastebasket in which to burn index cards. (You may want to consider doing this activity outdoors.)

Have the youth take out their index cards. Ask: "Which names do you really dislike and would like to change if you could?" In a lighthearted ceremony, have each person, one at a time, drop or burn these names. Next, on the newsprint with the Bible passage, have each person write the name by which he or she would like to be called from now on. This name may be the same name already used, or it may not.

Closing
Step 8. Prayer (2 minutes)

Close with volunteer prayers.

More Ideas and Activities
1. Another Banner Idea

Instead of making a banner of the name one likes most, make a banner of a "dream" name. Share why this name is chosen.

2. Names Research

During the week after the session, you may want youth to go home and ask parents and grandparents why they were given their names and whether there are special meanings behind their names. Have the youth share this information at the next session.

THEME 2

Relationships and Community

Human relationships at home, school, and in the neighborhood are important to youth. In these settings youth learn to balance the variety of expectations others have for them, develop social skills of relating with one another, and grow in acquiring the abilities needed to be Asian Pacific American youth living in America. Through these relationships youth begin to share in the responsibility of shaping just communities.

- Family Expections, *by Tim Tseng*
- Dating and Marriage, *by Tim Tseng*
- Discovering Our Neighborhoods, *by Brandon I. Cho*
- Racism and Me, *by Rodger Y. Nishioka*
- Racism and Institutions, *by Rodger Y. Nishioka*
- Being Socially Adaptive, *by Tim Tseng*

Family Expectations

by Tim Tseng

Goal:

- Youth will discover the role of family responsibilities and the need for them.

Introduction:

Although all young people have family responsibilities, expectations, and obligations, Asian Pacific American youth are particularly concerned about such matters. Their Asian cultures place a high value on family obligations because they especially value the extended family structure. For many Asian Pacific American youth, this tradition places much pressure on them. Sometimes they perceive that these expectations and obligations are extra burdens which their non-Asian Pacific American friends do not have.

For example, they may be expected to be home for an aunt's birthday instead of going to a church retreat. Or they may have to take care of a younger sister or brother. Or they may be expected to take parents to visit a relative instead of playing basketball with the youth group. In many immigrant families, such expectations sometimes cause youth to mature faster than their peers in other cultures. Furthermore, they are often expected to represent their parents by contacting local authorities, or the doctor, or the school principal, or the immigration agency, etc. They are needed to handle contracts and other transactions. In most of these cases youth are thrust into major responsibilities because of their parents' lack of English language skills or lack of time. But, even in families that have lived in the United States for a number of generations, Asian Pacific American youth are still expected to make the family primary in their lives, and other social relationships, including the church, secondary.

Why do parents have these expectations? There are historical and cultural reasons for them, based on the concept of the extended family. The extended family structure is not uniquely Asian or Pacific. Many European cultures share this feature too. The early American settlers valued extended families. Survival, preservation of culture and heritage, function and work roles, need, and similar factors explain why they valued extended-family structures so highly. In Asian and Pacific cultures, the values of extended families were originally brought from their "home" countries to the United States. Immigrants tried as much as possible to live as they did in their home countries. In a strange land they held on tightly to the most important values of their traditional cultures. (This preservation of cultural practices and values by people in a new land is a natural phenomenon. It happens to many American who live abroad. They maintain as much of their American identity and culture in these other countries as they can. They continue to read American newspapers and magazines, see American movies, speak English, and socialize with other Americans.)

Retaining the values of an extended family was more than just a carry over from the old country. It met a very practical need. Because of harsh conditions in America many immigrants needed these extended families to survive. They needed grandparents or older brothers and sisters to take care of the young while parents worked long hours six or seven days a week. They needed extra money which came from the earnings of the extended family. Family members depended on one another not only for financial support but also for moral reinforcement. In a strange country, where they were unfamiliar with the customs and language, and where they were often unwanted, they gave each other encouragement and incentive. The family gave each person a sense of self-worth as well as a sharing of obligations. When one family member did something wonderful, it was a source of pride for the whole family.

Much of this feeling still exists today. Although early white American culture thrived on it, the extended family in most white American society is no longer as functional as it once was. The individual, who in the past was in a balance with the corporate (the family), now outweighs the corporate. Families are separated by distances because of job situations and because of our mobility. This factor is not necessarily present with Asian Pacific American families. Even today, many Asian Pacific American families remain intact and the members live relatively close to each other geographically. The extended family structures still exist, therefore, and are highly valued.

This program session seeks to help Asian Pacific American youth to understand the need and role of their family obligations and the importance of their family's expectations in light of the fact that American society is so much more individualistic than theirs. Because Asian Pacific American youths often find these expectations burdensome, this session seeks not only to help them value family responsibilities but also to enable them to negotiate with their parents a balance between the desire of youth for individual freedom and their family duties.

The theological and biblical themes for this session are "healing" and "reconciliation." The church should be a place where both can take place, especially in Asian Pacific American families torn by parental authoritarianism and youthful resistance. The Christ whom the church confesses is "our peace, who . . . has broken down the dividing wall of hostility" (Ephesians 2:14). Later in the same Letter (Ephesians 6:1-4, reechoed in Colossians 3:20-21), the writer lists a household code which illustrates this principle:

> Children, obey your parents in the Lord, for this is right. "Honor your father and mother" (this is the first commandment with a promise), "that it may be well with you and that you may live long on the earth." Fathers, do not provoke your children to anger, but bring them up in the discipline and instruction of the Lord.

Whether Asian Pacific American youth belong to an extended family or only to a nuclear family (they will more likely be a part of the extended family), the gospel's vision for wholeness is the ideal.

Preparation:

• Make a video or audiotape of parents or grandparents who have had interesting experiences. Select some parents and grandparents and ask them to share their stories about their lives. Also ask them to share their expectations of the family and of their children. If translation is necessary, prepare for that as well.

• Bring plenty of newsprint and markers. These will be used throughout the program session as the youth brainstorm and make lists.

• Prepare youth to perform a role-play. Although situations may vary, youth must choose between family obligations and personal desires. The role-play may lead to a more structured play developed by the youth to be performed before both youth and parents. In such a play, expression of the youths' feelings about family expectations and the issue of negotiating responsibilities with parents will be central.

Procedure:

Opening
Step 1. Use a Tape *(10 minutes)*

Play the video or audiotape of the parents or grandparents that you have made in advance. Have the youth reflect for a moment on what they have seen/heard before asking them about their impressions of the tape. Have them list on a sheet of newsprint the family obligations and expectations that their parents or grandparents have expressed on the tapes. Then have them list other expectations that were not mentioned.

Discovering
Step 2. Do Role Plays *(20 minutes)*

Divide the group into subgroups of three or four. Each will role-play a family with a particular situation of tension between family expectations and the youth's personal desires. Ask the youth to suggest appropriate issues for role-playing, but be prepared to suggest some yourself if necessary. In any case, ask the subgroups to have fun with their role play and try to make the situations as realistic as possible. One subgroup might have the youth give in to family expectations, another may have the youth reject these expectations and still another may have the youth ignore them. *No subgroup should have the youth and the family work together to negotiate a compromise (not yet!).* If your group is too small to divide, then have the total group role-play two or three situations (it will only take more time). The only expectation is that each small-group situation must have different conclusions or resolutions.

Step 3. Reflect on the Role Plays *(10 minutes)*

After the role plays have been performed, have the students look at the list again and discuss the family expectations they perceived in the role plays. For discussion, ask questions such as:

(a) What do the youth consider negative or unrealistic family expectations and obligations?

(b) Are there any values to these expectations and obligations? What are they?

(c) When do youth fulfill their family's expectations? (For instance: Do they fulfill only the obligations they consider important? Do they fulfill them even if they appear unimportant?)

Step 4. Bible Study *(15 minutes)*

Given the fact that most youth will see some value in their family's expectations, what needs to be discussed now is how the faith of youth can give them an incentive to work out a resolution between family expectations and their personal freedom.

Introduce the groups to the Letter to the Ephesians. Note that it was probably addressed to all the early churches in the Greco-Roman world. What is most important is that one of its themes is the reconciliation that Christ brings between Jew and Gentile through his death and through his body, the church (Ephesians 2:13-22). Mutual submission in the family (Ephesians 5:21ff) is one way for the church to create a unity from two differing groups. Likewise, parents and children ought to have mutual respect and concern for each other (read Ephesians 6:1-4).

Ask:

What do you think Ephesians 6:1-4 tells us about our family expectations?

How can we obey our parents and how can our parents avoid provoking us to anger at the same time?

Do you think it is possible to negotiate with your parents so that you can satisfy their expectations and at the same time they can give you enough freedom?

Step 5. Do Role Plays Again *(15 minutes)*

Ask the youth to go back to their role-playing subgroups and perform their situation again, except this time they should resolve the tension situation through a negotiating process with the parents. Have them think about which youth freedoms and family obligations can and should be considered indispensable and which ones are negotiable (for example, taking care of one's younger brother or sister at certain times and setting aside time to attend church or do something else; or minding the store only on certain days if they are given other days free).

Step 6. Summarizing Learnings *(5 minutes)*

After the second role play have the group gather and list as many freedoms or obligations they can think of that are negotiable and those that are not. Try to come to some consensus about fairness with their family responsibilities and resolving conflicts with parents.

Closing
Step 7. Share Closing Remarks *(5 minutes)*

Family expectations, responsibilities, and obligations are usually valuable because they help the family

to survive. Sometimes, however, these expectations become too much for youth to deal with them realistically. What Asian Pacific American families need is to have a balance between these expectations and the youths' freedom. The Bible helps us by pointing out that both parents and youths need to have respect and concern for each other. Young people should try to be sensitive to the parents' concern that the family survive and prosper. Parents should attempt to understand the youth's need for freedom to grow. Thus, while youth should obey their parents, parents should not provoke their children to anger.

Under ideal conditions, both parents and youth should be able to work out their tensions. Ideal conditions seldom exist, however, and often one or both sides may be unwilling to work things out. The church can help by bringing both together through seminars, workshops, and shared meals to provide a better mutual understanding. Youth can help work towards this goal by helping the church sponsor these events.

Close with prayer.

Additional Activity
Put On a Play

Based on all that was discussed, have the group develop on newsprint an outline for a play that will express their feelings about family expectations and what they would like to see happen in their families to resolve the tensions that come with it. Assign a task force to write the play and another to produce it. If you have the cooperation of the parents, this play may be performed before the entire church. Perhaps the church can sponsor an "Understanding Your Teens" day when this play can be performed.

Dating and Marriage

by Tim Tseng

Goals:

• Youth will examine the meaning of their dating and marriage relationships according to Christian and societal values.

• Youth will affirm the need to develop a climate of acceptance and a sense of belonging in their youth group, in support of growing interpersonal relationships.

Introduction:

For Asian Pacific American youth, like most American youth, dating provides opportunities to experiment with and to develop intimate relationships with members of the opposite sex. They share with other American youth the same pressures to conform to society's ideas of romance, love, and sexuality. A great many of these ideas are perpetuated through the media (rock videos, magazines, and television) and the marketing of youth products such as clothing, records, and radios. Most of these ideas exalt Anglo-Caucasian (white) images and ideas of relationships and virtually ignore the real presence of Asians and other racial/ethnic groups. When Asians are portrayed, they are often viewed as exotic "China dolls" or insensitive, uncaring, inhuman male gangsters. Because many Asian Pacific Americans are influenced by these ideas of romance, love, and sexuality in dating, they may bring expectations to their relationships which are inconsistent with reality. Furthermore, some may also bring unhealthy racial/ethnic or sexual stereotypes which affect their perceptions of the ideal date or spouse and their understandings of dating and marriage.

However, Asian Pacific American youth often need to deal with issues not usually confronted by others. For example, how does one react to interracial dating? How does one deal with a companion with a different degree of "Asian-ness" or "American-ness" from one's own (more culturally oriented or less)? How do Asian Pacific Americans cope with marital breakups or divorces? (This question is especially important in some contexts where the break would be seen as failure and the "losing of face"—embarrassment to the family.) How does one cope with parents who do not permit dating until the youth becomes an adult? When using this program session, consider both the kinds of situations Asian Pacific American youth share in common with other American youth and those which are

distinctively Asian Pacific American. Also note that situations may differ because of confused expectations for youth and their relationships.

As Christians, youth will need to ask themselves whether their dating and potential marriage relationships are based on Christian values or on society's values. What is the meaning of Christian faithfulness in the face of social and sexual demands? Both parties will need to see the relationship in light of their commitment to Christ. Karl Barth said that we reflect the image of God more fully when male and female are in relation with one another, for each is incomplete without the other. Thus, Christian integrity in dating would involve rejecting unhealthy expectations about romance, dating, and loving, while finding wholeness in male-female relationships through Christ. As the leader, bear in mind that dating can be a time of excitement and Christian growth. It can also be a time of disappointments and frustrations. Asian Pacific American churches should therefore provide support and guidance for their dating youth and for young adults who are ready for marriage.

The second goal of this session assumes the value of youth's ownership and involvement in their youth fellowship. In this group they can shape a climate of acceptance. In some Asian Pacific American churches, where the adults adapt the traditional authoritative Asian family value relationship to youth ministry, the young people have little control of their youth group. Hopefully, in this part of the program session, youth will discover that they can contribute significantly to their own group's ministry. As a "family" member in Christ, each young person is encouraged to share something which helps determine the direction and climate of the group.

In social settings such as school and parties, young people often have very rigid dating patterns. Those who date and those who don't are likely to exclude each other in these settings. In other words, daters and nondaters usually do not interact with each other. The church, however, can provide through its informal youth fellowship a setting which is broad enough to include both daters and nondaters. In the church, youth can experience acceptance and the freedom to discuss the tight dating patterns of some youth circles. Christian kinship (being brothers and sisters) enables young people to feel a sense of belonging to each other. Thus youth learn that intimacy and friendship are not limited to dating relationships but can be shared in the wider, caring context of the fellowship groups. This session will address the question of how Asian Pacific American youth can help their group to become accepting and broad enough to include both those who date and those who do not.

To summarize, two themes stand out through this program session. First, there is something distinctive about Christian relationships that is different from the world's perception of relationships. In Christ we find integrity in dating and kinship relationships. Consequently, Asian Pacific Americans, in light of their diversity which runs across a continuum from very traditional to fully Americanized, will be able to identify and work through issues related to their ethnic identity with the knowledge and assurance that Christ has called them to be bicultural. Second, the church's youth can be more open to and accepting of the diversity in their group of daters and nondaters, Asian-oriented and Americanized persons.

Preparation:

• Prepare the following Scriptures as a dramatic reading, making copies for the participants.

Song of Solomon 1:2-4, 8-11:

Beloved: O that you would kiss me with the
kisses of your mouth!
For your love is better than wine,
your anointing oils are fragrant,
your name is oil poured out;
therefore the maidens love you.
Draw me after you, let us make haste.
The king has brought me into his
chambers.
Friends: We will exult and rejoice in you;
we will extol your love more than
wine. . . .
Lover: If you do not know,
O fairest among women,
follow in the tracks of the flock,
and pasture your kids
beside the shepherds' tents.
I compare you, my love,
to a mare of Pharaoh's chariots.
Your cheeks are comely with ornaments,
your neck with strings of jewels.
We will make you ornaments of gold,
studded with silver.

• Read over Romans 12:1-21 before the session.
• There are two options for Step 2 in this program. In the "Ideal Lover" option, ask your group what characteristics they would like to see in the ideal lover. You will need newsprint and markers for them to list these characteristics.

The second option is to generate a list of ethnic and sexual stereotypes and expectations for use in a continuum. In this list you might include statements such as:

"Blondes have more fun."
"Asians are not assertive enough."
"Men should be more sensitive."
"Asian women have an exotic Oriental mystique."
"Women belong in the home."
"My boyfriend (or girlfriend) should be _____ ."
Think up some of your own.

Procedure:

Opening

Step 1. Do a Dramatic Scripture Reading
(5-10 minutes)

After opening with a prayer, have a female and a male youth, respectively, read the parts of "beloved" and "lover" from the Song of Solomon passage while the rest of the group reads the "friends" part. Ask for some feedback, but let this be a brief time of reflection. Note how intense and explicit the language is. Male-female love in the Bible is not to be repressed, but is seen as an opportunity for God to work in and through the lives of the lovers.

Discovering

Step 2a. Brainstorm the Ideal Lover
(30 minutes)

Divide the group into male and female subgroups and have each group separately list the characteristics of their ideal lover on newsprint. Then gather the group together and have each subgroup share their lists. Have the youth discuss both lists. Pay attention to racial/ethnic and sexual stereotypes and expectations and ask about them with questions such as:

Why does she have to be able to cook?

Why is he supposed to be the head of the household?

What characteristics do you like and/or do you dislike about Asian Pacific Americans whom you've dated? Why?

What difference would it make to you if your ideal lover were non-Asian?

OR

Step 2b. Do an Opinions Continuum
(15 minutes)

Have the group stand up. Tell them that, as you read each statement, those who agree with it should position themselves at the right side of the room and those who disagree to the left side. Since it is a continuum, the young people can position themselves anywhere along the line to express their degree of agreement or disagreement. After each statement is read, ask individuals to explain why they stood at that point on the continuum which they chose. As in option 2a, bring up issues on racial/ethnic and sexual stereotypes and expectations.

Step 3. Discuss the Issues *(15 minutes)*

Once the open-ended discussion about sexual ethnic stereotypes and expectations has been concluded, move on to youth expectations in dating and marriage. The discussion could follow a pattern something like this:

Why do we have these expectation of our dates and companions?

How are these expectations influenced by this society and our peers?

What makes Christians different from others in their ways of relating to their lovers?

What makes Christian expectations different from other types of expectations? (One difference is that we don't have to be influenced by society's expectations or ideas about romantic relationships; rather, we can accept who we are as a part of God's calling for us. We can be free to relate to one another not as the "world" does but as Christ commands.)

How far should Christians go in their dating relationships (i.e. hugging, kissing, necking, petting, premarital sex)?

Step 4. Discuss a Case Study *(20 minutes)*

Read this open-ended case study to the group and discuss the questions which follow it.

Joe and Jane are Asian Pacific Americans who have been dating for about two years. Joe is a senior in high school, and Jane is a junior in a different high school. Jane's family lives in the suburbs. Her father, an engineer, earns enough that her mother does not need to work outside the home. Jane's family is quite active in the church. However, Joe's family lives in Chinatown. Both of his parents work long, hard hours each day and are not Christians. They speak little English. Both Joe and Jane attend the same church regularly and used to be very active in church activities before they started going out together. They are recognized as "going steady" by the other youth. As in many churches, there are some members in this church who are dating regularly and many who do not date at all. Very little about dating and relationships has been discussed in the church and so far, there have been no breakups. There is a visible gap between people who have dates such as Joe and Jane and those who do not date. Neither group really interacts with the other. In fact, once a couple pairs off, they spend very little time with the fellowship group. However Joe and Jane are about to break up. Joe complains that Jane is too self-centered and much too outspoken. Jane complains that Joe is too insensitive and too old-fashioned.

Ask the following questions:

• If they break up, do you think they will continue to attend the same church?

• If you were one of the two, what would motivate you to keep attending church even if you have to see the other person each week?

• If you were one of the members of the youth group, what kind of advice would you give them?

• How has our group handled these types of situations in the past?

• How should the youth group respond to this situation?

Step 5. Being an Accepting Group *(10 minutes)*

Read the "friends" part of the Song of Solomon passage and Romans 12:3-21. Ask:

From these Bible passages, how do you think we can make our group more supportive of couples?

How can we better accept both daters and non-daters?

What steps can each of us take to make this group more inclusive?

After the steps have been listed, have the group decide which are the most important and ask them to use these as the basis of a covenant to which they will commit themselves. Write the steps down and have each member sign it, acknowledging that the climate of the group is their personal responsibility.

Closing:

Step 6. Close with Sentence Prayers *(5-10 minutes)*

Help youth to see that dating and marriage are never simply private affairs between two lovers, as our society might lead us to believe. Nor are they always exciting or romantic or free of responsibility. In every Christian relationship, God plays the most important part—God encourages us not to pretend that we must have the kind of relationships that our society or our peers idealize, but to make our faith in Christ and our commitment to the Christian community central to our relationships of intimacy. Dating and marriage thus will often involve you in greater responsibility not only for your companion but also for the community of Christians you belong to.

Close with sentence prayers of affirmation for the covenant to make the group a more open fellowship.

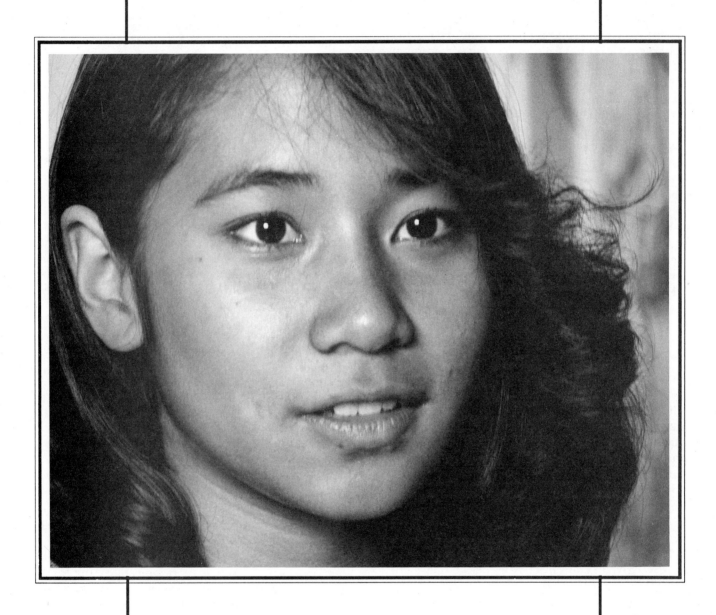

Discovering Our Neighborhoods

by Brandon I. Cho

Note: This program may take two sessions to complete. Session One may concentrate on a photo walk exercise. Session Two can be used as a sharing reflection and wrap-up session. If you want to do it in one session, you need to complete the Session One steps prior to your scheduled meeting.

Goals:

• Youth will sharpen their awareness of their surrounding neighborhood (e.g. racial/ethnic make-up, various cultures and religions, economic and social characteristics, lifestyles, etc.)
• Youth will clarify their understanding of the term "neighbor" in our pluralistic society.
• Youth will explore ways to serve their neighborhood in Christ.

Introduction:

Most of us are living in a radically individualistic high-tech society where it is easy to lose contact with our neighbors. Our American lifestyle adores individual achievements far more than the general welfare of all. The sense of competition takes precedence over community building. We need to recapture the meaning of neighborhood in our lives. This program arises out of this concern.

The program includes a number of group activities. Your youth group will be led to understand their immediate community through a neighborhood study activity. They will share their findings in the youth group meeting. Then they will engage in a reflective exercise on the term "neighborhood," and discuss some concrete ways to serve their neighbors.

Preparation:

• A neighborhood map for each team of two or three
• A 35-millimeter camera for each team, with film cartridges for slides. (If this is not possible, another kind of camera with print film may be substituted)
• A note pad and a pen for each team
• A slide projector and a screen (if slides are used)
• Newsprint and felt-tipped markers (or chalkboard and chalk)
• Copies of Bible passages (see Session Two, Step 2)

Procedure (Session One):

Opening

Step 1. Introduction *(5 minutes)*

Explain about the program's theme, "Discovering Our Neighborhoods." Some of preceding material can be used for this introduction.

Discovering

Step 2. Mission Impossible Photowalk Exercise *(1 1/2 hours)*

Subdivide your youth group into teams of two or three each. Explain to them that their job is to explore their neighborhood and take pictures. Assign each team a specific area of the neighborhood for a photo walk. Each team needs a map of their assigned area, a camera, a note pad, and a pen. Before they go out, have each team select its captain.

Feel free to use the following instruction for this exercise. You can either make a copy for each group, or record it on a tape cassette recorder for each with the "Mission Impossible" theme song on the background.

MISSION IMPOSSIBLE PHOTOWALK
Dear Photowalk Team:

You have just been chosen as a team of news reporters for (add here the name of your youth group). Your job is to disclose some of the hidden characteristics of your assigned area in our neighborhood. Here is what you do:
• Work as a team, not as individuals.
• You have only one hour and fifteen minutes to complete your mission. So plan well with your teammates. Decide how you will cover your assigned area.
• Use your imagination. As you look for the things that are characteristic of your neighborhood, be sensitive to what you see and hear.
• Be aware of the people you see and meet, especially their ethnic backgrounds. Notice their language, culture, and behavior patterns.
• Also observe the buildings, landscape, and facilities, as well as the activities that are going on around you. I encourage you to enter into shops, hospitals, or other buildings for closer observation. Get the manager's permission if you feel the need for it.
• Take pictures (the more natural the pictures, the better they are) and jot down your observations on a

writing pad. Guard your camera!

• Remember, you have only an hour and fifteen minutes to complete your mission. Be back by (time).

• If you have any problem or question, call me at (000-0000). Enjoy the mission, and may the "force be with you!"

Step 3. Informal Sharing (15 minutes)

Note: If your group is combining the two sessions, skip Steps 3 and 4.

Get some refreshments ready to serve to your teams on their return from their photowalks. After the refreshment time, bring them together as a whole group for a time of informal sharing. For a starter, ask what they found out about their neighborhood. This should be a simple, light sharing time. More extensive sharing will come during the next session.

Closing

Step 4. Wrap-Up (5 minutes)

Sing a song related to neighborhood or community, such as "They'll Know We Are Christians by Our Love" or "You Are the Light of the World."

Step 5. Develop Films into Slides

Assign each team captain to have his/her team's films developed. Otherwise, collect them and take them to a local film shop yourself for development. Keep in mind that you need the slides for the next session.

Close the session with a prayer.

Procedure (Session Two):

Opening

Step 1. Discussion on "Neighborhood" (20 minutes)

Ask the whole group: "How do you define a neighbor?" "Who is your neighbor?" "Would you consider those who speak a different language, have different customs, and eat different foods your neighbors as well?" "Why or why not?" Write their answers on newsprint.

Next, have your group share freely the stereotypes held by themselves and other people for various racial/ethnic groups, and write them down as well. You can subdivide the Asian Pacific Americans into Chinese, Indochinese, Japanese, Korean, Vietnamese, Philippine, and any other groups. Using two different-color markers, check off good and bad stereotypes for each group.

Discuss why people have stereotypes for others who are different from themselves. What are the effects of such stereotypes when people relate to one another in their neighborhood, in their school, in their work areas, in public policy, etc.

Discovering

Step 2. Biblical Reflection on "Neighborhood" (20 minutes)

Divide your group into small discussion subgroups of no more than six persons. Give each subgroup a copy of a Bible passage about neighbors. Here are some possibilities: Leviticus 19:16b-18, Proverbs 3:29-30, Matthew 5:43-48, and James 2:2-4. For more references, consult a Bible concordance.

Have each group deal with the following questions:

• What does the Bible say about our neighbors?

• What does Jesus say about our neighbors?

• What criteria do people look for when they relate to their neighbors? (For example, money, car, vocation, house, and so on.) Share your personal experiences. As Christians, what should be our attitude?

• As Asian Pacific Americans, we have inherited a culture which advocates close-knit family lifestyles. As Christians we have also been taught to treat our neighbors like our own family members. Do you think this kind of relationship is possible in America? If your answer is yes, why? If your answer is no, why not?

Read the following thoughts aloud to your youth:

Our American life is largely influenced by the "bigness syndrome." We have learned to respect bigness and minimize the importance of smallness. We accept the fact that "big bucks" speak and "big people" influence our society. Even the fast-food restaurants appeal to us with "Big Macs," "Jumbo Jacks," and "Double Whoppers." We adore big things, but we ignore and ridicule smallness.

This bigness syndrome has distorted our image of human relationships, particularly our interracial ones. The majority often believes that its way is better and right, failing to consider the rich contributions that can be made by minority groups in America. Racial tensions in North America are not limited to white-black or white-ethnic relationships; they also take their toll among the minority groups themselves. Racial/ethnic groups often compete with other racial/ethnic groups—even to the point of conflict. For example, do you suppose it is right that some Asian Pacific Americans label the Indochinese refugees in America as "F.O.B." (Fresh Off the Boat)? Or that they discriminate against these newcomers as third-class citizens because they are recent immigrants, have fewer numbers than other Asian Pacific American groups, and possess less economic or political power?

Listen to the words of James in the Bible: "If you show more respect to the well-dressed man and say to him, 'Have this best seat here,' but say to the poor man, 'Stand over there, or sit here on the floor by my feet,' then you are guilty of creating distinctions among yourselves and of making judgments based on evil motives" (James 2:3-4, TEV). When we discriminate against our fellow human beings because of their outward appearance or background, aren't we alienating ourselves from God's kingdom?

Together as a whole group, discuss the bigness syndrome. Give each discussion subgroup a chance to share their biblical reflections. Jot down the major ideas on the newsprint or chalkboard. Encourage personal sharing.

Step 3. Slide Presentation *(45 minutes)*

Have each team of reporters share with the whole group through a slide presentation of what they have seen in their assigned area. (If the photos are in the form of prints, share these by passing them around and discussing them.) During their presentations have the teams respond to neighborhood-related questions such as: Who are the racial/ethnic groups (blacks, Hispanics, Asian Pacific Americans, Native Americans) that make up your neighborhood? What is the percentage of Anglo-Americans in your neighborhood? What kind of things do they do in your area? What kind of needs did you sense in the neighborhood and the lives of its people? Did you find any community issue that needs to be addressed?

Allow ample time for a question-answer period.

Closing
Step 4. Mission Project *(10 minutes)*

Ask your group, "Is there any mission project we can do for our neighborhood?" If your youth saw a real need in their neighborhood, it could be the basis of an exciting mission project for your youth group. Explore that possibility, by all means. Select a few key youth as a task group to do more study on the project. Have this group report next week on how some form of involvement can possibly take place.

Step 5. Wrap-Up *(5 minutes)*

Sing "Kum Ba Yah," or "We Are One in the Spirit."

Form a complete circle for a time of community prayer. Encourage each youth to pray about one thing for the neighborhood. After each prayer, the whole group responds by saying, "God, hear our prayer."

About the Next Two Sessions

Introduction

Racism is alive and well in America. Race-related violence against Asian Pacific Americans is increasing. The media continue to perpetuate racist stereotypes. Asian immigrants are victims of discrimination in employment, housing, and education.

Yet many Asian Pacific Americans, especially the older-generation Japanese, Chinese, and Korean, still question that racism even exists. Some have adopted the slogan "God helps those who help themselves" or "Tell them to pull themselves up by their own bootstraps."

It is simply not that easy. While the work ethic still operates in America, minority-race people are facing examples of personal and institutional racism, both intended and unintended; both overt and subtle.

These next two sessions are designed to raise the awareness of young people to the evidence of racism around them. The first session addresses personal racism, while the second session focuses on institutional racism. Both sessions are difficult to work through, and the leader should be familiar enough with the procedure to be able to explain it in his or her own words.

Racism and Me

by Rodger Y. Nishioka

Goals:

- Young people will understand what personal racism is.
- Young people will identify specific ways in which racism exists today and how it affects Asian Pacific American youth.
- Young people will see that racism is contrary to the will of God.
- Young people will discover ways to cope with racism in their lives.

Introduction:

Personal racism makes its appearance whenever someone is put down because of his or her racial/ethnic heritage. Not all Asian Pacific Americans will say they have personally experienced racism. Some genuinely believe they have not, and others are not able to admit that they have.

This session is based on the assumption that young people already understand what is meant by stereotypes, and it then moves the group to understand how those stereotypes help to create racist attitudes and actions.

The leaders of this session must be prepared to risk by sharing some personal examples of racism in their own lives.

Preparation:

Supplies needed:
- newsprint or chalkboard
- markers or chalk
- masking tape
- large sheets of newsprint to trace a silhouette of a person
- Bibles
- copies of the situation cards for role plays

Procedure

Opening
Step 1. Getting Started *(5 minutes)*

Open the session with prayer. If there are new youth in your group, take some time to get acquainted. Have the goals for the session posted somewhere around the room. Refer to the goals now, so the participants will know what to expect.

Discovering
Step 2. Create a Silhouette *(15 minutes)*

Divide the group into fours and give each of these smaller groups a large sheet of newsprint. One person of the four is to lie down on the sheet and be traced in outline by another. When the tracing is completed, the small group should label the silhouette "Stereotype Asian Pacific American." *Note:* You may choose to encourage the group to name the silhouette, and perhaps label which Asian heritage group it represents.

For the next few minutes, the participants should fill the silhouettes by writing in all the images, words, phrases, and symbols that reflect stereotypes of Asian Pacific Americans. Encourage them to focus on different areas; including physical appearance, academic/intellectual skills, social behaviors, emotions, family relationships, spiritual affiliations, etc.

Step 3. Sharing the Silhouettes *(10 minutes)*

Mount the silhouettes on the wall and ask individuals from each small group to read through all the stereotypes listed.

After each group has shared, ask all to look back at their silhouettes, with all the stereotypes, and to quickly count the number of positive and negative characteristics they have identified. Most groups will probably count many more negative stereotypes than positive ones.

Step 4. Defining Stereotypes and Racism *(10 minutes)*

In the total group discuss the following questions:
What is a stereotype?
Can any stereotype be positive?
Why do people form stereotypes?
Racism is based on stereotypes. Post and read this definition to the group: "Racism is any attitude, action, or institution which [puts down] a person or group because of color. Racism is not just a matter of attitudes; actions and institutions can also be a form of racism." (from *Racism in America and How to Combat It*, U.S. Commission on Civil Rights, 1970). Discuss this statement with the youth and ask how they feel about it.

Step 5. Personalizing Racism *(10 minutes)*

Explain that anytime you are put down because of your race, it is an act of racism. Be ready to share a personal example of racism in your life. Discuss with the group:

Have you ever been put down intentionally or unintentionally because of your race?

What happened?

How did you react?

Have you ever put someone else down because of their race? If so, are you a racist?

Step 6. Bible Study *(10 minutes)*

Have the youth turn in their Bibles to two passages and read them together: Genesis 1:26-28 and Galatians 3:26-29. One of the passages is describing the creation and the second is a letter from Paul to the church at Galatia, but both have the same clear message about stereotypes.

Discuss with the group:

What is God saying to us through these two passages about stereotypes?

What does it mean when it says there is no difference between Jew and Gentile, slave and free, men and women?

Who was created in the image of God?

What are the implications for us if everyone is created in the image of God?

Step 7. Coping with Racism *(20 minutes)*

Even though we reject the idea of stereotypes and any form of racism, we will still have to cope with the reality in our daily lives. Divide the group into pairs and distribute the *A* situation cards and the *B* situation cards (see page 111). One person in the pair plays person A. The other person plays person B. Explain the situation and allow no more than ten minutes for the role play. You may choose to switch roles after a few minutes.

Finally, ask for a volunteer pair to role play his or her situation in front of the whole group. Not all groups will have the same role play.

Closing
Step 8. Debriefing Role Plays *(5 minutes)*

From the role play, list on newsprint some specific responses that are helpful when we confront personal racism. What kinds of things should we say? How can we respond, remembering that we are all images of God? Try to list at least four or five ways we can respond. What kinds of responses were helpful in the role plays? Be ready to share some of your own ideas.

Step 9. Relooking at the Goals and Endings *(5 minutes)*

Review the activities in the session by referring again to the goals. Did you accomplish these? Close with prayer.

SITUATION CARDS FOR ROLE PLAYS

Duplicate enough for each person to have a card.

Person A.—Situation One

You are a high school teacher. You are the chairperson of the math department. In your honors calculus class, everyone is getting *A*'s except this one student, an Asian Pacific American. You can't understand it. All Asian Pacific Americans are great in math. This one also is talking too much. You can't understand that either, because they are all supposed to be quiet and polite. You are now in a conference with the student to try and straighten the situation out.

Person B.—Situation One

You are a high school student. Your worst class is calculus where you are barely pulling a *C*. You're satisfied with that, because it's a tough class and you're working hard. Your best friends are also in that class, so it's fun for you. Besides, math has never been your favorite subject. The teacher, who is basically arrogant, has never really liked you. The teacher has asked for a conference with you. You don't know what this is all about.

Person A.—Situation Two

You are new to this part of the country. You've moved from an area where there were no Asians. Your whole high school had only twenty-seven people in it, and four of them were teachers. You've also never met an Asian Pacific American before. They look kind of like the Indians back home, but their eyes are funny and their skin is lighter. You've seen some of them on cable TV but never met one face to face. You've heard all kinds of things about them from parents and TV. On your first day at this new school, you meet one at lunch. You want to find out more about Asian Pacific Americans, but you're cautious and skeptical. You aren't sure you should trust these "foreigners." You begin remembering Pearl Harbor.

Person B.—Situation Two

You are minding your own business at school and eating lunch. Your friends have just left, and you're about to finish and join them when this new kid you saw in your last period class sits close to you. The newcomer is from someplace far away—North Dakota or someplace like that. You don't know anything about the person, but you want to appear friendly and welcoming. You have had a hard day, though, and you're a little bit edgy and uptight.

Racism and Institutions

by Rodger Y. Nishioka

Goals:
- Young people will understand what institutional racism is.
- Young people will identify ways by which institutional racism exists today and how it affects Asian Pacific American young people in particular.
- Young people will discover ways to cope with institutional racism.

Introduction:

Institutional racism is a difficult topic. Many young people are not sure what it is—let alone, whether or not it exists.

The Marble Game is a simulation activity designed to show young people how a system, through its design, might unfairly favor certain people.

In American society, virtually every institution is characterized with racism, because the institutions themselves were designed by a white majority population to serve that population. The fact that Asian Pacific Americans have demonstrated a remarkable ability to adapt to these institutions and survive makes them no less racist or discriminatory.

This session, then, is designed to help young people recognize, discuss, and cope with institutional racism.

Preparation:

This session is designed for a ninety-minute program. For the Marble Game, see the "supplies needed" and "before the game" sections on page 115.

Other supplies needed for this session are:
- newsprint
- marking pens
- masking tape

Procedure:

Opening
Step 1. Beginnings *(5 minutes)*

Begin the session with prayer. Welcome any new members to your group.

Discovering
Step 2. Play the Marble Game *(40 minutes)*

Following the directions listed in the game. You will need to set up the room; also to make copies of the rules and the marble market bulletins for each client.

Step 3. Discuss Learnings from the Game *(10 minutes)*

After the game, discuss what happened by asking the following questions:
- What did you understand to be the goal of the game?
  - Was that the real goal?
  - What actually happened?
- What promises do you think were made to you at the beginning of the game?
  - Were those promises kept?
  - How do you feel about your role in the game?
  - Who had the most power in the game?
  - Was the game fair?
- Can you see any parallels to this game in real life?

Read aloud the background section printed at the beginning of the game to explain the purpose of the game and its teachings about institutional racism.

Step 4. Defining Institutional Racism *(10 minutes)*

Post or write the definitions for "institution" and "institutional racism" somewhere around the room. Review the meanings with the group.

Institution: A stable social arrangement or practice through which collective actions are taken. Examples: Courts, governments, businesses, unions, schools, churches, police, etc.

Institutional racism: A situation in which a system or practice (institution) rewards one group in particular and excludes others on behalf of race.

Some other helpful explanations:

"Institutions have great power to reward and penalize. They reward by providing career opportunities for some people and foreclosing them for others. They reward as well by the way social goods are distributed—by deciding who receives training and skills, medical care, formal education, political influence, moral support and self-respect, productive employment, fair treatment by the law, decent housing, self-confidence, and the promise of a secure future for self and children.

"One of the clearest indicators in institutional racism is the exclusion of black members of society from positions of control and leadership."[1]

"Some of the most conspicuous examples of [institutional racism] are in housing patterns; segregated schools; discriminatory employment and promotion policies; segregated churches; white control of newspapers, radio and TV; routes selected for construction of expressways or freeways, and textbooks which ignore or distort the role of black people."[2]

Step 5. Looking for Examples *(10 minutes)*

Next, choose an institution and discuss in what ways it is racist (favors the white majority). For example, how does the educational system benefit white students in particular? Here are some possible answers:

• Textbooks emphasize white perspective and history.

• Standardized tests are designed with the white experience in mind.

• Home economics labs teach how to bake bread, which is not used in some nonwhite societies.

• Quiet students are encouraged to talk more.

• Aggressive or assertive behavior is often praised.

Step 6. Coping with Institutional Racism *(10 minutes)*

Finally, ask the group about ways by which we can cope with institutional racism. What can we do about it? Try to list a few tangible, practical steps.

Using the example of school, Asian Pacific Americans could do a report for history class on Asian exclusion acts or the internment of Japanese-Americans.

Closing
Step 7. Summarizing Learnings *(5 minutes)*

Summarize the two major points:
1. Institutional racism does exist and it affects our lives.
2. We can work to change racist systems. Close with prayer.

---

[1]Knowles and Prewitt, *Institutional Racism in America,* (Englewood Cliffs: Prentice-Hall, 1969).
[2]*What Curriculum Leaders Can Do About Racism.*

The Marble Game

Goal: To earn the highest number of points by collecting the best color combination of marbles.

Time: The game will run approximately forty minutes. The game is divided into four five-minute rounds. Each round contains one minute of discussion time.

Supplies needed:

- chalkboard or newsprint for scoreboard
- ten marbles for every two people (include at least five different colors)
- paper cup for each set of ten marbles
- bell or buzzer to signal the beginning and end of each round
- watch to check time
- game prizes (optional)

Before the game:

- set up the chairs in the room as depicted on the diagram
- divide the marbles into the cups, mixing the colors, but with different combinations in the various cups
- post the rules
- prepare the scoreboard
- duplicate a copy of the Marble Market Bulletin for each team for each round

Background:

This game is designed to simulate a racist system or institution. Racist institutions say that everyone is equal but provide special advantages or privileges to assure that one particular group succeeds.

In this game, the rhetoric is that all marbles are equal. They are not. But the point values of the marbles are simply a distraction from the real inequity of the special privileges. The special privileges are examples of ways the *system* or *institution* assures that one group will get ahead regardless of how hard the others work. In this way, the game provides a simplistic view of institutional racism.

Procedures:

1. Explain the goal and rules of the game. Post them on the wall in the room.
2. Explain the procedure.
3. Divide the group into pairs, which will function as teams. Clients (A) sit on the outside of the circle facing in. Brokers (B) sit on the inside of the circle with their backs toward the center of the circle (see diagram).
4. Give each team a cup of ten marbles. List on the cup how many points would be awarded for that combination of marbles, but do not explain how they are calculated. Actual points begin with the first round.
5. Distribute the first Marble Market Bulletin. No talking until the round begins.
6. Begin Round One. Pairs consult for one minute, then trading by the brokers may start.
7. After four minutes of trading, call time. Subtract points if any broker is still in the marble exchange area or if any marbles were dropped.
8. Ask each client to report his or her marble combinations. Figure the new value in points, based on the point scale, but again do not explain the values.
9. After all points have been awarded, give the privilege bonus to the team you have selected (see privilege scale). Give the group some made-up explanation which may or may not make sense.
10. Proceed with Rounds Two, Three, and Four. Distribute the appropriate Marble Market Bulletin, in each round. Distribute the Special Flash with Bulletin Three.
11. Following each round, award the points earned in that round and grant the special privilege bonus to the privileged team. Again, do not explain the point system, and give some made-up explanation for the privilege bonus.
12. Following Round Four, the last round, record the total points, award the special privilege bonus, and declare the winner. If you choose to, you may award prizes.

Marble Game Rules: *(Post these around the room.)*

1. No talking until the round begins.
2. Only the Brokers may enter the Marble Exchange Area.
3. Brokers remaining in the Marble Exchange Area when the round is up will lose ten points.
4. Teams will lose one point per marble if a marble is dropped.
5. Consultations between Broker and Client may happen only while both are seated.
6. Client may not leave his/her seat.
7. Only Client may read the Marble Market Bulletin.
8. No stealing marbles.
9. Brokers must maintain ten marbles at all times.

Point scale:

1. Choose two different-colored marbles—for example, light blue and red.
2. Give the light blue marble a point value of two points and the red marble a point value of three.
3. All other marbles are worthless.
4. At the end of a round, if a Client holds ten marbles with (for instance) a combination of three white, one yellow, four black, one *red,* and one *light blue,* the value of the marbles is five points.
5. If in the next round, the Client changes all of the marbles except the one red and one light blue and gains no more marbles of those colors, the value will remain five points.
6. Therefore, at the end of two rounds, the Client will have earned ten points.
7. You may choose to change the values in the middle of the game if you desire. Point values really do not matter.

Privilege scale:

1. The key to this game is the privilege scale. Remember that the goal of this game is to illustrate how institutional racism works. That is why participants are constantly told that "all marbles are of equal value." While society may say this, it is not always true.
2. Choose one group to be given special privileges for the whole game. You will need to be creative in making up reasons to give this group the special privilege bonus. Award the special privileges after the points have been totaled. If the special privilege affects the point totals, change them.
3. Be sure you try to justify the special privileges always going to the same group with specific reasons. Toward the end of the game, your reasons may become more and more ridiculous.

Privileges:

Round One — Team receives a bonus of six extra points.

Round Two — Team may trade any number of marbles for any color with any other team.

Round Three — Team may "zap" any other team to take away up to six points without trading marbles.

Round Four — Team may trade any number of marbles for any color with any other team.

Marble Market Bulletin One:

Dear Client:

The Marble Market is remarkably healthy. The Federal Marble Reserve Board has just issued a bulletin saying that all marbles are equal. Everyone knows, however, that the real system does not run that way and certain marbles are worth more than others. Trading is expected to be heavy during this first round.

Marble Market analysts report that clients who keep a variety of marbles will be safest. Some other analysts, however, insist that the smart client will lean toward the lighter colored marbles.

Good trading, Clients!

Marble Market Bulletin Two:

Dear Client:

The Marble Market opened to good trading last round. Trading for this round is predicted to be just as good, although some clients may try to hold on to their marbles.

Market analysts recommend that clients maintain a diversity of marbles, not trying to corner the market on any particular marble color yet.

The Federal Marble Reserve Board says that all marbles are equal.

Good trading, Clients!

Marble Market Bulletin Three:

Dear Client:

Trading was moderate last round, with some clients playing conservatively and keeping their marbles. Some clients are complaining about others receiving more privileges for no apparent reason.

Market analysts were unreachable. Apparently all are busy checking their sources about a wild rumor of a marble embargo.

The Federal Marble Reserve Board says that all marbles are equal.

Good trading, Clients!

Marble Bulletin SPECIAL FLASH!

Market analysts are alarmed by a series of unconfirmed but consistent reports of a sudden embargo on dark-colored marbles. Experts predict that the costs of dark marbles will skyrocket, changing the marble value scale entirely. Holders of light marbles may risk high losses as the value of light marbles may plummet.

Marble Market Bulletin Four:

The market rose and fell last round following a bizarre rumor apparently begun by holders of too many dark marbles.

The rumors were completely unfounded.

Market analysts are unsure as to how to best secure the highest point value. Analysts still tend to lean towards light marbles. Experts are completely confused by an apparent privilege scale which seems to award certain privileges to certain persons no matter whether deserving or not. Experts are critical of the privilege scale saying it tends to favor only a few.

The Federal Marble Reserve Board is still insisting that all marbles are equal. Market experts agree that members of the FMRB lost their marbles three rounds ago.

Good trading, Clients!

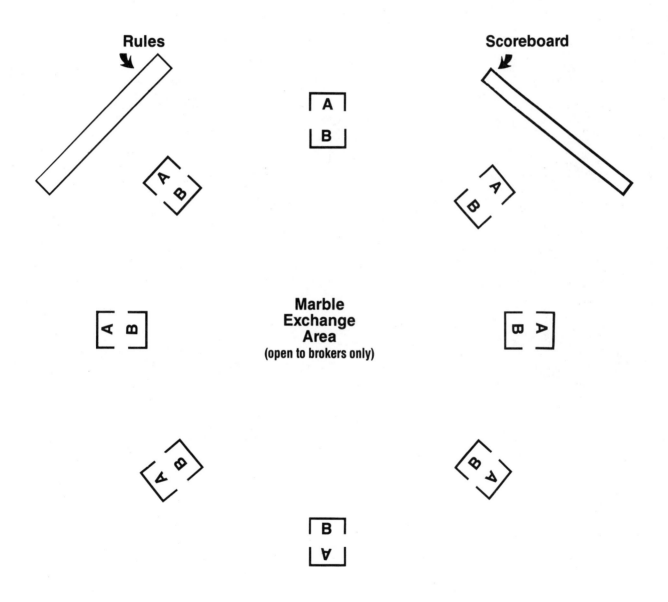

Being Socially Adaptive

by Tim Tseng

Goals:

• Youth will identify and appreciate the various cultural settings and modes of behavior they are experiencing.

• Youth will develop a criterion or plan that affirms their socially adaptive behavior and bicultural experiences in light of their Christian identity.

Introduction:

Asian Pacific American youth live in at least two cultural settings: American and Asian Pacific. They are often uncomfortable with this experience. This uneasiness is due in part to the way American society is usually portrayed. When the word "American" is used, one usually thinks of white Anglo people and values. The cultural experiences of Asian Pacific, black, Hispanic, and Native American people are not recognized as a reality in a monocultural society. Thus, Asian Pacific American young people often feel alienated from this Western context. Furthermore, many of them, having been raised in this American environment, are also distant from their inherited Asian cultural contexts. The world in which their parents or grandparents live is equally alienating for Asian Pacific American youth who do not share all the norms and traditions held by their elders. They are caught in the middle. Thus, they experience discomfort and even severe stress because of their marginal status.

Of course, there will be those in a given youth group who are either "assimilated" (those who have consciously or subconsciously rejected their Asian identity and accepted the ways of white American society) of "insulated" (those who have managed in large part to retain ethnic identity.)[1] However, such clearly defined identities are rare among Asian Pacific Americans. Most are somewhere along the continuum between being culturally Asian and culturally American and are able to move back and forth.[2] This ability to move back and forth between two cultures in terms of one's behavior and attitudes is called "social adaptivity."

Bicultural young people need to realize that being "socially adaptive" is a gift to be appreciated. In light of the gospel message, they do not *have* to act one way or another. They can be "all things to all [people]" (1 Corinthians 9:22), because in Christ "there is neither Jew nor Greek . . . slave nor free . . . male nor female" (Galatians 3:28). This realization has helpful insights for a dynamic intergenerational church which ministers to both the newly arrived immigrants and the second- and third-generation Asian Pacific Americans. As people called to be Asian Pacific Americans, these youth will be encouraged to search more deeply and affirm both their inherited and their adopted cultures.

This program session seeks to enable youth to realize their calling and gift of biculturality. Through individual reflection, role play, and group discussion, they will connect their everyday experiences with this program session. A Bible study will further help them to discover for themselves this calling and gift. The second objective—developing a criterion or action plan to affirm their bicultural identity and behavior—will be attained through discussing and planning a project.

The session is flexible enough to be used with suitable adaptation, for either teenagers or young adults or even for a group that includes both. The role-play situations and discussion questions would need to be adjusted, depending on the make-up of the group you are working with. Such variations will be discussed further in the preparation section.

Preparation:

Although this session may be conducted without recruiting additional leaders, you may find it more helpful to select three discussion group leaders a few weeks in advance. These persons can lead the role-plays and the project planning. Go over the session with them first.

You will need the following materials:

• A chalkboard, chalk, and eraser; or newsprint and markers
• Paper
• Pencils
• Bibles (different versions are optional)
• Movable chairs that can be grouped into three small circles
• A room large enough for a single large circle and at another time for three small circles

On the newsprint or chalkboard, draw two large boxes, one to the right and the other on the left.

[1]Donna Dong, "The Asian-American Bi-cultural Experience," in Roy Sano, (compiler), *The Theologies of Asian Americans and Pacific Peoples: A Reader* (Berkeley: Asian Center for Theology and Strategies, Pacific School of Religion, 1976), pp. 12-13.

[2]Gail Law, A Model for the American Ethnic Chinese Churches," *Theology, News and Notes,* December, 1984, pp. 21ff.

Between the boxes, draw a line connecting them. Do not write anything else until the session begins. You should have a diagram that looks similar to this:

One box represents the "insulated" Asian Pacific American who has retained his/her ethnic identity, and the other represents the "assimilated" Asian Pacific American who has rejected his/her ethnic identity. The line represents the Asian Pacific American who has been "marginalized" (or "acculturated") and lives in a bicultural experience.

Although you will be making lists of behaviors and attitudes during the session, it would be helpful for you to do some advance thinking about them. Consider these elements:
• Behaviors or attitudes that uniquely characterize immigrants from Asia and the Pacific Basin.
• Behaviors or attitudes that uniquely characterize white Anglos living in the United States.
• Responses of "assimilated," "insulated," and "marginalized" ("acculturated") Asian Pacific Americans to a situation where Asian and American peoples interact and confront each other.

Study Galatians 3:26-29 and I Corinthians 9:19-23. Note the contexts in which Paul wrote these Letters. A good Bible commentary will be a helpful reference at this point.

Procedure

Opening
Step 1. Reflection *(15 minutes)*

Have the group sit in a large circle. Pass out the sheets of paper and pencils to each person. Read the following paragraphs to them (or you may find another quotation which describes a different Asian Pacific experience which may be more relevant for addressing the problem of identity to your group):

I was Chinese-American, whatever that meant. That I was not an individual, not just a human being. Just a human being in this culture, in this society, is a white man, he can disappear. I couldn't disappear, no matter how enlightened I was, no matter how straight my English was. Someone, just because they saw my skin color, would detect an accent. Someone would always correct me. And well, then I began to look at my writing, what I'd been writing about in my letters and everything was just to this point. The Chinese-American, well, schizophrenia. That I'd been playing a kind of ping-pong game, you know. Now, I'm Chinese, now I'm American. But up against real Chinese . . . I saw that I had nothing in common with them. That they didn't understand me, and I didn't understand them. We both use chopsticks okay, that's recognizable. But that's mechanics, not culture.
I identify with my father. My father tried, in his own way he tried as hard as I am to make it in his terms in this country. Yeah, I think he failed and I think he thinks he's

failed. But in his eyes I'm irresponsible. I'm fooling around and I'm an insult to him. . . .
We live in different worlds. And when my world comes in contact with his we just destroy each other. I look at the way he tunes the television set, it's all wrong. The people look like they're dead. They come on looking dingy, gray, the color of Roquefort cheese. But that's the way he sees the world. And he lives in Chinatown, so it's in Chinatown, his world, and he can't see that it's partly my world, too. So you know, I'll never have his respect. And I could win a Nobel prize, you know, and prove that my writing's been worthwhile and he'll say, "you dress like a bum." And then I see that I've broken the guy's heart. So I feel bad about that.[3]

[3]Dong, *op. cit.,* pp. 12-13.

Tell each person: "Write two paragraphs in response to this quotation. In the first paragraph, write how you feel about what this person has said. In the second paragraph, write how you feel about being an Asian Pacific American."

After five to ten minutes of reflection and writing, ask persons to share their ideas and feelings with the entire group.

Discovering
Step 2. Line Diagram *(10 minutes)*

Show the diagram you drew earlier. As you explain what each of the figures represents, write "insulated," "assimilated," and "marginalized (or acculturated)" on the diagram. You may want to explain the diagram this way:

"Generally speaking, there are three kinds of Asian Pacific Americans. First, there is the person who retains his/her ethnic identity and is insulated from American society. We'll call this person the 'insulated.' Second, there is the one who has become so assimilated into American life that he/she has rejected his/her ethnic identity either consciously or subconsciously. We'll call this person the 'assimilated.' Third, there is the person who lives in both the Asian Pacific and the American world. This individual cannot fully identify with either world and often feels left out. We'll call this person the 'acculturated' or the 'marginalized.'

Step 3. Role-Playing *(20 minutes)*

Divide the group into three subgroups. Have each subgroup form a circle, using different parts of the room. After they have settled down, give each group an identity as "assimilated," "insulated," or "marginalized" (or "acculturated"). Explain:

"Each group represents one of three kinds of Asian Pacific American. In each group, pretend you are either an 'isulated,' 'assimilated,' or 'acculturated' person, as assigned. Spend some time listing the types of responses you would give as that person in response to one of the following situations. Choose one.

- You have been asked to go to the prom by a person not of Asian Pacific American background.
- You have been invited to go to a ski (or camping) trip with a mixed group of white Anglo, black, and Asian Pacific American friends."
- You have an Asian Pacific American friend who is marrying a white Anglo American. You've been invited to the wedding and reception.

"In replying tell: (a) How you would respond to the invitation. (b) Assuming that you go, how you would behave or interact in the situation."

Step 4. Processing the Role Play (10 minutes)

Gather the three groups together into a large circle and discuss the responses. The following questions may be helpful for further discussion:

a. Which type of person found it easiest to deal with the situation? The most difficult? Why?

b. Which person would have the most difficult struggle as an Asian Pacific person in America? Which do you identify with?

c. List on newsprint or chalkboard some characteristics, behaviors, and customs unique to Asian Pacific people and some characteristics, behaviors, and customs unique to Western white Anglo-American people.

d. How do you feel about being part of two worlds and two lifestyles?

e. How do you feel about the tasks of adapting your behavior in various social groupings as an Asian Pacific American?

Step 5. Bible Study (15 minutes)

Have two group members read Galatians 3:26-29 and 1 Corinthians 9:19-23. Then discuss the following questions either as a large group or in the same three subgroups (you may want to make use of the subgroup leaders if you have prepared them.)

a. Compare and contrast these two passages. Both were written by the apostle Paul.

b. What does our Christian identity tell us about our American and Asian Pacific identities?

c. How and when would it be more important to be or behave as an Asian Pacific person? An American person?

Step 6. Action Planning (15 minutes)

Before closing, break the group into the same three subgroups again.

Ask each subgroup to plan or design a project in which they may better appreciate both their Asian Pacific identity and their American identity. In this project they should study the customs, behavior, characteristics, and values of both Asian Pacific people and American people.

Some suggestions: Listen to and record the stories of parents and grandparents who immigrated to America. Study what the word "America" means and should mean. Attend either an American or an Asian language worship service (or perhaps both).

Ask them to meet again as the same group at a later time, after they have completed the project, for follow-up.

Closing
Step 7. Prayer (5 minutes)

Gather the entire group together for closing prayer. In the prayer, affirm the calling and gift of the ability to interact in both an Asian Pacific and an American setting.

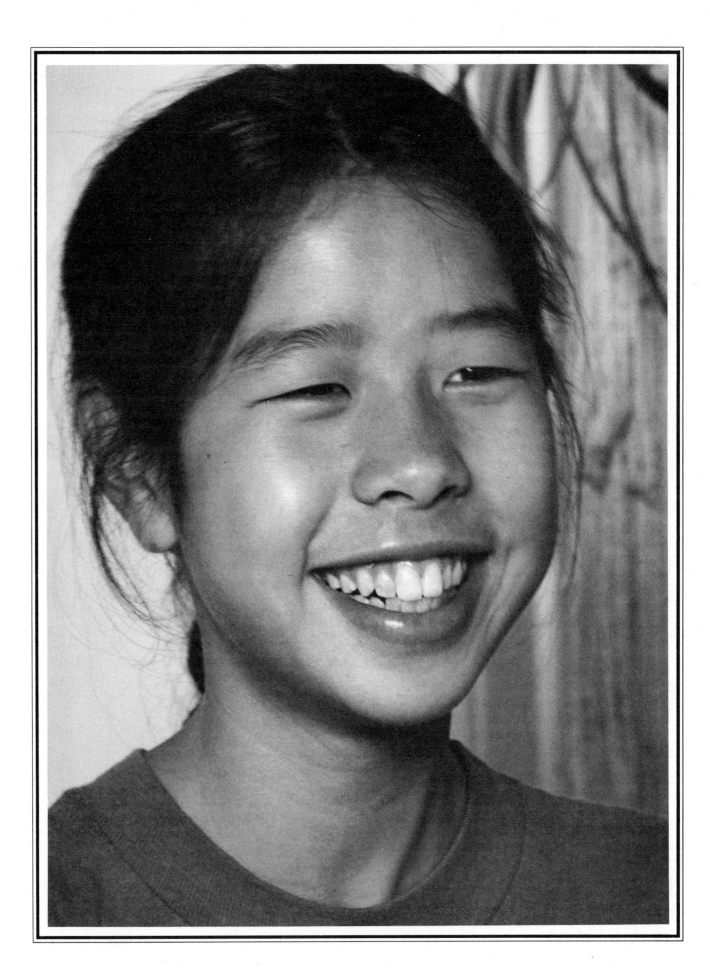

THEME 3

Beliefs and Christian Faith

To find and claim beliefs that fit together is the object of an ongoing search for most Christians today. Asian Pacific American youth in particular often see the Christian faith as differing from their traditional cultural values and struggle to relate them to each other. Helping youth see the dynamic relationship that exists between faith and culture will celebrate the contributions Asian Pacific American Christians have made and will make to the church and its mission. Through this understanding, youth can explore their active role as the younger laity in the church.

- Knowing Your Values, *by Kathryn Choy-Wong*
- Faith and Cultural Influences, *by Kathryn Choy-Wong*
- Faith in Our Setting, *by Kathryn Choy-Wong*
- The Role of Culture in Faith, *by Kathryn Choy-Wong*
- The Role of Youth in the Church, *by Kathryn Choy-Wong*

Knowing Your Values

by Kathryn Choy-Wong

Goals:

• Youth will examine what white American and Asian Pacific American values they hold and why they hold them.

• Youth will begin making vocational and other life choices based on their values.

Introduction:

There are positive values in both white American and Asian Pacific American cultures. White America offers the values that youth are important persons in their own right and can contribute to the general society; that each person has a mind of his/her own and has basic human rights; and that each person can make his/her own choices.

Earlier Euro-American generations embraced many of the same values as Asian Pacific American cultures, such as the importance of the land and hard work, striving for success, the need for family and community, and responsibility toward others.

Similarly, in traditional Asian Pacific American cultures we value family, the interdependence of persons with each other, the community and the environment, conservation, group decisions, and honor and respect for elders and authority.

As Asian Pacific Americans we can select and recover the best values in both cultures. We therefore have an opportunity to utilize what we have to benefit not only ourselves but others and society as a whole. We have many opportunities which others may lack, and therefore we have a responsibility to use our skills and resources to the fullest for the benefit of all.

Many Asian Pacific Americans enjoy a middle-class lifestyle. Our parents or generations before them have made sacrifices that enable us to live better lives today. Our parents have instilled in us the desire to "strive for success." Asian Pacific American youth are pressured to "succeed," usually in the form of materialism, consumerism, "moving up the ladder," or "staying on the top of the ladder." Such achievements are often understood as the measure of "success."

The Bible has very distinct warnings about the overemphasis on materialism, worldly goods, and wealth. Matthew 19:16-30 stresses the importance of spiritual matters above economic success, and the final verse of this passage says many that are first shall be last, and the last first. That is God's justice and mercy; there will be a reversal of status and position in life. Matthew 20:26-28 teaches us to be servants and not to be served. And Matthew 20:1-16 shares a message that in the end we will all be treated equally, no matter how hard we worked or when we started working.

Asian Pacific American youth need to begin making vocational and other choices in light of these considerations. They need to begin making personal choices, sometimes in spite of family or group choices. What is true success? How can success be measured? What values do Asian Pacific American youth want to convey to others? What might they want to transmit to future generations?

Preparation

The program is for a sixty- to ninety-minute session. You will need to:

• Make copies of "Values Opinion Survey"
• Make copies of "Vocational Choices"
• Have pencils or pens on hand
• Print each Bible passage on separate index cards—
  Matthew 19:13-30, Matthew 20:26-28,
  and Matthew 20:1-16
• Arrange the room to allow for movement

Read over the Bible passages. Fill out the "Values Opinion Survey" and "Vocational Choices" for yourself. Ask yourself: What values do I hold? Are my values more "Westernized" or more toward the "Pacific and Asian" cultures? Do I feel my values are in harmony with, or in conflict with, the biblical passages?

What is beginning to look like my own vocational choice? What factors have encouraged me to go in this direction? What are my other options?

Pray for the session to go well.

Procedure:

Opening

Step 1. Become Acquainted *(10 minutes)*

Start the session by sharing updates with one another. Explain what the youth will be doing in this session by reviewing the program's goals.

Step 2. Take a "Values Opinion Survey" *(10 minutes)*

Give each youth a "Values Opinion Survey." Ask the youth to place an "X" on the continuum toward the value or words they feel more positive about, or which better describes them or their personality. For example, I might draw an "X" on 15, because I have a more positive attitude toward family than individual.

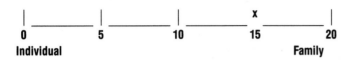

Or, I might put an "X" between 5 and 10, and mark the "X" #7, toward sports rather than schoolwork, because I prefer sports over schoolwork.

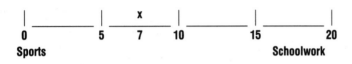

Be sure to explain that there are no right or wrong answers, that the survey is not a complete list, and that the distinctions between Western culture and Pacific Asian culture may not be that clear, especially if the traditional cultures have undergone changes themselves. Also within Pacific Asian cultures, as well as Western cultures, there are variations and differences in values. However, the survey is an exercise to help you begin to explore the origins of the values they hold.

Discovering

Step 3. Share Your Responses *(10 minutes)*

Have the youth form pairs to share their responses. Encourage them to compare and contrast their responses.

Step 4. Score Your Responses *(10 minutes)*

In order to get a picture of each person's likely tendency, have everyone total up the numerical values to his or her responses. Having a few calculators for use would make the additions easier. If you scored between 0 and 75, you strongly reflect Western values. If you scored between 75 and 150, your values are somewhat Western. If you scored between 150 and 225, your values are somewhat Asian Pacific. If you scored between 225 and 300, your values are very Asian Pacific.

Step 5. Use the "Vocational Choices" *(15 minutes)*

Pass out the "Vocational Choices" form to be filled out individually. Circle all the vocations you prefer.

Answer the questions following the exercise. Share your answers in the total group for discussion.

Closing

Step 6. Review the Scriptures *(15 minutes)*

Go over the Bible passages briefly with the youth. Time permitting, have them join the partners they had at the beginning of the program to discuss what the Bible passages tell us about our values. Do you feel the choices and discoveries you have made today reinforce or conflict with these passages? If they conflict, how might you resolve this difference?

Close with a prayer that calls for understanding and clarity of what our values might be and what we might choose for our future.

More Ideas and Activities

Step 1. Do a Values Situation Game *(40 minutes)*

Instead of the "Values Opinion Survey" and the "Vocational Choices" exercises, you might want to do a values situation game. The situation is: "The world is coming to an end. There is one spaceship left for a small group of you to leave the 'doomed' planet Earth. Your task is to build a new civilization on another planet. The civilization will be based on five values. What would these values be and why? (Values could include respect for human life, stewardship of all God's creation, love, the individual's right to pursue happiness, etc.) Which of these values are more Asian Pacific? Which are more Western? Which are more biblically based?"

You can divide the large group into smaller groups to decide on the five values, then share these in the larger groups.

Step 2. Picture an Ideal Person *(30 minutes)*

Instead of the "Values Opinion Survey," you might want to do an "Ideal Person" exercise. Have each person draw a picture of his/her ideal person. Go beyond physical appearances and also describe what values this person would have.

Discuss which of these values are more Asian Pacific. What are more Western? Which are biblical?

Values Opinion Survey

Values are not necessarily good or bad, right or wrong. They reflect your preferences, which are based on your own personal history and background.

The following is a list of words which reflect traditional Asian Pacific values or Western/American values. Place an "X" on the line at the point between the two values which best represent your thinking. You may have varying degrees of preference. These are indicated by the vertical lines and numbers. The "X"

should be at or close to the number which coordinates with your degree of preference.

When you have finished, go back over the scale and add up all the numbers where you have placed an "X." Then look at the chart at the end of this exercise.

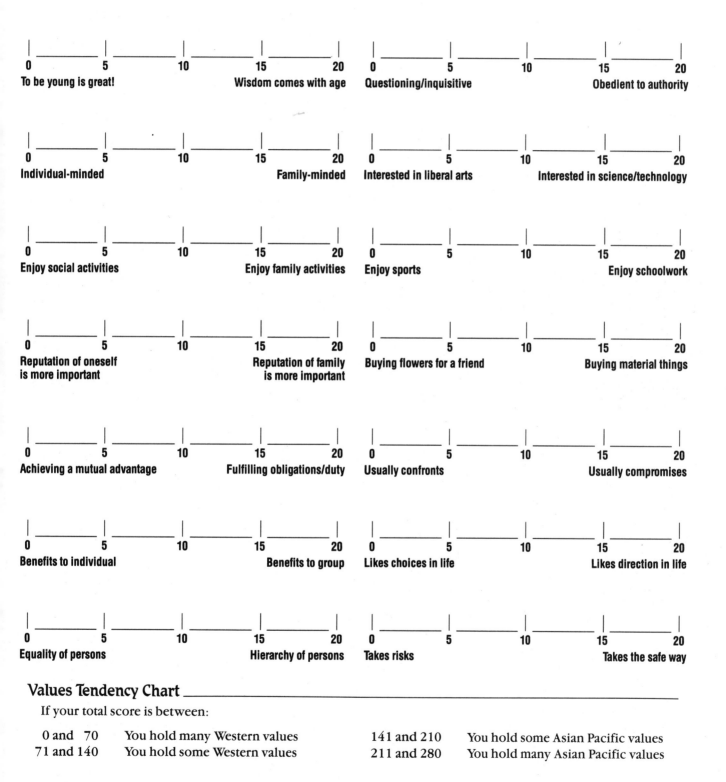

| 0 | 5 | 10 | 15 | 20 |

To be young is great! — Wisdom comes with age

Questioning/inquisitive — Obedient to authority

Individual-minded — Family-minded

Interested in liberal arts — Interested in science/technology

Enjoy social activities — Enjoy family activities

Enjoy sports — Enjoy schoolwork

Reputation of oneself is more important — Reputation of family is more important

Buying flowers for a friend — Buying material things

Achieving a mutual advantage — Fulfilling obligations/duty

Usually confronts — Usually compromises

Benefits to individual — Benefits to group

Likes choices in life — Likes direction in life

Equality of persons — Hierarchy of persons

Takes risks — Takes the safe way

Values Tendency Chart

If your total score is between:

0 and 70	You hold many Western values	141 and 210	You hold some Asian Pacific values
71 and 140	You hold some Western values	211 and 280	You hold many Asian Pacific values

VOCATIONAL CHOICES

WHAT VOCATIONS DO YOU PREFER? Circle all the vocations which you prefer. Then answer the questions at the end. Add any that are not listed and circle.

Engineer	Carpenter	Administrator	Ski instructor
Teacher	Plumber	Translator	Politician
Minister	Electrician	Paralegal	Accountant
Social worker	Stockbroker	Lawyer	Policeperson
Dancer	Real estate agent	Dentist	Mechanic
Singer	Secretary	Dental assistant	Postal clerk
Actor	Farmer	Doctor	Artist
Writer	News reporter	Nurse	Athlete
Computer programmer	Fashion designer	Pharmacist	Musician
Corporation executive	Inventor		

1. Are the vocations you have chosen influenced by family? Friends? Society?

2. Are the vocations you have chosen popular among Asian Pacific Americans? Which ones are and which ones aren't?

3. How do you define success? What is more important to you in your vocation—money? Job enjoyment and fulfillment? Upward mobility and advancement? Service to humanity? Service to God?

Faith and Cultural Influences

by Kathryn Choy-Wong

Goals:
• Youth will analyze the effects of culture on Christianity.
• Youth will see that faith is often expressed culturally according to each person's particular context.

Introduction:

The Christian faith is handed down through the centuries from generation to generation, from culture to culture. The Bible is full of illustrations of the cultural experiences of the Hebrew people as they try to live out their faith. The Gospels tell us the story of Jesus through the eyes of ancient Middle Eastern, Jewish, and Greek persons. The words they use, the examples they share, the stories they tell, come from their real-life experiences, which, of course, are entrenched in their cultures. So the Bible itself conveys many cultures.

Thus in the Bible you discover that it was the custom of widows to marry their husband's next of kin. You learn that the Jews did not associate with Gentiles, and that they observed strict dietary laws. You find that it was very unusual for men to talk to women who were not their wives, and for women to be educated. You learn that tax collectors were hated and that demons were common. Some of these cultural characteristics are now gone, but others remain today.

This session will help youth discover a few ancient cultural practices and influences so that they can read the Bible with open minds. By understanding the relationship of ancient cultures to biblical tradition, youth can discover how cultural traditions have aided in determining people's view of God. They can begin discovering the intent of biblical passages which are interwoven in the cultural traditions of Bible times. It is hoped that tools can be developed so youth can continue this ongoing process of uncovering cultural heritages and biblical truths.

Preparation:

The program is for a sixty- to ninety-minute session. You will need to:
• Make copies of "Archaeological Dig"
• Have pencils or pens available
• Have Bibles on hand
• Make copies of the Bible passages: Matthew 1:18–2:15 and Luke 2:1-20.
• Make copies of the role-play descriptions of Mat-
thew and Luke
• Arrange the room to allow for movement

Prepare yourself by doing "Archaeological Dig" ahead of time. What did you discover? Read over the role-play descriptions and the Bible passages. Think about each passage in your mind. How is each passage different from the others? Are these passages reflective of the authors? How? Pray for the session.

Procedure:

Opening
Step 1. Begin with Introductions
(5 minutes)

Start the session by getting in touch with one another. Introduce the goal for this session.

Step 2. Play "Archaeological Dig"
(20 minutes)

Begin with the "Archaeological Dig" exercise. Divide the class or group into teams, representing rival groups from different universities trying to discover ancient secrets of the Bible. The winning team to finish with the most correct answers will receive a large funding grant from a private foundation. See the instructions for the game for more information.

Discovering
Step 3. Discuss Your Findings (20 minutes)

Have the groups share their answers and discuss them together (for correct answers see pages 132-133). Also share these questions with the group:

Do you see any traces of the biblical culture of the Hebrews in our society today?

In our practice of Christianity today are there traces of biblical culture present? Name some.

What differences or similarities do you see between biblical Hebrew culture and Asian Pacific cultures?

Step 4. Do Role Plays (15 minutes)

Now divide into two subgroups. Assign each group a birth narrative passage (Matthew 1:18–2:15, Luke 2:1-20) and provide each subgroup with the appropriate description of the passages' authors (see pages 133-134). Ask each group to read their passage and description, then role-play the events of the passage.

Step 5. Discuss the Differences
(10 minutes)

Discuss the differences between the two passages. What is important to Matthew about Jesus' birth? What is important to Luke? Why do the passages differ? How do these passages reflect the cultural backgrounds of the authors?

Closing
Step 6. Conclude with Worship *(5 minutes)*
Close with a hymn and prayer.

ARCHAEOLOGICAL DIG

Just imagine that you are on an archaeological dig in the Middle East. Your task is to take a hard look at today's literature in order to discover what people were like in the days of Jesus' time. You are what we call a cultural anthropologist. Cultural anthropologists look at many evidences from ancient sites and cultures to trace the cultural traditions of ancient peoples. You are to do so today by looking at passages in the Bible and finding the correct answers to the questions.

However, just to add a little pressure, you are a member of one of two teams with the same task. Your responsibility is to help your team discover the ancient cultures before the other team, thereby winning the prize and a larger funding grant for your university.

Good luck and BE CAREFUL!

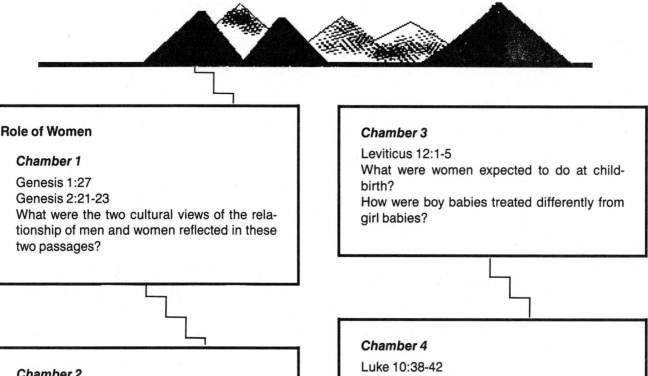

Role of Women

Chamber 1

Genesis 1:27
Genesis 2:21-23
What were the two cultural views of the relationship of men and women reflected in these two passages?

Chamber 2

Genesis 12:10-20
Genesis 19:8
Exodus 20:17
Judges 19:24
How did the ancient Hebrews view women in these passages?

Chamber 3
Leviticus 12:1-5
What were women expected to do at childbirth?
How were boy babies treated differently from girl babies?

Chamber 4
Luke 10:38-42
What were the two views of women's role in society during Jesus' time?

Chamber 5

John 4:27
What cultural tradition did Jesus break?

Chamber 6

1 Corinthians 14:34-35
What was the cultural view of women's role in the early Christian church?

Marriage

Chamber 7

Deuteronomy 24:1-4
What was the Hebraic view of divorce?

Chamber 8

Ephesians 5:22-33
What was the view of a "proper" relationship between husband and wife?

Widowhood

Chamber 9

Matthew 22:24-28
How did society handle widowhood?

Slavery

Chamber 10

Exodus 21:1-6
Ephesians 6:5-8
Philemon 10-18
What cultural views of slavery do you find?
Was slavery condoned?

Justice

Chamber 11

Exodus 21:23-25
Matthew 5:38-39
What cultural views of justice are expressed in these passages?

Chamber 12

Joshua 7:24-25
How was justice given?

Dietary Laws

Chamber 13

Leviticus 17:10-14
Deuteronomy 14:6-8
What could a person eat and not eat?

Ancestral Importance

Chamber 14

Matthew 1:1-17
Luke 3:23-38
What role did one's ancestors play in a person's life?

View of Outsiders and Foreigners

Chamber 15

John 4:7-9
What was the Jewish view of Samaritans?

Chamber 16

Acts 10:9-20
What was the early Christian view of Gentiles?

Chamber 17

Acts 15:1-5
Galatians 5:6
What was the early Christian view of circumcision? Did all Christians agree on this?

View of Youth

Chamber 18

Jeremiah 1:6-8
What were youth considered to be capable of?

Chamber 19

Matthew 19:13-15
Luke 18:15-17
How were children viewed by Jesus?

Chamber 20

1 Timothy 4:12
How did the writer of this book view youth?
How did he want youth to view themselves?

Answers to Archaeological Dig

Chamber 1

One view is that men and women were created equally in God's own image.

The second view is women were created to be the helpmates of men, and are created out of men (Adam's rib).

Chamber 2

Women were viewed as the property of men, like land and oxen.

Chamber 3

Women needed to purify themselves after childbirth. They could not touch anything sacred or enter into the temple's sanctuary.

If a woman had a girl baby, it took longer for her to purify herself than if she had a boy baby.

Boy babies were required to be circumcised.

Chamber 4

One view of women was that they were housekeepers and servants to men. The other view was that they should be learners.

Chamber 5

Jesus talked to a woman.

Chamber 6

Women should keep silent in the church.

Chamber 7

Men could divorce women for any reason as simple as displeasure, but women could not divorce men.

Chamber 8

Wives were subject to their husbands.

Chamber 9

Widows were expected to marry the next of kin.

Chamber 10

Slaves were considered property, along with their families. However, slavery was not a permanent status in life. The New Testament does not condone slavery, nor does it speak out against it. Rather, it speaks of treating one another, slave and master, justly and kindly. Slaves were treated equally in the eyes of God.

Chamber 11

The Old Testament view was that the punishment should fit the crime, but Jesus taught his followers to be merciful.

Chamber 12

When an individual committed a crime, it affected his/her entire family and household (animals, property, etc.), so all were punished.

Chamber 13

One could not eat blood. Animals that were killed must have the blood drained first.
One could eat animals that have parted hoofs and chew cuds, except camels, hares, and rock badgers. Pork was forbidden.

Chamber 14

Ancestors played an important role in a person's identity. Matthew traced Jesus' ancestry to David and Abraham, two great fathers of the Hebrew people. Luke traced it to the universal father of all people, Adam. Thus Matthew emphasized Jesus' Jewishness and Luke his universality.

Chamber 15

The Jews despised the Samaritans and regarded them as inferior.

Chamber 16

The Gentiles were considered by the Jews as unclean. Jews had as little to do as possible with the Gentiles.

Chamber 17

In the earliest years of Christianity, when the Jewish influence was still strong, males were required to be circumcised. However, later in the church's life, as more and more Gentiles became Christians, circumcision was no longer a necessary consideration. Faith became the important thing.

Chamber 18

Youth were considered capable of many things, especially with God behind them.

Chamber 19

Jesus loved the children and saw them as belonging to the kingdom of God.

Chamber 20

He said that one should not despise youth. Youth, in turn, should set examples by their conduct of love, faith, and purity.

Two Role Plays

Divide the total group into two smaller groups. One group will take the birth narrative from Matthew, and the other the birth narrative from Luke. Decide in the small group which parts people will role-play. Then act these parts out before the entire group. Discuss the role-plays together after each group does its presentation.

Matthew 1:18–2:15

The author: The evangelist Matthew is a person who comes from the Jewish tradition. That is, he comes from the same Jewish background as Jesus. His deep concern is with the new Christian church and its mission to the Jews. He climaxes his Gospel with the "Great Commission" (Matthew 28:19-20). He is also concerned with how the Christian church differs from Judaism. Matthew views the birth of Jesus as the fulfillment of ancient Jewish scriptural prophecy. It is important to Matthew to link Jesus to his Jewish heritage and the Jewish history. Thus you find the birth narrative beginning with a genealogy tracing Jesus to King David and Abraham, two great fathers of the Hebrew people. You find stories of going into Egypt and the killing of male infants. (See the stories in Exodus, e.g. Exodus 1:8-22.)

Luke 2:1-20

The author: Luke is a companion of Paul's. Luke's background is Greek. He is a well-educated man, a physician. He is also the author of Acts. Luke's concern is the emerging Christian church, which is in constant dialog and dispute with Judaism. He is concerned with the new Gentile Christians and the relationship between Christianity and the Roman Empire. Luke views Jesus as the divine savior. He is concerned with Jesus' promises for the future, not the fulfillment of ancient Hebrew prophecy. Luke is also concerned with Jesus as the savior for *all* peoples—of different nationalities and ethnicity, of different ages, of different gender, of different social status and classes, etc. Luke is concerned with justice in God's kingdom. You can find these concerns reflected in Luke's birth narrative. You can also find many stories of women, in addition to the long passages of Elizabeth and Mary, such as Mary and Martha (Luke 10:38-42), stories about the rich such as the parable of the Rich Fool (Luke 12:13-21), stories about sinners such as Zacchaeus (Luke 19:1-10) and the Prodigal Son (Luke 15:11-32), stories about other ethnic groups such as the Good Samaritan (Luke 10:29-37), and stories about justice such as the teaching on humility (Luke 14:7-14).

Faith in Our Setting

by Kathryn Choy-Wong

Goals:

• Youth will examine how their own church has incorporated culture into the practice and expression of Christian faith.

• Youth will identify forms of culture which affect their own understanding of faith.

Introduction:

Cultures have played a part in shaping the church as we know it today. Christianity, after spreading from the Holy Land throughout the Eastern Mediterranean part of the Roman Empire, moved northward into Western Europe. People began to practice their Christian faith within their cultural realities. Many Western European cultural practices became incorporated into the practice of the Christian faith. Church traditions, hymns, and Communion practices were shaped by the predominant cultures. Cultural folksongs were turned into Christian hymns. Advent, as a season of preparation for Christmas, began in France.

In similar fashion in the United States, the large white American culture shaped the practice of Christianity which had come first from England and then from the Continent. Thanksgiving became an important part of the Christian calendar in the United States, celebrating the experiences of the Pilgrims in New England.

There are times, however, when the values of the host cultures may clash with the Christian faith. War, individualism, pollution, and peer pressure to put down others are examples of cultural practices that clash with the essence of Christianity.

Just as Christianity incorporates a blend of culturally influenced biblical interpretations and practices, so does each local church. Every church is influenced by the larger culture around it, as well as by its own history and traditions. Examples of this are the customs of Boy Scout Sundays and Girl Scout Sundays or Fourth of July Sundays. Memorial Day Sundays or even Superbowl Sundays may be other examples.

As Asian Pacific Americans we too are not isolated individuals. Our practice of faith is also influenced by our cultural background. Our youth are influenced by youth cultures, both Asian and American, which may affect the practice of their faith. Culture can help us understand our faith, as well as make our faith more alive and meaningful.

Preparation:

This program is for a sixty- to ninety-minute session.

You will need to . . .

• Make copies of the handout "Hymn Tracing"

• Have the music to the hymns available on cassette tape, or have someone play the hymns (optional)

• Have newsprint available for hymn writing

• Have felt-tip markers available

• Gather together copies of old church bulletins, old programs of special events and celebrations, annual reports, newsletters, etc.

• Print the Bible passage, Matthew 15:1-9, on newsprint for all to see

Read over the Bible passage. What was Jesus talking about when he addressed the Pharisees and the scribes? What does this passage mean to us today? Is it a warning that we must be careful about incorporating our traditions and customs into our practice of the faith? Read over the handout "Hymn Tracing." If you have time, you might want to design a sample hymn to share with the group or class. Review the copies of old church bulletins, programs, newsletters, etc. Identify from these: (1) the traditions of the church; and (2) the cultural/societal influence in the church. Pray for this session.

Procedure:

Opening:

Step 1. Begin the Program *(15 minutes)*

Start the session by getting in touch with one another. Introduce the topic of today's program.

Distribute and read the handout "Hymn Tracing." Discuss the significance of hymns coming from the ordinary lives of persons and the traditions of culture. Ask the youth for examples of contemporary youth songs that reflect a particular cultural perspective.

Discovering

Step 2. Composing Your Own Hymns *(20 minutes)*

Break into pairs or groups to design your own hymns. Have the work recorded on newsprint. You may want to share a sample hymn. They may want to take popular songs, or jingles from commercials as the tunes for the hymns. Encourage them to be creative and have fun writing their own words. After everyone has completed the hymns, share them with one another. The group might even sing them.

Step 3. Researching Traditions (25 minutes)

In the same pairs or groups, distribute the old church programs, newsletters, bulletins, etc., that you have brought. Ask the youth to review these and to list on newsprint (1) some traditions of the church; and (2) any examples of cultural or societal influences in the activities of the church, such as Boy Scout Sunday, Thanksgiving Service, or Mother's Day.

Have the pairs or groups share the discoveries. Discuss what each pair or group learned. Ask: "What role does culture or society play in our own church's practice of faith?"

Step 4. Exploring the Scriptures (10 minutes)

Have one of the youth read the Bible passage, Matthew 15:1-9, out loud. Ask: "What was Jesus talking about to the Pharisees and scribes? What does this passage say to us today? Is there a warning about bringing our cultural traditions and social customs into our practice of the Christian faith? Is it right or wrong? Can anyone say that these are parts of the Christian faith that are not culturally tainted?"

Closing
Step 5. Summarizing Learnings (5 minutes)

It is all very natural and valid for us to express our faith with the influences of our customs and traditions, as our collection of hymns does. However, we must be careful and know that we are using our culture to express and share our faith, and that this in itself is not the faith or the gospel itself. Ask for a volunteer to close this session with prayer.

More Ideas and Activities
1. Identifying Traditions

Instead of looking at the programs, bulletins, newsletters of the church, you may want to observe a worship service in your own church and then compare this with an observation of another church's worship service. Ask the youth to write down their reactions, what is similar, and what is different. Why? Have the youth bring these reactions to the session for discussion.

2. Researching Traditions and Symbols

You might want to try finding out where some of our Christian traditions and symbols originated. Some examples: the symbol of the fish, the bread and cup, our particular practice of baptism, the Christmas tree, Easter egg hunt, Maundy Thursday. A good Bible dictionary can be helpful in providing some of the answers, and perhaps an encyclopedia or a polity book from your denomination will also be helpful.

Hymn Tracing

Many of us have heard of the story behind the writing of the United States' national anthem by Francis Scott Key. Just as "The Star Spangled Banner" has a story, so do the Christian hymns. Hymns sung by the congregation became popular with Martin Luther when he utilized German folksongs and added to them Christian messages and words. Today, behind every hymn there is a story. The following are just a few hymns and their stories. . . .

Amazing Grace

"Amazing Grace" was written by John Newton, who was a child of a sea captain. He had a very colorful life. At the age of seventeen, he had already committed a number of sins and had deserted his ship. He later ended up imprisoned, abused, and suffering under cruel slave owners in Sierra Leone. One day, during a storm at sea, he cried out to God for help and mercy. His life was changed from that moment on. Later, he became an ordained priest. This hymn is thus the life story of one person's salvation by the grace of God.

A Mighty Fortress Is Our God

This hymn was written by Martin Luther in a year of protest against the Roman Catholic Church. It was the time when the word "protestant" began to emerge. In 1530 Luther wrote this hymn to comfort his friends during those stormy times of protest. It comes from Psalm 46.

Blest Be the Tie That Binds

This hymn was written by Dr. John Fawcett, an English pastor of a small church, who had received a call to serve a larger congregation in London as their minister. This would have been a prestigious position. However, the tears of his current congregation and his love for the people convinced him to stay. The hymn was written to commemorate this event.

Break Thou the Bread of Life

The words were written by Mary A. Lathbury and the music by William Sherwin in 1877. The two collaborated at the invitation of the Chautauqua Literary and Scientific Guild of New York, and Bishop Vincent. The hymn is United Methodist.

The Old Rugged Cross

This United Methodist hymn was based on John 3:16. It was used in revival campaigns at Pokagon, Michigan, but the song was perfected and the words written by Rev. George Bennard. It was finally introduced in 1913 in a church.

The Wounded Chief

This is on the record *Pacific Worship* and the words are from the *Issue Series* "Worship the Pacific Way" by Lotu Pasifika Productions, Suva, Fiji, 1973. The song is a Pacific Island Easter song and was especially written for Christmas. The words are the following. . .

There was fury that long weekend,
Caiaphas was trying to be Caesar's friend.
Yes, brother, don't pretend
That we weren't there at all;
We both saw him crucified
And on the cross he died.
Yet at Easter dawn there's a silver sea.
Christ is risen and we are free.

Grabbed in the garden, lashed in a cell,
The officers were brutal and the crowd as well.
Our chief, Jesus, went through hell,
And weren't we there at all?
We both saw him crucified,
And on the cross he died.
Yet at Easter dawn there's a silver sea.
Christ is risen and we are free.

Blood on the pavement and on the road,
Blood as he carried his heavy load
Precious blood on the hillside flowed,
And weren't we there at all?

We both saw him crucified,
And on the cross he died.
Yet at Easter dawn there's a silver sea.
Christ is risen and we are free.

He rose in a garden at break of day,
He took our fears and all our sins away
Mary heard; she heard him say,
"I live, and love you all."
So in the end the crucified
Is living by our side. . .
Yes, at Easter dawn there's a silver sea.
Christ is risen and we are free.

I Have Decided to Follow Jesus

This hymn comes from a folk melody from India. It was sung in Assam, India. The words are. . .

I have decided to follow Jesus,
I have decided to follow Jesus,
I have decided to follow Jesus,
No turning back, no turning back.

Tho no one join me, still I will follow,
Tho no one join me, still I will follow,
Tho no one join me, still I will follow,
No turning back, no turning back.

The world behind me, the cross before me,
The world behind me, the cross before me,
The world behind me, the cross before me,
No turning back, no turning back.

Kum Ba Yah
(Come by here)

This hymn is from Angola, Africa.

Kum ba yah, my Lord, kum ba yah.
Kum ba yah, my Lord, kum ba yah.
Kum ba yah, my Lord, kum ba yah.
O Lord, kum ba yah.

The Role of Culture in Faith

by Kathryn Choy-Wong

Goals:

• Youth will be able to identify some Pacific Asian cultural and religious practices that may cause conflict or may challenge the Christian lifestyle.

• Youth will be able to design a worship experience with Asian Pacific symbols and rituals.

Introduction:

As Asian Pacific Americans we have inherited many rich traditions from our roots. We have an interesting task of incorporating these into our lives, making our lives rich as we blend two or more cultures. The same principle applies to our Christian faith and the ways we practice it. In order to make our faith meaningful to us, we have had to include some of our cultural practices in our faith practices. Sometimes the attempt to harmonize these cultural elements in our faith and practice can create conflict.

As we have stated in the other programs on faith and practice, all Scripture is understood through cultural glasses. There is no right or wrong way to practice the Christian faith. Understanding the Christian faith from the perspective of Asian Pacific Americans is therefore possible and legitimate. Faith is dynamic; it constantly integrates and blends with the culture surrounding it.

Blending culture with faith and practice is always happening. It happened with the early Christians, the Gentiles, Europeans, and North Americans. Integrating culture with the Christian faith can also happen with Asian Pacific Americans today. Shaping a faith experience by incorporating Asian Pacific American culture with it can create a new and exciting Christian expression. God made us who we are for a purpose. Our Asian Pacific qualities and heritages are gifts from God, to be used by God and for God. No one group of people has the complete truth and picture of God. Each group can add a different dimension and perspective of God to the rest of Christianity, so that together we gain a fuller picture of God and of God's kingdom. The four Gospels in our Bible are a perfect illustration of this. Each Gospel offers a different view or perspective of Jesus. Each enhances the others and gives us another picture of Jesus. Without any one of the Gospels, we would miss a major part of the picture.

Thus culture has the capacity to express faith, and the variety of cultures helps each of us see the truth and unique God.

Preparation:

This program is for a sixty- to ninety-minute session. You will need to. . .

• Make enough copies of the "Cultural Practice and Faith" handout for each youth

• Have copies of last week's worship bulletins

• Provide newsprint and markers

• Provide pencils or pens

• Print the Bible passages, 2 Corinthians 4:7-9 and 5:17-19, for all to see.

Read over the Bible passages. What does it mean to be "in earthen vessels"? Could this refer to our race or ethnicity? What is the treasure in our earthen vessels? In reading 2 Corinthians 5:17-19, do you think this means we should forget our identities and cultural past? Or does this mean that as Christians we create new identities and build upon our faith from the richness of our cultures and our gifts?

Become familiar with the "Cultural Practice and Faith" checklist, by doing it yourself. What did you discover about yourself? Look over the "Basic Worship Design." What cultural elements might you add to enhance your worship experiences? Pray for this session.

Procedure:

Opening

Step 1. Begin the Program (5 minutes)

Start the program by getting in touch with one another. Explain what today's topic is about, by presenting in your own words, the material in the introduction.

Step 2. Do a Checklist (30 minutes)

Have your group do the "Cultural Practice and Faith" checklist exercise. For example, in traditional Chinese culture, when women were seen as primarily supporting the men, the view of females under "Gender Roles" would conflict with the practice of my faith. So I would check off the box under "Conflicts with the Practice of My Faith." Or under "Age and Status" the traditional Chinese cultural view of older adults would enhance my faith, so I would mark the box entitled "Enhances the Practice of Faith."

After all have completed the checklist, discuss their learnings and discoveries in the large group.

Discovering:

Step 3. Creating a Worship Service (30 minutes)

Pass out copies of last week's Sunday worship bulletins. Explain that most of the elements it lists are basic to the worship experience. However, their order in the worship can vary, as can the way the elements are expressed. Break into smaller groups, and have each group design a worship experience. Ask the youth to utilize elements or expressions from their own culture or background that they feel would enhance this worship experience. For example, a call to worship might be offered with the use of a conch shell. This might symbolize "calling the people to gather for worship."

The use of the conch shell has significance in many Pacific Island cultures. Have the groups do their work on newsprint so that all can see later.

Have each group share their worship experiences with the larger group. Discuss any cultural expressions included in the worship services. Are they appropriate and helpful in planning a worship experience?

Closing:

Step 4. Summarize the Topic (10 minutes)

Close with a look at the Bible passages. Ask the youth to share their thoughts about what is meant by "earthern vessels." What is the treasure we all have? What does it mean to be a new creation? Is it possible for us to utilize our culture, talents, and gifts as new creatures in Christ? End with some sentence prayers by having each person offer a prayer.

CULTURAL PRACTICE AND FAITH

PACIFIC/ASIAN CULTURAL PRACTICE & TRADITION	CONFLICTS WITH THE PRACTICE OF MY FAITH	ENHANCES THE PRACTICE OF FAITH	HAS LITTLE EFFECT ON MY FAITH
View of. . . Gender Roles			
males			
females			
Age and Status			
children			
youth			
adults			
elderly			
authority			
Sexual Relations			
premarital sex			
extramarital sex			
marital relations			
Family Relations			
parent/child			
individual/family			
sibling			

PACIFIC/ASIAN CULTURAL PRACTICE & TRADITION	CONFLICTS WITH THE PRACTICE OF MY FAITH	ENHANCES THE PRACTICE OF FAITH	HAS LITTLE EFFECT ON MY FAITH
Work Importance of money			
Working hard			
Self-expression			
Religion How religion relates to everyday life			
How religion relates to youth			
How religion saves or redeems persons			
Beauty What is human beauty?			
What is earthly beauty?			
What is artificial beauty?			

The Role of Youth in the Church

by Kathryn Choy-Wong

Goals:

• Youth will be able to discover their gifts and ways to use them in the church.

• Young people will be able to recognize the importance of their role in the church and identify ways to become involved.

Introduction:

Being young is a gift. This adolescent stage in life can offer a church much meaning and opportunity to grow. Learnings can come not only from church elders but also from the young. There are many biblical examples of this truth: Jeremiah, the young people who came to Jesus, and Jesus himself both as a lad at the synagogue (Luke 4) and as a young man in his thirties. Young people can make contributions to the church as individuals or as a youth group.

What qualities and talents do the young people in your church have? How can these be utilized in the church? In what positions can youth be legitimately asked to serve?

There are many benefits that result from youth serving in the church. The young people themselves will gain from the experience and exposure, and the church will gain from the interaction. Youth can bring a different perspective to things, new ideas, and changes in approaches. Youth can bring new enthusiasm and hope. To them, all things are possible. "So what if it didn't work before? We'll try again."

Asian Pacific American young people can play a vital role in the church. Their ability to be bilingual and bicultural makes them natural bridges for many first-generation immigrants in the church seeking to relate to American society. They can help interpret the language and culture of the Asian Pacific American churches, help bridge denominational differences, and help reach other Asian Pacific American youth and children. They can help first-generation members understand their American-born or American-raised children or the dominant expectations of American society.

And in nonimmigrant Asian Pacific American churches, young people can help sensitize adult members to the particular needs of Asian Pacific American communities and youth. They can take an active role in their denomination, bringing an Asian Pacific American perspective and interpretation to religious life. They can contribute to American society with their unique Asian Pacific American culture.

Preparation:

This program is for a sixty- to ninety-minute session. You will need to. . .

• Make enough copies of the "Gifts Inventory" (see page 143) for the group
• Have pencils or pens available
• Have index cards and tape available
• Have newsprint and felt-tip markers available
• Have the Bible passages printed on newsprint for all to see; (Jeremiah 1:4-10, 1:17-19; and Luke 2:42-47; 3:23; 4:18-19)
• Have Bibles available

Read over the Bible passages to become familiar with them. Who was Jeremiah? How old do you think Jeremiah was? Why was he chosen to be a prophet? What is a prophet? How did people react to Jeremiah? For some of these answers, you may want to do some research in a Bible dictionary or in a commentary such as the *Interpreter's Bible*. These may be available from your church library or at a public library. Expand your understanding of the prophet Jeremiah by reading other passages in the book of Jeremiah.

Read the passages about Jesus. What contributions did Jesus make to the world as a young person? How old was Jesus when he died? How did the world react to Jesus?

Try the "Gifts Inventory" handout yourself. What gifts do *you* bring as a member of a congregation? In what ways can you utilize these gifts within the church? Within your denomination? Ecumenically?

Talk to your pastor. Beforehand, find out possible mission projects the youth can do in the church or outside the church. Keep this list in mind to suggest to the youth.

Procedure:

Opening

Step 1. Begin the Program *(10 minutes)*

Start the program by getting in touch with one another. One way is to have each person share the best gift that he/she has received from Christmas, last birthday, or a special day. Why was this particular gift special? Introduce today's program by sharing in your own words some of the materials in the introduction.

Step 2. Discuss the Scriptures *(20 minutes)*

Divide into two subgroups. Assign one subgroup the references in Jeremiah, the other the passages on Jesus. Have the groups discuss the following questions:

1) How old do you think this person was?
2) What contribution was this person to make?
3) How did people respond to this person?

Discuss briefly these answers with the entire group.

Discovering:

Step 3. Fill Out the "Gifts Inventory" *(10 minutes)*

Have each person do the "Gifts Inventory" handout. Next, on three separate index cards, have each person write down one gift he/she brings to the church, one gift he/she can contribute outside the church, and one gift he/she didn't know existed or was surprised about.

Step 4. Combining Our Gifts *(10 minutes)*

Post three sheets of newsprint, with the following titles on one of these sheets: "Gifts We Bring to the Church," "Gifts We Can Contribute Outside the Church," and "Gifts We Have Just Discovered." Have each person tape his/her index cards to the appropriate sheet of paper. Have everyone look at these for a few minutes. Discuss the great potential a group can have when it combines all these gifts into one effort or project.

Step 5. Consider a Mission Project *(30 minutes)*

Now introduce the idea of doing a mission project. Mention that, after discovering the gifts we have, God has called us to use these gifts—just as God called Jeremiah and Jesus. Get into a brainstorming session on all possible mission projects that can be done in or outside the church. List these on newsprint. Remember, brainstorming means listing all responses. Persons should not critique or make comments about these suggestions. Now go back over the list and "star" the projects that seem to fit the gifts of the youth group.

Where should it be done? How can it be done? Are there contacts to be made? Is permission needed? Are supplies and other resources needed, such as money, transportation or adult leadership? Make assignments and deadlines. (After the project is accomplished, there should be an evaluation, so that everyone can learn from the experience.)

Closing:

Step 6. Committing Gifts for Service *(5 minutes)*

From the newsprint, have each person take an index card home marked with a gift he/she wants to utilize. Have each person put his/her name and today's date on the back of this card. Ask each to place this card somewhere at home where it can be seen as a reminder of his/her commitment to utilize this particular gift. Close with prayer.

More Ideas and Activities

1. Instead of planning the mission project, you might want to conduct an all-church survey to seek the opinion of church members on how youth can contribute to the church. Design the survey, the method of conducting it, and the process of evaluation. The survey may suggest ways youth can more appropriately be involved in the church.

2. Instead of planning the mission project, the group could plan a youth worship service or an appreciation lunch/dinner for the leaders of the church.

3. You may want to check with your denominational offices on possible mission projects beyond your church community. Many youth groups have participated in work projects in needy areas under denominationally sponsored programs.

4. Plan an intergenerational event for the entire church, focusing on the richness of the total church community (children, youth and adults) learning and growing together.

GIFTS INVENTORY

The following are some gifts you may have which can be of great service to your church, denomination, or community. Check off the ones you think you have. Write down any additional ones you may have, but are not listed.

I am good in. . .

_____ music

_____ art

_____ dance

_____ drama

_____ writing

_____ singing

_____ speaking

_____ reading

_____ humor

_____ organizing

_____ visitation

_____ being up-front in events

_____ cleaning

_____ painting

_____ performing maintenance

_____ using my hands

_____ doing research

_____ record keeping

_____ understanding history

_____ working with statistics or numbers

_____ dealing with money

_____ fund raising

_____ greeting persons

_____ meeting strangers

_____ negotiating

_____ handling conflict situations

_____ leading Bible studies

_____ leading prayers

_____ teaching

_____ leading groups

_____ translating

_____ cooking

_____ writing calligraphy

_____ working on computers

_____

_____

_____

_____

THEME 4

Vocation and the World

Finding one's purpose in life is a major youth agenda item.

Every youth is asked the question, "What do you want to be?" The Christian message proclaims that each person is a gift from God with a purpose to live faithfully and responsibly. Asian Pacific American youth, like all young people, are called to be witnesses in their workplaces, communities, and the world.

- God's Call to Me, *by David Ng*
- My People's Call to Me, *by David Ng*
- Vocation, My Work and Social Justice, *by David Ng*
- How Have I Spent My Life? *by David Ng*

About These Four Sessions:

This study unit is about *vocation.* Vocation–God's call–is a key issue in every young person's life. Christians believe that life is a gift of God meant to be lived in faithful response to God's call. A Christian expresses faithfulness and gratitude to God by the way she or he lives and works. Vocation can be expressed for Asian Pacific American young people through these stages of thought:

1. God is the Creator.
   (Genesis 1:1; Psalm 19:1; John 1:1-3, 10)
2. God created a good world.
   (Genesis 1:31; Psalm 19:1; Psalm 65:9-13)
3. God created us humans.
   (Psalm 100; Genesis 1:26-27; 2:4-9)
4. Our human identity is related to our creation by God and God's call to us to be creative and to work.
   (Genesis 1:28; 2:7-8; Psalm 104:1-4, 14-15, 19-24, 33-35; 2 Thessalonians 3:6-12)
5. We are partners with God in creation and in work.
   (Genesis 1:28; Psalm 8:3-9; Colossians 3:23-24)
6. As worker-partners with God we are called by God to be:
   - stewards of God's world
   - engaged in serving others
   - ministering through the church
   (Psalm 8:3-9; Colossians 3:23-24; 1 Corinthians 3:8-15; Romans 12:6-8; 1 Corinthians 12:27-28)
7. Asian Pacific American youth are called by God to be creative, to work, and to minister.
   (Galatians 3:28-29; Romans 12:4-8; 1 Corinthians 12:27-28; Ephesians 4:11-13)

All young people are engaged in important decision making in their lives. They are deciding about their values and their identities. They are also deciding about what they will do with their lives. They are making choices about jobs and careers. As Christians their decisions are influenced by the faith they know through their understanding of Scriptures and their involvement in the church. *This study unit is aimed at young persons who are making these important decisions about faith, life, and work.*

This unit can be studied in four sessions of between sixty and ninety minutes each. Other combinations of time are possible to accommodate the pace and abilities of a particular group of young people. This unit can be studied in a regular youth group discussion meeting, in church school, or in a weekend retreat or youth conference.

With guidance from adult leaders the young people themselves can plan and conduct the study sessions by following the suggestions given in the session plans which follow.

Preparation

A simple way to call attention to the seven concepts listed in this introductory section is to have young persons create *seven posters to be displayed throughout the study.* The seven posters will provide a visual and conceptual framework for the study, specially if they are posted on the walls to surround the participants with their messages. At the close of each study session the participants will look at the posters to help them reflect on the discussion and to draw together their learnings. The seven concepts will help the Asian Pacific American youth to organize and summarize what they have learned.

Making the Posters

The posters should be large enough for the entire group to see from wherever they sit in the room. For example, a group of twelve persons would need posters that are about 24 by 36 inches or more in size. Use of color and special artistic or decorative effects such as symbols and calligraphy can add interest, if there are young persons with such skills to create the posters.

Each poster can have the same basic format even if there are artistic variations:

- a statement of a biblical perspective about vocation
- passages from the Bible which exemplify the statement
- a call for young people to state the implications of this statement for their own life and work

For example, a poster could look like the following:

GOD CREATED US HUMANS
Psalm 100

Genesis 1:27-28; 2:4-9

Implications for My Life and Work
as an Asian Pacific American Person. . .

Allow a little space below the third statement about implications for the participants to "fill in the blank" in their own minds.

Personal Preparation

To prepare yourself for leading the group in this study of vocation, read this guide thoroughly, including the Bible passages listed. Take time to reflect on the concepts presented here.

God's Call to Me

by David Ng

Goals:

- Participants will consider their personal ideas about themselves—their talents and interests, and their reasons for working.
- They will be challenged to consider the needs of the world and how their work might address those needs.
- Four "classic calls to the Christian" will help the participants understand how God might be calling them to faith and work.

Preparation:

- As directed in "About These Four Sessions," (page 144), have some young persons create and put up seven posters which state the concepts of this study unit.
- Make copies for the participants of the exercises which will be used in the session as described below.
- Have pencils available.
- Have a chalkboard or newsprint ready for writing the four "classic calls to the Christian."
- Have Bibles available for looking up the passages on the posters.

Procedure:

Opening
Step 1. Introducing the Unit of Study
(10 minutes)

Begin the meeting with prayer. Especially if this is the first time this group has met, spend some time greeting each other.

Ask the young people what might be some of the most important decisions they will be making in the next several years. Invite several participants to elaborate on their responses. Then ask them to comment on the importance of their decisions about what they will do with their lives—their work and their careers. Ask what problems they face as they make decisions about their careers. Jot on the chalkboard or on newsprint some notes of the problems they identify.

Tell the participants that choosing a job or a career is an act which the church is greatly concerned about. Suggest that the church has some resources and some ideas about how to make such decisions. Point to the seven posters on the walls as examples of the perspectives the church offers on the subject of vocation. Ask about or explain the meaning of vocation—the calling of God to a person, to fulfill one's purpose in life as God intends it.

Tell the participants that the posters will be on the walls throughout the study, to offer guidance on the subject of vocation.

Discovering
Step 2. My Reasons for Working
(20 minutes)

A method for opening the discussion about vocation is to involve the participants in a personal way. Make copies of "My Reasons for Working." Give each participant a copy and a pencil and have each fill in the exercise and discuss their rankings with two other persons as instructed on the copy. After the small-group discussion ask for a few sample responses.

Step 3. Considering Gifts and Choices
(10 minutes)

Choose either Exercise A or B.

(A) *God's Gifts—My Traits, Talents, and Interests* (10 minutes). Use copies of the list below to help the participants become more aware of their traits, talents, and interests, and to see these as gifts of God to them.

(B) *Personal Factors to Consider* (10 minutes). Another exercise which can be used to help the participants become more aware of themselves and their potential as workers is shown below. If you want the group to use this, make copies for each participant. Have them read the material and jot notes under each section.

(Have the participants discuss their findings about themselves in groups of two or three. Assure them that they need not reveal anything they do not wish to, nor do they need to show anyone what they have jotted down.

After the small-group discussions, call the entire group together and ask for some sample responses to the question, "What did you find out about yourself and your potential for work?"

Step 4. Four "Classic Calls to the Christian"
(30 minutes)

In an influential book, *The Purpose of the Church and Its Ministry*, H. Richard Niebuhr described how God's call to each Christian can be experienced in four dimensions:

- the call to be Christian
- the inner call
- the providential call
- the church's call to ministry

These four dimensions of God's call can be used as guidelines in evaluating an occupation a person is considering. The group can consider these guidelines as follows:

Write this statement on a chalkboard or newsprint: "Hypothesis: God calls every Christian to a job." Ask the participants what they think this statement means and what it implies about choosing an occupation.

This hypothesis claims that, for the Christian, the job she or he chooses should be one which is pleasing to God and of benefit to humanity. What is implied is that every job is a "calling" and involves the Christian in some form of ministry.

Now write on a chalkboard or newsprint Niebuhr's statements of the four dimensions of God's call and explain them.

- the call to be Christian
- the inner call
- the providential call
- the church's call to ministry

• *The call to be Christian* is the call to discipleship. Every Christian is called to follow Jesus Christ faithfully in every aspect of life and relationship, including his or her work.

• *The inner call* is what a person feels personally and directly as the will of God.

• *The providential call* suggests that, when God calls someone to a task, God provides the talents needed for the job. The other aspect of this statement is that, when a person is gifted with certain talents, God may intend these talents for use in a certain "calling" or occupation.

• *The church's call to ministry* is the invitation by the Christian community to the work of ministry. This does not necessarily mean "church work" or ordained ministry but it does imply the witness and service performed by the church and its members. Whatever a Christian's occupation may be, it ought to be a form of ministry.

Ask the students to comment on how they understand these statements. Provide further comments to add to their understanding.

A way to test out this list of four dimensions for young persons considering an occupation is to see how the list relates to a decision concerning say, a computer salesperson.

Ask the participants to suggest several other jobs and run them through this same process. How do they fare? Additionally, try some jobs which would not be compatible with the four dimensions, such as bank robber or dope peddler. Also try some jobs that are difficult to evaluate, such as bartender, prison executioner, or designer of nuclear weapons.

Closing
Step 5. Looking at Learnings *(5 minutes)*

Ask the participants to read several of the seven theological posters on the walls. Suggest that they recall what has been discussed in this session and that they think about how some of the statements on these posters apply to the discussion.

Close with prayer.

God's Gifts—My Traits, Talents, and Interests

In each section circle any words that describe who you are. Since you are a unique person, write in each section at least three additional words that further describe who you are.

Traits	Talents	Interests
Physical strength	Organizing	Cooking
Finger dexterity	Analyzing	Writing
Mental concentration	Directing	Fixing
Patience	Deciding	Speaking
Persistence	Taking apart	Building
Inquisitiveness	Putting together	Growing
Aggressiveness	Creating	Drawing
Quietness	Listening	Expressing
Concern for people		

My Reasons for Working

_____ To please my parents

_____ To do what my friends are doing

_____ To provide for my family

_____ To buy things I enjoy

_____ To help persons in need

_____ To be a part of God's creative activity

_____ To stay busy and not become bored

_____ To become famous

_____ To improve the world in which we live

_____ To obey God's law

_____ To use my talents

Instructions
A. Read the entire list of reasons for working.
B. Rank for 1 to 11 the reasons you would want to work, number 1 indicating the best reason and number 11 the worst reason. Write in your rankings on the lines provided.
C. Discuss your rankings with two other persons. Listen to what they have to say about the reasons they consider the best for them, and about those they consider the worst for them. Share your feelings and learn from each other.

(Adapted from _Work and Worth,_ Living the Word, Christian Education: Shared Approaches. Used by permission.)

Personal Factors to Consider in Choosing an Occupation

Read each section and jot down some notes in response to the questions raised.

1. What are your interests, abilities, and skills?

You probably already have some knowledge of what kinds of activities you do well, and what kinds of work you might be best suited for. For example, artists show artistic ability and interest early in life. Carpenters and similar workers often show manual and mechanical skills when they are young. What are your interests, abilities and skills? What kinds of occupations make use of these traits?

Jot some notes here in response to the questions above:

2. How adaptable are you?

One of the biggest challenges you will have in your future occupation is to be able to adjust to changing conditions. The duties in a job often change; entire companies get reorganized and workers are reassigned; workers are required to move themselves and their families to other locations; new technology requires the development of new skills. Do you think you prefer a job that hardly changes, or one which is likely to have changes like those mentioned above? How adaptable are you?

Jot some notes here in response to the questions above:

3. How well do you get along with other people?

All occupations involve working with other human beings. Every job has possibilities for tension as well as cooperation and harmony between workers and persons served by workers. Workers often must submit to authority and supervision, or must provide oversight to others. Do you want a job in which you lead, or one in which you accept the leadership of others? Or a job with both types of leadership? Do you see yourself working in close proximity to others? In a setting with many workers or just a few?

Jot some notes here in response to the questions above:

Computer Salesperson

The call to be Christian.

• Everyone who is a Christian is called to discipleship—to be a Christian is all he or she does, including as a computer salesperson.

The inner call.

• A person who wants to sell computers for a living should feel that this job is right and is what God wants him or her to do.

The providential call.

• The talents and personal traits which God has given the person should suit him or her to be a competent computer salesperson.

The church's call to ministry.

• The Christian who wants to sell computers should be confirmed by the Christian community in this choice. The church, in its doctrines and support for the person, would confirm that selling computers is a good job for this person and would contribute to the betterment of humanity.

My People's Call to Me

by David Ng

Goals:

• Participants will consider their responses to vocation—God's calling—in light of the needs of society and the call of the church to ministry.

• They will consider the unique situation of Asian Pacific American Christians and the opportunities which come from such a background.

Preparation:

• Check to be sure that the seven wall posters from the previous session are still on the walls. If desired for the sake of variety, the posters could be moved into new positions on the walls.

• Have the handouts copied and ready for distribution according to the suggestions given in the "Discovering" section.

• Have pencils available.

• Make posters of the four "reaction statements" as suggested in Step 4.

Procedure:

Opening
Step 1. Getting Started and Reviewing (5 minutes)

Start the study session with greetings. If you used the preceding session in this unit, ask a few questions to remind the participants about the previous discussion and to help those who were absent last time to "get on board." For example: "Last week we began to talk about vocation. Soo Jung, can you give us your definition of 'vocation'?" "We talked about the 'four calls to the Christian' which are. . . (name four calls). Lydia, how would you describe 'the call to be Christian'?"

Discovering
Step 2. Questions About Jobs (30 minutes)

Make enough copies of "Questions to Ask About Any Job" for each participant. Begin by having each participant write on the top space on the worksheet two or three occupations he or she might like. When participants read the three sections they can then question in their own minds what these jobs would be like according to the three questions which follow.

Have the participants read the questions and think about them. Then they can discuss their thoughts with two or three other participants. A general time of sharing can follow.

Especially with younger groups, the leader could help the participants get started by going through the exercise with a common occupation such as schoolteacher or grocery clerk as example. What would such an occupation be like in terms of the three questions below? Discuss this example first, and then have the participants work on their worksheets.

Step 3. These Jobs Call for Pioneers (30 minutes)

At the end of this session plan is a reading for young persons, "These Jobs Call for Pioneers." This reading can be duplicated for distribution to the participants for reading and discussion during the study session. Alternatively, it can be used as a handout for reading at home.

The reading can be discussed by asking the participants to brainstorm (generate ideas) about occupations that deal with each of the twelve "dynamic forces that are changing our society." These forces are listed as headings for each section of the reading.

List the headings on newsprint or the chalkboard. Ask the participants to brainstorm by calling out jobs that can be beneficial to society, grouping them under the appropriate headings. For example, for the heading "The Population Explosion," some beneficial jobs would be pediatricians, nurses, family-planning workers, counselors, etc. For "Urbanization" some jobs would be urban planners, social workers, architects, recreation directors, traffic engineers, etc. For "Automation," some jobs would be career guidance counselors, union organizers, industrial designers, etc.

After a number of beneficial jobs have been identified—perhaps thirty or so, ask the participants to express some opinions about how the jobs they will take themselves might benefit society. Ask if they want their future jobs to do more than just satisfy themselves or their parents. If so, why and how?

Step 4. Dealing with Stereotypes of Asian Pacific Americans (20 minutes)

Very likely the young people are already aware that as Asian Pacific Americans they are thought of by others or even by their own people in stereotypical ways. Teachers, parents, or others expect them to behave in certain ways or choose certain jobs on the basis of stereotypes of what Asian Pacific Americans can or cannot do.

Mount on the wall four posters, each making a "reaction statement." These statements are strong opinions held by some people, neither completely true nor completely false. They can cause people to react and to state opinions of their own. Discuss them with the group. The four "reaction statements are these:

!?! All Asian Pacific American men excel in math and sciences!?!

!?! All Asian Pacific American women are artistic!?!

!?! All Asian Pacific American women are destined for careers in medicine or social work!?!

!?! All Asian Pacific American men are destined to become engineers!?!

Notice that the !?! marks suggest that these reaction statements are possible opinions meant to draw out reactions or opinions from others.

One way to use these statements is in face-to-face discussion. Ask the participants to read them and to discuss one of the statements with another person for about three minutes. Then, as a whole group, obtain some sample reactions and discuss some of the reactions. In the end ask: "How do we as Asian Pacific Americans deal with the stereotypical expectations of others? How can we as Christians make free choices about our work and careers?"

Remind the participants that the seven posters on the wall offer guidance.

Step 5. Brainstorming the Needs of Asian Pacific American Society *(20 minutes)*

Earlier in this session the participants were asked to brainstorm the needs of society in general. Now as a final activity, ask them to brainstorm the special needs of their own Asian Pacific American community or society. This part can be done in two steps.

A. Discuss what are some needs within Asian Pacific American society. A way to think about these needs is to imagine a typical immigrant family and what they must do to get established from the time they arrive in this country until the time their children are educated and ready to enter the job market. Ask each participant to imagine all of this process, and ask two or three to describe what they have imagined. Then ask the participants to identify specific needs of such a family. Answers might include help with the English language, finding housing, applying for school, getting counsel on social benefits, and finding jobs.

B. Given the needs which have been identified, what kinds of vocations might help the immi-

grant family? Examples: social workers, teachers, job counselors, employment agency workers, municipal clerks, ministers, health workers.

As in the earlier discussion about the needs of society, ask the participants if they can imagine themselves doing work which will be of service to the people of their Asian Pacific American community.

Closing
Step 6. Closing Remarks *(5 minutes)*

Remind the participants to scan the seven wall posters for ideas that help them think about what was discussed. Also point out that in this study session we have considered the *needs* of Asian Pacific American society and in the next sessions we will consider the *contributions* Asian Pacific Americans can make.

Close with prayer.

These Jobs Call for Pioneers[1]

Vigorous young people in every generation have looked for exciting tasks to perform, dragons to slay, new worlds to conquer. Your grandfather may have felt that his opportunities for adventure were curtailed when the cowboys won out over the Indians and the West was settled. Your father may believe that the coming of television, jet planes, and earth satellites has narrowed the field for new explorations.

You probably know that the inventions of the last one hundred years have changed life on earth more than the innovations of all the preceeding millennia, and that far more startling changes lie ahead.

Following is a list of some of the dynamic forces that are changing our society, and the resultant tasks that need to be done. As you read and think about and your place in it you will find new tasks to add to this list of pioneering jobs.

The Population Explosion

It took from the beginning of human life to the year 1830 for the earth's population to reach one billion. In 1930 the population reached the two billion mark. It reached three billion in 1963 and is expected to reach seven billion in the year 2000. The primary cause of the rapid increase is not an unusual rise in the birth rate but the lowering of the death rate. This dynamic increase in the population calls for workers who will:

• increase the supply of food, clothing, and shelter around the world.

• build more houses and apartments.

• build, equip, and staff more schools.

• develop more recreation facilities.

• utilize more fully the arable land of the world.

- discover more effective methods of family planning.
- educate people for more responsible parenthood.

Urbanization

Throughout most of its history the U.S.A. has been predominantly a rural nation. It was not until 1920 that more than half (51.2%) of its people lived in urban areas. In 1950 the percentage had increased to 64. It is predicted that more and more people will live in metropolitan areas. The rapid urbanization of life calls for workers who will:

- build attractive, livable houses and apartments at prices people can afford; and eliminate slums.
- create architecture that lifts the spirit of people as well as serves their physical needs.

- develop systems of transportation that will avoid traffic congestion, and enable people to move about with ease.
- plan urban areas that are attractive and functional.
- develop parks and recreation areas that are accessible to all people.
- increase understanding and appreciation of differences in racial, cultural, and religious background.

Centralization of Agriculture and Industry

Despite the phenomenal rise in agricultural production between 1930 and 1950, the number of farms in the U.S.A. decreased from 6,289,000 to 5,382,000 during that time and the trend has continued to the present time. The slight increase in the number of busi-

Questions to Ask About Any Job

Think of two or three occupations you might want for yourself in the future. Write them down in this space:

1. What does this job (or field of work) contribute that is useful to humanity?

In the Bible God is portrayed as a worker for the benefit of all God's creatures. God commands that people shall work, and God blesses their labor.

2. How does this occupation include challenge and responsibility?

The great social issues of our time—poverty, war and peace, economic justice, public health, etc.—require people who are committed to problem solving. Struggles to find solutions to these problems will take place in the workaday world. How much opportunity for challenge and responsibility will your occupation offer?

3. How does this occupation give me the opportunity to live with integrity?

You undoubtedly hold certain values or principles such as honesty and fair-mindedness. Christians hold high standards of conduct. Would your occupation enable you to practice these principles? Or would compromises with your values and principles be expected?

(Adapted from "You and Your Occupational Choice," a brochure produced by The United Presbyterian Church in the U.S.A.)

ness firms during that period did not keep pace with the rise in the population or the growth of production. The tendency is for more and more Americans to work for salaries and wages and for a smaller proportion of them to be self-employed. This trend calls for workers who will:

- develop more effective procedures for handling disputes between labor and management, democratically and with justice.
- find ways for workers to share more fully in developing the policies of the firms for which they work.
- discover ways of representing the public interest and the welfare of consumers in economic affairs.

Automation

The Industrial Revolution substituted machines powered by steam and electricity for the muscle power of men and animals. The worker became a machine tender. Automation, sometimes called the "Second Industrial Revolution," is in process of changing the machine tender into a supervisor of an automatically controlled operating system. The worker does not operate the machines; he merely sets the controls and reapirs the equipment when necessary. This trend in our society calls for workers who will:

- invent more machines that can be used to reduce human toil.
- adjust economic practices so that automation brings the boon of shorter hours to all workers, rather than unemployment for some and too much work for others.
- train displaced workers to operate the new machines.
- develop procedures for distributing the work fairly, so that all persons who seek employment can find it.
- adapt technological advances for use in underdeveloped parts of the world.
- develop a philosophy which can make the economic practices of the West more beneficial and which can give guidance for coping with abundance.

Regional Development

The Tennessee Valley Authority (TVA) and similar projects have shown the value of regional development. One coordinated program, operating in a river system that was once a menace in time of floods, now controls the floods, develops navigable waterways, provides water for irrigation, produces electric power, reforests marginal land, and conserves the soil. Scores of regions of the world are in desperate need of this kind of regional development. Workers are needed who will:

- educate people concerning the need for regional development.
- develop more effective technical processes in the many fields involved.
- encourage governments to instigate the necessary projects, finance them, and give them adequate powers.

Atoms for Peace

The earth's supply of coal and oil will one day be exhausted. These fuels are now in short supply in many parts of the world. Atomic energy should be developed, with adequate safeguards, as a source of power and for medical purposes. Workers are needed who will:

- educate the people concerning the needs and opportunities for peaceful uses of atomic energy.
- discover more efficient and less hazardous ways of developing atomic power and disposing of waste products.
- establish private and governmental projects for harnessing atomic energy.

Use of Leisure

Most of the inhabitants of the earth, and all their ancestors back through history, have devoted most of their time to toil for their daily bread. The Industrial Revolution gradually reduced the hours of labor to the present 30- to 40-hour week. The "Second Industrial Revolution" will soon reduce it to 20 to 30 hours. Workers are needed who will:

- help adults find meaning in lives no longer dominated by toil.
- teach adults to use their newfound leisure in creative ways.
- prepare young people for lives in which a few hours a day are devoted to work while others are free for meaningful leisure-time activity.

Health

Tremendous strides have been made toward eliminating many diseases that have plagued mankind, yet many still elude science—the common cold, cancer, arthritis, heart diseases, and many others. Because of AIDS, the high cost of medical services and the maldistribution of doctors, nurses, and hospitals, many persons still suffer and die of diseases that can be cured. Thousands of communities in the world are without doctors and dentists. This situation calls for workers who will:

- discover the cause and cure of many diseases not yet conquered.

- use their medical, dental and nursing training in the communities and areas of the world where their services are most needed.
- discover more adequate ways of paying for health services so that no one will suffer from incurable diseases for lack of money.

Children, Youth, and the Aging

These groups around the world need special care. Many children are unwanted and lack adequate care. Many young people fail to get the understanding they need, and become delinquents. Many aging persons are lonely and suffer from poverty and disease. Workers are needed who will:

- discover how to reclaim children and young people who, lacking adequate care, have become delinquents.
- discover how the needs of the elderly should be met.
- devote themselves to the care of persons in these groups.
- persuade Congress, churches, and private agencies to provide more adequate resources for meeting the needs of persons in these groups.

World Affairs

Rapid means of travel and communication have placed all nations in close proximity to one another, and their vast differences in cultural and economic development cause more friction among them now than when they were separated by great distances. The future of civilization depends upon workers who will:

- learn the languages and cultures of other nations and thus increase understanding among them.
- assist underdeveloped nations in moving from primitive cultures to modern ways with as little social disruption as possible.

- restrain powerful nations from aggression against and exploitation of smaller nations.
- serve as missionaries and help to make the gospel of Jesus Christ known to all nations.
- work as governmental officials in the foreign service of their own nations and in international organizations.

Local, State and Federal Government

Many of the most important decisions concerning our common life are made by governmental officials. They are too important to be left to poorly trained, self-seeking individuals. Government service calls for workers who will:

- develop a philosophy of government commensurate with the problems of a dynamic, interrelated world.
- make laws that will deal fairly with the economic realities of the "Second Industrial Revolution."
- make laws that meet the needs of the people for health, education, welfare, and justice.

Meaning and Values

Old values are always disrupted in periods of rapid social change. The ever-increasing mobility of Americans has contributed to such change and has resulted in much uncertainty concerning the meaning of life. Workers are needed who will:

- help discover essential meanings and values in life.
- express meaning through painting, sculpture, literature, architecture, dancing, drama, music, and the other arts, as well as through religion.
- use the means of mass communication (books, magazines, newspapers, radio and television) to impart information truthfully, to interpret meaning and values, and to add zest and humor to life.

[1]Fern Babcock Grant, *Facing the World of Work* (New York: United Church Press, © 1965). Used by permission.

Vocation, My Work, and Social Justice

by David Ng

Goals:

• Participants will see one's work in the light of Christian concern for social service and social justice. These concerns are social and corporate, not merely personal and individual.

• Participants will begin to think about contributions that Asian Pacific Americans can make for themselves and for all of society.

Preparation:

• Check the seven posters to be sure they are still on the walls; move them around for the sake of variety if you wish.

• According to the suggestions given in Step 2, collect newspaper and magazine articles and pictures for use during the discussion.

• Have Bibles available for the participants, preferably in a modern translation such as the Revised Standard Version, or Today's English Version.

• Have pencils and four-by-six-inch cards for each participant.

Procedure:

Opening

Step 1. Getting Started and Reviewing
(5 minutes)

Open with greetings and a few comments and questions to help the participants recall the topics discussed previously. For example, ask: "What do you recall about the needs of Asian Pacific American society? About the kinds of jobs we might take to benefit our community?"

Discovering

Step 2. Social Problems and Society's
Victims *(20 minutes)*

Help the participants to get a sense of the social problems and injustices which victimize people, including Asian Pacific Americans. One way to lift up some examples is to display a wall exhibit of articles and pictures which show such problems. Prior to the meeting, with the help of some young persons, clip from newspapers and magazines some articles which report current events related to economic justice and human rights, such as the exploitation of workers, militarization, oppression by multinational corporations, and so forth. Post these clippings on the walls of the room.

Ask the students to name some of the "big problems that cause injustice and harm to people in our world." Likely they will mention such things as war, poverty, prejudice, homelessness, drugs, and public health issues (e.g., AIDS). Give each participant a four-by-six-inch card and a pencil, and ask each to list two such social problems after walking around the room and looking at the clippings on the wall. When all have written two problems on their cards, they are to discuss with someone the nature of their listed problems and how these affect Asian Pacific Americans.

After about five or ten minutes of walking around and discussing, call all the participants together to share their notes and findings. Guide a discussion of how these problems affect Asian Pacific Americans or even victimize them. For example, in the area of economic justice they might talk about unemployment, underemployment, low wages, and exploitation of recent immigrants; also about poor working conditions and long working hours in sewing factories, restaurants, and other industries. In the area of human rights the problems of refugees, exploitation of workers, and women's roles and rights are among those that could be discussed.

Examples of the problems of militarization relate mainly to the exploitation of Pacific and Asian nations by military powers such as the United States. Other issues include nuclear weapons, the economics of military spending, and the constant threat of war which create serious problems of insecurity and anxiety for Asian and Pacific nations and their peoples.

Multinational corporations in and of themselves are not necessarily evil, but often their largeness and singleminded devotion to profits lead them to exploit poor nations and to dominate their economic systems. Again, Pacific and Asian nations often are the victims. On the other hand, Asian Pacific American persons sometimes are involved in such businesses and thus become partners in exploiting the poor.

A question which can help tie together this discussion is this: "How are our people (Asian Pacific Americans) victimized by the social problems of the world?"

156

Step 3. Considering the Church's Corporate Witness *(10 minutes)*

Having identified social and corporate problems, the participants need to consider ways to deal with such large issues. Refer to the seven wall posters and ask what help any of these statements might offer. These statements reflect biblical perspectives: that God created a good world and intended people to live in it peacefully as partners with God in establishing a just society. As partners with God we are to work to establish community and well-being for all. It is God's will that the people of this world live in peace and well-being. The church, as God's people, is to work to bring about this type of society.

Other questions to ask are these: "In the face of these immense social problems, what can we do as individuals?" "What can we do as a church together?" Help the participants to think about the corporate witness of the church.

Step 4. Learning from Our Asian Pacific American Values *(25 minutes)*

The participants can now consider the contributions that they and their communities can make in the face of the social problems discussed. Write on newsprint or on a chalkboard the following three cultural characteristics shared by many Asian Pacific Americans:

– a sense of community (rather than individualism)
– support from an extended family
– a sense of responsibility to an extended family

Ask the participants to discuss these characteristics—to give examples from personal experience of these characteristics in Asian Pacific American life. Ask if they can think of other cultural characteristics which are also valuable for dealing with daily living.

Then ask how these characteristics might affect the way we deal with social problems such as economic injustice and the others discussed earlier. For example, how does an Asian Pacific American sense of community help a person deal with the exploitation of workers? Can it make us work to prevent exploitation? Can it lead us to *become* exploiters? Discuss reasons for your answers.

After some discussion of the value of Asian Pacific American cultural characteristics, ask the summary question: "How can Asian Pacific Americans help bring about a more just and peaceful world?"

Step 5. Learning from the Wall Posters *(15 minutes)*

In the time remaining, look for learnings from the statements on the wall posters and the related Bible passages. Select one or more statements for the participants to think about, discuss, and learn from. Posters 4 to 7 are especially appropriate.

For example, poster 7 states, "Asian Pacific American youth are called by God to be creative, to work, and to minister." Have the participants read the statement and discuss how it affects their thinking about the type of work they might choose, and the way they will do their work. Have them look up the Bible passages to discuss how these passages speak to the topic.

Invite participants to raise any questions about a poster or to comment on a statement on a poster.

Closing
Step 6. Reading Together *(5 minutes)*

A way to close is to have a unison reading of one of the Bible passages listed on the posters (such as Romans 12:4-8 or Ephesians 4:11-13), followed by a prayer.

How Have I Spent My Life?

by David Ng

Goals:

• Participants will reflect on how their faith can affect choices about careers and work.

• Issues of social concerns and the effect of Asian Pacific American identity on one's work will be reviewed.

Preparation:

• Be sure the seven posters from the previous session are on the walls.

• Prepare copies of "How Will I Spend My Life. . ." and Reunion Exercise for distribution.

• Have pencils available.

Procedure:

Opening

Step 1. Beginning Words (2 minutes)

Greet the participants and tell them that the first activity of this session calls for some imagination and creative thinking. Then lead them in the Reunion Exercise described below.

Discovering

Step 2. The Reunion Exercise (28 minutes)

Through this exercise the participants can review what has been discussed in the previous sessions and begin to make some personal applications. Explain to the group that they will reflect on all they have learned so far through an imaginary reunion of the group. Ask them to relax and to allow their imaginations to flow freely. They are to imagine what they might be doing ten years from now. They are to imagine that they are attending a happy reunion party. At the party they will "catch up on news about each other and share news about their current jobs."

Hand out copies of the Reunion Exercise, which is printed at the end of this session plan. Explain the handout and have the participants fill in responses on as many of the questions asked as possible. Then have them move around the room as though they were at the ten-year reunion party. They can greet each other (as though they hadn't seen each other for ten years!) and ask each other questions such as the ones listed on the handout. For example, "How are you?" "Are you married?" "What kind of work are you doing now?" "How do you like it?" "How does your work help others?" "What is your goal in life?"

After about fifteen minutes of walking around and talking with each other at the reunion, have the participants gather to discuss what they learned about each other and what they learned about themselves. You can guide this discussion with questions like these:

a. What kind of person did you turn out to be?
b. How did you like the kind of person you became?
c. How did you like the kind of work you chose?
d. Did any choices surprise you?
e. Did you hear any examples of how someone's faith greatly influenced his or her choices?

Step 3. Reflecting on Vocation (15 minutes)

Provide an opportunity for personal reflection on vocation, work, witness, and Asian Pacific American issues. Explain that the participants are called on to use their imagination again. In the reunion exercise they have imagined freely without much regard for reality. Now they are to imagine their futures, but in realistic terms. What do they really think will happen to them in the future?

Use the following questions to guide the thinking of the participants. (If each participant has a personal copy of the questions, he or she can write in notes and keep the handout for future reference.)

Closing

Step 4. Sharing Reflections (15 minutes)

Allow time for the participants to jot notes in response to the questions above. Allow time for personal reflecting. Invite anyone who wishes to do so share a few thoughts brought out by the exercise (but do not push or pry for responses).

Lead the participants in a unison reading of the seven wall posters, in numerical order. Then close with a prayer which incorporates the concepts in the posters.

How Will I Spend My Life as an Asian Pacific American Worker?

Jot down some notes in response to each question below:

A. What questions and concerns do I have about my career?

B. What questions and concerns do I have about social justice?

C. What questions and concerns do I have about the needs of Asian Pacific Americans?

D. What contributions do I think we Asian Pacific Americans can make to society?

E. How can I be helped by biblical perspectives as I choose a job and a career? (See the seven wall posters.)

F. What are some clues. . . connections. . . possibilities. . .?

G. Things for me to do as I make my decisions. . .

Reunion Exercise

Imagine yourself at a reunion of this class ten years from now. Imagine the kind of person you will have become. Don't worry about whether or not anything is possible—with your imagination, everything is possible!

By yourself, jot down some notes in answer to these questions about yourself ten years from now.

1. Where do you live?

2. Are you married, single, or divorced?

3. Do you have any children? Describe them briefly.

4. What work do you do?

5. How did you decide to do this type of work?

6. What satisfactions do you get from your work?

7. Who benefits from your work?

8. How does your faith influence your work, if at all?

9. What would you like to accomplish before you retire?

10. What do you do in your spare time?

Adapted from "Where Will You Be When You Get Where You're Going?" by Richard P. Olson, *Respond,* Vol. 5, Judson Press.